Sousan Azadi now lives with her son in Canada, where she designs and sells jewellery. An unwilling exile, she knows it is unlikely she will ever return to Iran.

Angela Ferrante is an award-winning Canadian journalist who has in the course of her work travelled widely in the Middle East. She is currently assistant managing editor with *Maclean's Newsmagazine* in Canada.

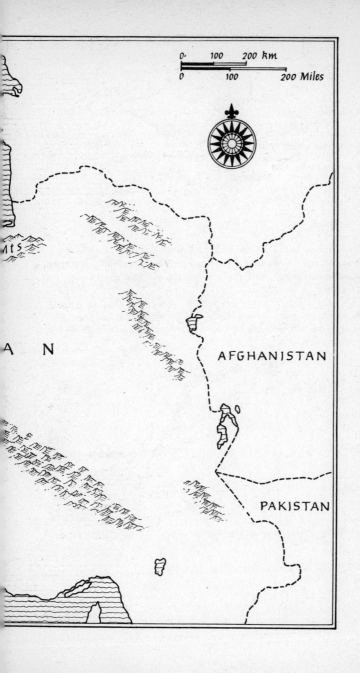

FOR HOMA

without your inspiration and determination, this book
would never have been written.

Merci Kali mamnon

Sousan

I wish to thank my uncles, J, J and K, and my aunts S, H and F, for all
their help and support and for always being there when I needed them.
Special thanks to Pavine, Diana and Syrous for the help they have given
with the book.

Thanks, too, to my agent, Lucinda Vardey and my lawyer, Michael
Levine, and especially to Angela Ferrante for her hard work and efforts in
co-writing my story.

OUT OF IRAN

One Woman's Escape From The Ayatollahs

SOUSAN AZADI WITH ANGELA FERRANTE

Futura

A Futura Book

First published in Great Britain in 1987 by
Macdonald and Co (Publishers) Limited,
London and Sydney

This edition published by Futura in 1988
1st reprint 1989
2nd reprint 1990
3rd reprint 1991

Reproduced, printed and bound in Great Britain by
Cox & Wyman Ltd, Reading

ISBN 0 7088 3926 6

Futura Publications
A Division of
Macdonald & Co (Publishers) Ltd
165 Great Dover Street
London SE1 4YA
A member of Maxwell Macmillan Publishing Corporation

Contents

Prologue

Allah is the Patron of the faithful. He leads them from darkness to the light. As for the unbelievers, their patrons are false gods (the taghout*), who lead them from light to darkness. They are the heirs of Hell and shall abide in it for ever.*

THE KORAN

 The *taghout*. Satan. A ruler who has transgressed the limits of his authority. Such was Ayatollah Ruhollah Khomeini's title for Mohammad Reza Pahlavi, King of Kings, Shah of Iran. And we, the Shah's loyal subjects, were condemned by Khomeini as the *taghouti*, the followers of Satan. In 1979, a revolution brought to power in my country a fundamentalist Shi'a regime under the Ayatollah. From the moment he stepped back onto Iranian soil after a long exile, he branded those who had opposed his return as *taghouti*. We were the rich of Iran, the ruling elite, the nation's leaders. We did not want to accept a vengeful religious leader as our new master. In his view, because we were rich, we must have been corrupt. Because we were Westernized, we must have been immoral. I have known what it is like to be hated just because I wanted basic rights as a woman in a Moslem country. Within three years I found myself an unwilling exile, purged by a society that I barely recognized as my own. Before I managed to escape, I was hunted by the regime's revolutionary committee, the Komiteh; my son was brainwashed by the new school system; and my family was under continual threat from the state. I even spent time in one of Khomeini's new prisons.

And yet my life began with great promise and privilege. I was the great-granddaughter of a Shah of the Qajar dynasty — the two-hundred-year-old dynasty that the Pahlavis over-threw. My father was a wealthy landlord and my mother the cherished child of one of Iran's great entrepreneurial and philanthropic families. Later, when I married a powerful businessman, we became leading members of the new and glittering oil-rich Iran. The change — from a protected, charmed life to that of a hated outsider in my own country — occurred so suddenly that I barely had time to understand the historic events that swept me along. Because of my hus-band's highly religious family, I experienced first-hand how cruel could be the fervour of Shi'a fanatics to those they despised. I saw the whip marks of the regime on my friends' backs. As the *ayatollahs* tightened their grip on my country, friends disappeared; others escaped. I watched as family friends — former politicians, owners of large companies, landowners — went into hiding and lost all their property while we, the young, became even more reckless, knowing that soon our way of life would end. It is estimated that almost a million people, most of them from the upper and middle classes, left Iran in the years after the revolution. More than ten thousand people are believed to have been executed. My story is only a small part of a much larger national tragedy — the obliteration of a country, of the Iran I loved.

I have written my story to awaken others to what is hap-pening to my countrymen, and to defend the *taghouti*. Once, not long ago, I was skiing with some Iranian friends in California, enjoying a moment of fun. I was pretending that the revolution had never happened and that life had not changed. Some Americans overheard us talking in Farsi. One of them said to another loudly enough to be overheard, "It's because of people like *them* that there was a revolution in Iran." The words stung terribly. Why were we responsible? Because we dared to be rich in a poor country? Or because we looked so much like people from the West in a veiled society? Even outside Iran I was being condemned for what I represented and not for the individual I was.

I have changed as much as my circumstances. I am no longer rich, although I am not poor. Once I allowed men to protect and care for me, and in return I accepted the subservience that my society demanded. Once I lived in so small a circle that I never saw the poverty and resentment that bred so many martyrs for the revolution. But now that I have to support and rely on myself, I see what I was once blind to.

I still have family in Iran, and it is to protect them that many of the people and places in this book have been given fictitious names. Every now and then I call friends or family members still living there. Their lives have only become sadder since I left. In North Teheran, where the remnants of the old elite still hide in their mansions, there are pockets of Westernized living. Wine, bought on the black market, is served with dinner, and music, smuggled from abroad, plays on the stereo. Although it is illegal and expensive, opium is much in use because the young are permitted so few pleasures. Sometimes it is the *mullahs* themselves who get the payoffs that permit such illegal joys. Khomeini accused us, the *taghouti*, of corrupting our country and debasing Islam. But behind the façade of spartanism and religious rigour in the new Iran, a society is rotting.

Chapter One

Roses and Thorns

So my land had suffered at Fate's ruthless hand
There is now an inferno where once was my land.

KHAGANI SHIRVANI

 It was the fourth of July, 1982, and in my cousin Fariba's house in the wealthy Teheran suburb of Saltanatbad, there were still no signs of morning approaching.

Quietly, I rolled over on the makeshift bed on the floor of her living room and tried to make out the figure of my son Farhad as he slept soundlessly just a few feet away. I looked at him long and deeply, just barely making out his dark curls and the small fists held tightly under his chin. Only seven years old, I thought, and about to grow up quickly. Am I doing the right thing for you, I wondered. Here, you are sure to grow up to be a rich man. Your grandparents, no matter how much they hate me, will raise you with all the privileges and comforts that Iranians give their sons. But what future am I choosing for you? An uncertain one. Much less money, certainly. Loneliness, perhaps.

Turning carefully, I cast a furtive glance at Kamal, my new husband of just a few weeks, a stranger more than a mate. Would our hastily arranged marriage survive the day? His forehead was smooth in unperturbed sleep. He had won me, much as I had tried not to be won. But now I could see the first pale signs of another hot Iranian summer day on his long, slim face. There was no time left for doubt. The alarm clock was set for 5:00 A.M., and before it could sound, I got up quickly and stealthily.

Soon others in the household began to stir. Throwing his blankets off with one decisive movement, Kamal stood up, suddenly wide awake. "What time are we expecting Marjani?" he whispered.

"At a quarter to six."

"Are you sure that everything is ready? The money, the contact?"

"Everything." I tried to sound confident.

Upstairs I could hear my father and Fariba and her husband getting ready to come down. We had slept only two hours. The night had been for saying goodbye. Fariba was the first to emerge, her hair uncustomarily dishevelled, her eyes still sleepy and full of worry. She went quietly into the kitchen to prepare our last Iranian breakfast. In the half-light I dressed quickly. A pair of blue jeans. A pair of plain, dark, walking shoes — not running shoes; they would have been too noticeable. An ordinary-looking belt. I felt it carefully to see if the jewellery I had stitched inside it was still in place; I counted mentally twelve thick, gold chains, ten diamond rings, four sets of diamond earrings and four matching bracelets. Portable assets. One set of matching necklace and earrings alone was worth about $20,000 U.S.

I slipped on a long-sleeved shirt and instantly felt its surprising weight. There were two long Iranian chains, 22-carat gold, left to me by my mother and the best of Iranian workmanship, sewn into one of the shoulder pads. A heavy diamond bracelet with several large stones that my former husband had given me was stuffed into the other, and many fine, gold chains were sewn into the collar. Over the shirt, I wore a forgettable blue jacket. Finally, I pulled a large, deep-coloured *hejab* over my head so that it covered my long, gold-coloured hair and most of my forehead.

Then I checked our bags. Each adult was allowed one small bag. I unzipped a small grey nylon carrying case and checked our one change of clothes. That was all we were taking, except for the clothes we were to wear for the day. The other bag was for food: cans of juice, mineral water, fruit and sandwiches. Who knew if we would be able to stop to eat?

Finally, as gently as I could, I roused Farhad. He mewed little complaints while I uncovered him and led him into the bathroom to wash and dress.

"Why do we have to get up so early, Mummy?"

"I told you last night, luvijun," I said, using his pet name. "We're going on a picnic."

"But it's so early."

"Look. Kamal is all ready to go and so am I. You can sleep in the car."

We sat, subdued, at the breakfast table, not wanting to look at each other. My cousin would now be the last of our generation of the family still in Iran. My father, who had already lost his land, his home and his status, was now about to lose what was left of his immediate family. Unless absolutely forced to, as I was, neither my father nor Fariba would leave the country. Ravaged though it was, Iran was still their home.

I still remember that last breakfast in Teheran. Laid out on the dining-room table was a sumptuous meal: Fariba's home-made jam from the famous fist-sized apricots that grew in the wild hills of the northern province of Azerbaijan, honey from Mount Sahand, warm, fresh barbary bread and fresh juice from the oranges of the orchards by the Caspian Sea. But we ate without appetite, and before long we heard the expected knock at the front door.

With newly acquired caution, Fariba looked out of the window before answering the summons. There stood Marjani, as promised. He was short, stocky and suavely dressed, and next to him was the tall, gaunt Kurd who was to give us our freedom—for a price. After ushering them in quickly, Fariba looked out to make sure that no one had seen our unusual visitors. We could not afford to be noticed; in the Teheran of Ayatollah Ruhollah Khomeini, any movement so early in the morning was suspect. There were no servants about. My cousin and most of her neighbours had stopped employing live-in servants long before — too many of them had turned out to be spies for the new regime.

"Did you bring the money?" I asked Marjani.

"You'll get the Turkish lire in Tabriz tonight."

"And what about the marks?"

"Damn. The marks. I completely forgot about them. We'll have to go back to my apartment and pick them up."

It was a bad way to start the day. Driving through the empty streets of Teheran we would be in danger every minute. We would be too noticeable and too easily stopped by one of the watchful Komiteh. That was the name of the special re-volutionary committees at the service of the *mullahs*. The *mullahs* were the clerics of the Shi'a faith who now ruled the country; the highest ranking was the *ayatollah*, or "reflection of Allah."

I did a mental calculation. Twenty minutes to get downtown to his apartment; another twenty minutes to come back to the northern part of the city to pick up Shery, an old friend who would be travelling with us. We would lose forty precious minutes — forty minutes that might be worth more than the German marks. And yet the marks — about

$10,000 worth — were the only European currency we had been able to buy on the black market.

I decided. "All right. Let's go get them."

Now that the moment had come to say our last goodbye, I could not let go of my father. He laid his hand on my shoulder and I felt, rather than heard, him cry.

Then I hugged Fariba. "If we are stopped, we won't tell them where we spent the night and if by any chance the Komiteh comes here, just say you haven't seen us. Do you hear? Take no chances."

Farhad jumped joyfully into my father's arms. His mind was already on the picnic we had promised him.

"Don't come outside, any of you," I ordered. "You might be seen."

"Nonsense," said Fariba. "I don't care who sees us. We are coming out to say goodbye and that's that."

Despite our warnings, they came to watch us get into Marjani's brown Range Rover. As we drove off, they kept waving to us, almost defiantly. We looked back until the car made a right-hand turn and they disappeared from sight.

"Don't worry," said Marjani. "Everything will be fine. I've done this any number of times. I promise you by midnight tonight you will be in Turkey. You will be free."

Free. Turkey tonight — and then maybe Paris tomorrow. They had told us nothing of how we would escape. The details were kept a closely guarded secret even from those of us who were risking our lives to do it. We knew only that we were to drive that day to Tabriz, the city of merchants, the old Mongol capital, seven hundred kilometres northwest of Teheran, in the heart of Azerbaijan. After that, there were only my wild imaginings and the promises of Marjani and the silent Kurd. We had to make it. There would be no second chance.

We arrived at Marjani's place without incident. The Kurd ran upstairs and, in a minute, came back down carrying an envelope. After stuffing it into some hidden niche under the front seat, Marjani set the car moving again. Twenty minutes later we arrived at the apartment house where Shery's sister lived. As we drove up the street I could see a woman leaning out of a window, keeping a lookout.

We made no signal but waited in the car, and presently a woman hiding deep inside a *chador* came out the front door of the apartment building. The woman wore her *chador* pulled down low over her forehead, with a piece of the heavy black cloth tightly clasped between her teeth. She was the perfect image of a devout Moslem woman, a black bird born without features. But when the woman uncovered her mouth to reveal a jaunty smile, I gasped. It was Shery under the *chador*, my elegant sixty-year-old friend, a tireless worker, who had run a string of schools for the handicapped and who had never broken down under the pressure from the *mullahs* to wear a *chador*. And now that she was finally leaving all the threats behind, she had chosen as her disguise the uniform of the regime.

She got in the back seat with the three of us and we set off once again, finding our way through the city, down quiet side streets, each one of us locked in our private farewells. The city that I had loved so much, that had been so full of excitement, was now just a backdrop for violent posters. Even now, long after the Shah Mohammad Reza Pahlavi was dead, there were exhortations to kill him. "Death to the Shah, Death to America," the signs said and the red paint was made to drip like blood. Banks, cinemas and store fronts stood gutted and boarded up. The streets were full of garbage. Occasionally, a small bonfire smoked in a street gutter. In the distance, we caught sight of armed revolutionary guards riding shotgun as they cruised the city in their Range Rovers. The few people in sight walked purposefully, their heads bowed down.

My God, how I had loved my country, how happy a family we had been, how lucky to have been born Iranian! And now Iran was no longer mine. I thought of the house that my first husband Bijan had built for me, standing empty in the hills overlooking the city, its rose garden growing wild, its orchard untended. I could see Farhad's collection of stuffed animals, hastily left behind in his room, my closets full of clothes, the family albums and home movies, the balcony where Bijan and I often took our breakfast. I would no longer make the drive to the villa on the Caspian Sea and watch the mountains change colour on the way.

The car circled the Shahyad, the Shah's monument to 2,500 years of Persian monarchy, which stood at the main entrance to Teheran.

"Goodbye to all that," said Shery, looking up at the city's most famous landmark.

I looked back one more time, and as I did so, I fingered the right-hand cuff of my shirt. There I could just barely feel something hard beneath the surface of the fabric. It was a ring, an ancient turquoise that my grandmother Roghieh had handed down to me, the ring that she herself had once worn on her wild bid for freedom sixty-five years before. She, too, had fled a revolution. Give me luck, grandmother, and let me find a new life as you did, I prayed. Then I turned and looked resolutely ahead at the highway to Tabriz.

Roghieh. I have always had an image of her as a young woman on the run. Galloping on horseback through the lawless lands of Caucasia in southern Russia in the spring of 1917, with one small child, only six months old, strapped on her back, and another sitting in front. Her only companion was her sister, who was in charge of her own son and Roghieh's third child. Carefully concealed in a pouch under her *chador*, she carried a family fortune in jewels: her magnificent Russian emeralds, a scattering of diamonds and rubies and ropes of pearls. I could picture the dust rising around them as they made their way through the hills controlled by armed nomadic tribes.

Years later, when she was an elegant old woman with her once long, dark hair streaked and tied in a bun and hidden under a *hejab*, a long, thick scarf that covered her head, forehead and shoulders, I would ask her what it was like on that harrowing two-month ride from Caucasia to Tabriz. She always shook her head and smiled privately.

"That was a long time ago, child. We hardly dared stop. Two women travelling alone like that, never knowing when someone might point a rifle at us — no, best not to dwell on that."

But she did tell me about how she and her sister crossed the fast-flowing Aras River that separates Iran from the Soviet Union.

"We came to the river and we thought, 'How can we cross over? What shall we do now?' We couldn't walk across: it was too deep and, besides, the water would have swept off the children. We couldn't ask for help: the Russians were everywhere and the Armenians would have slit our throats. So we thought and thought and then we saw a farmer crossing with some animals on a barge, so we decided to make our own. We found odd branches — thick ones — here and there and we used strips of cloth to tie it all together. It wasn't much of a thing, but it floated with all of us on it and we just pushed off, not knowing if we would get to the other side."

My grandmother was running from a revolution that was to change much of Asia radically. Caucasia, the Turkish-speaking part of southern Russia, was a much-disputed land tucked between the Caspian Sea and the Black Sea. My mother's parents were Shi'a Moslems, a breakaway sect of Islam that spurned the orthodox Sunni faith of the Moslem majority and believed that a great "imam," a messiah who had gone into hiding over eleven centuries ago, would one day return to bring about the triumph of good. It was a radical faith, imbued with a devotion to martyrdom and self-sacrifice.

My grandparents were Turkish-speaking and lived in the town of Baku, where relations with the local Christian Armenians had always been uneasy. My grandfather, Mahmoud Salman, was a builder and a businessman, who married the local beauty, my grandmother Roghieh. When the upheavals of the Russian Revolution finally invaded Caucasia, the Salmans began to fear for their lives. The Communists were beginning to confiscate property, and wealthy Moslems were becoming targets of Armenian threats. They finally decided that their only hope was to leave behind everything that they owned — several houses, tracts of farming land — and try to make a new life in Iran to the south, a land of Shi'a Moslems like themselves, where they would never have to fear for their lives again and where they could be at home forever.

Roghieh was to head out first and travel to Tabriz, a city that Mahmoud knew well from numerous business trips. He would join her and the children after he had sold off what property he could. It took him two years to rejoin her permanently. My Aunt Tootie, who was four years old at the time, remembers how he arrived carrying two large suitcases filled with Russian currency. But within weeks, that currency became valueless.

"Here," said my grandfather with disgust, handing over the suitcases to the children. "Play with it. It's only play money now."

My grandmother's jewellery became the foundation for their new lives and slowly each piece was sold off to start and maintain a construction business and to buy a house. They lived in Tabriz until 1933 and had five more children, including my mother Sima who was born in 1928. By the time they moved to Teheran, the sprawling capital city at the foot of the Alborz Mountains, my grandfather had already established himself as a reputable contractor. In Teheran the 1930s were years of great change. Under Reza Khan, the father of Iran's last Shah and the founder of the short-lived Pahlavi dynasty, the city was quickly becoming the most important commercial centre in the country. Reza Khan had embarked on a campaign to modernize and rebuild Iran after years of war and upheaval. And Mahmoud was one of those Iranians who were ready to help him. My grandparents owned one of the largest houses in Teheran: it boasted one of the few indoor bathtubs in the country and a circular drive, an uncommon feature in the capital.

Because they had come from Russia, my grandparents were more progressive and more willing to accept novelties from abroad than were the indigenous Iranians. In a country still emerging from its tribal origins and fearful of all foreign influences (and quite rightly, too, because Britain and the Soviet Union were the powers behind the throne), my grandparents were symbolic of the new Iranians who were interested in the outside world. They always looked to the West. Each of their children was given French and English tutors. Each child also had to learn a musical instrument—an unusual custom in Iran in those days.

By the end of the 1930s, although they had been in Iran fewer than twenty years, the Salmans lived the life of the elite. And in Iran, that elite was a very small one, close-knit, family-centred, living a life of its own, cut off almost totally from the rest of society. Even after years of oil wealth and the rise of a middle class, Iran was still that way when I left it. In Teheran, my mother and her brothers attended the very best schools in the country. They catered to an exclusive group. One of my mother's classmates, for instance, was the last Shah's sister, Fatimah.

Mahmoud and Roghieh were also among the first big wave of Iranians to send their children abroad. My Uncle Kamel, the oldest, travelled two months to go to Ann Arbor, Michigan, in the United States to study engineering. My Uncle Kurosh went to Paris, to study engineering at the Sorbonne. There he made friends with men who would later have important roles in Iran; Mehdi Bazargan, the first prime minister under Ayatollah Khomeini, and Shapour Bakhtiar, the Shah's last prime minister, were among them. They would prove useful when my uncles expanded their father's already famous Salman construction firm and took their places in the new hierarchy created by oil wealth. Uncle Fayegh went to Germany to study engineering and also joined the family firm. Uncle Amir, who, along with Uncle Ardeshir, studied dentistry at the University of Michigan, remained there and eventually became an American citizen and a well-known innovator in his field.

As progressive as they were, Mahmoud and Roghieh could not imagine sending their two daughters to school abroad, and Tootie's and Sima's education ended with the equivalent of high school. But after marriage, my Aunt Tootie went on to study dentistry, and she became the first woman dentist in Iran. My relationship with my austere aunt was never warm, but I have always admired her for carving out a new role for an Iranian woman — and doing it, apparently, without any personal strain.

It is probably difficult for outsiders to understand the Iranian elite's fascination with the West. But Iran in the 1930s was a deeply religious country still struggling to emerge from backwardness and illiteracy. Even now, over half the population cannot read or write. The first university, the University of Teheran, was not opened until 1934. Much of what was taken for granted in more developed countries was novel in Iran. For instance, there was no pumped water in the city of Teheran until 1956. There were few cars — royalty owned most of them — but my family had one of the earliest ones, a 1932 Ford. My mother and her brothers were also among the first to ski. One uncle brought back ski equipment from the United States and because skis could not be bought in Iran, my uncles had their own made by artisans who copied the American product. There were no resorts or ski lifts, but the brothers and sisters rented a bus and invited friends to go to the mountains just north of the city. Those same mountains now have luxurious resorts — and Iranians are mad about skiing. For the small group that had wealth, the West was a powerful attraction, a symbol of progress, an enticement, something to be aped. We were not worried then about losing the values that made us Iranians.

My father Jahangir's family was pure Persian establishment. The Azadis were landowners, related directly to one of the real Shahs—not to the upstart Pahlavis—and they have always been proud of their ancestry. My grandfather, Salim Azadi, was a nobleman who was responsible for collecting taxes in the large, important province of Azerbaijan—and this function gave him great power and wealth. He was also a big land-owner, who, under the old feudal system of Iran, owned many villages. When Mohammad Reza Pahlavi, Iran's last Shah, undertook the so-called White Revolution that reformed land ownership in Iran, he was attempting to move the country out of a primitive feudal system and into the modern era. My grandfather—and my father in the early years—had almost total control of their villages, including dealing with many matters of criminal and civil law. They were father figures, either benevolent or harsh, depending on the personality. Even though my father, greatly against his will, was to lose much of his land and most of his power during the White Revolution, he was never quite able to lay aside an imperious manner formed by having many servants and a quasi-monarchic hold over his people.

Under the old system of land ownership, the farmers worked the land and gave a percentage of their produce to my grandfather. He had absolute ownership of six villages— which meant that he even owned the land that the houses were built on. The villagers grew tobacco, wheat, fruits and vegetables, and raised sheep and cattle. As landowner, Salim had to provide water, that scarce commodity in a country of extreme temperatures, which he did by maintaining the *qanats*, the underground tunnels that carried water from sub-terranean streams to the fields.

Owning land in Iran was a sacred sign of social status and wealth. My family taught me that ruling landowners, *khans*, were the first rank of the elite, above the merchant class and even above the relatives of the new royal dynasty who were descended from a modest northern Iranian family of small farmers.

"Remember who you are, little one," my father would say. "The daughter of a *khan*."

I thought everyone lived as we did, with happy servants and the latest in clothes and comforts. I was never really permitted to see the world around me, with its poverty and its resentment, until it was too late for me to understand those forces. I assumed that everyone had been assigned to a particular place — there were servants and those whom they served — and I thought that was how it would be forever.

But only a few decades after my grandfather ruled so absolutely over his villages, owning agricultural land became an expensive liability. It was families such as my mother's, who established themselves in the cities and built new companies, who were to benefit most from the new Iran.

My grandfather, Salim Azadi, made a good match. He married his wealth and land power to the somewhat impoverished but nonetheless royal daughter of a prince of the Qajar dynasty that had ruled in Iran from 1786 to 1925. Her name was Ashi, and her father, Reza Ghili Mirza, a prince, had lived in Tabriz and ruled over Azerbaijan. She remembered her father as a soft-hearted romantic who loved poetry.

Ashi was fourteen years old when she married Salim. Although they had several residences scattered around the province, they preferred to live in Rezayeh, a resort town on Lake Rezayeh in the far northeastern corner of the country. They loved the city because it was much more easy-going socially than other Iranian centres. Inhabited largely by Christian Armenians who enjoyed their lives openly, the city was a haven from the strict Islamic code of behaviour that prevailed in the rest of Iran. A good Moslem did not drink alcohol, play cards, eat pork or dress provocatively. But in Rezayeh, people tended to have more European habits. In a country that was wary of public entertainment and where, as a result, people had to make their fun in the privacy of their homes, Rezayeh was remarkable for its restaurants and night life. In the evenings, the residents would stroll about and sit in outdoor cafés, eating ice cream — a pleasure rarely indulged in even in the capital. When the first movie theatres came to Iran (theatre-going is frowned upon in Islamic society and banned in post-revolutionary Iran), Rezayeh was one of the first towns to enjoy one. It was also a city where the women felt free to walk in public uncovered, unencumbered and unfettered by the *chador*.

The *chador* — the formless swatch of black cloth that is worn over regular clothing. Even now I cannot say that word without feeling darkness descending over me. A heavy blanket of darkness that settles first on the head, then the shoulders and falls to the ground. In those moments I like to think of my grandmother Ashi. It was 1936. In Rezayeh, most of the guests had already arrived at one of the social highlights of the year — the Azerbaijan governor's ball. Suddenly, there was a polite but unmistakable commotion at the main entrance. It was Ashi. She had just heard of the edict of the Shah, Reza Khan, ordering all women to throw off the *chador*. That night she showed what she had always thought of the Moslem custom of hiding women so that the mere sight of their skin could not arouse men. There she stood, her husband proudly beside her, dressed in a brightly flowered dress with a matching hat. When she entered the ballroom, the guests gasped, not only because of the burst of colour in the hall but also because of Ashi's startling beauty, which up to then had been a secret known to only the most intimate family members. "If you could only have seen their faces," she often told me, still savouring her triumph.

For the past fifty years, the wearing of the *chador* has been an important barometer of the political mood of Iran. The *chador* can send out a complexity of signals about a woman's attitudes to the outside world, her social status, her religiosity and even her political stance. One of the bravest things Reza Khan did in his ambitious drive to turn Iran into a modern country was to abolish the *chador* for women of all ages and of all classes. Seeking with one stroke to reverse centuries of tradition, he challenged the powerful religious establishment. That year, his own wife and two daughters appeared in public for the first time with their faces uncovered. Roghieh, a religious Moslem who had always worn a *chador*, took to wearing a *hejab* that covered her hair. Many women clung to the *chador* because they felt it protected their purity. Just the sight of a woman's hair or her ankles or wrists might arouse a man and cause grief. A pure woman was one who did not tempt a man. The *chador* was one of the ways in which the society of the time repressed any public signs of sexuality.

But under Reza Khan it became a serious offence to wear a *chador*. The king had ordered his soldiers to pull the covering right off any woman caught wearing one. Many religious women stayed indoors rather than be defiled. Later, when Reza Khan's son, the last Shah, softened the decree and made the wearing of the *chador* a voluntary matter, my grandmother Roghieh returned to wearing one occasionally.

Having been brought up during Reza Khan's enforced liberalization, my mother, Sima, never took to wearing a *chador* in her normal day-to-day life. She wore one only for funerals or on a rare visit to the mosque, and even then the *chadors* worn by the women in her circle were black, lacy ones, delicately patterned, and see-through so that the arms and legs showed. Despite the decree, Reza Khan never completely succeeded in eliminating the *chador*. Eventually the garment came to identify a woman's place in society: the poorer, older, more religious and less educated women clung

to their stultifying but also protective coverings. Even in the
Shah's day, when some streets in Teheran could be mistaken
for those of a European capital, a woman would rarely venture
into the bazaar without a *chador*. In those narrow little lanes
where so much of the nation's wealth was traded over a
handshake, conservatism prevailed.

I never willingly wore a *chador* except as a child when I
went to the mosque with my grandmother Roghieh. A colourful orange flowered one—children were permitted to wear
bright colours—it made a perfect prop for play. I could use it
as a tent or perhaps as an awning in the garden, suspended
from a tree. But the time would come when my toy would
become a weapon — to be used against me.

Ashi created the gracious ambience in which my father's father
lived. A true princess, she shared her father's passion for the
arts, especially for poetry. Under Islamic law, a man may take
four wives, although a woman may take only one husband,
and Salim took advantage of this law to marry another woman
as well, a woman of much lower social status, by whom he
had two children. But there was no question about who ruled
the house. Ashi was the only one who dined with my grandfather Salim. The other wife was relegated to the kitchen,
where she supervised the servants and all the children, including my father and his two sisters. Matters concerning the
day-to-day running of the household were always referred
to her to spare Ashi the annoyance. And when Salim went
out in public with his family, it was only Ashi and her children
who accompanied him. By the time I was a grown woman,
the practice of multiple marriages had almost disappeared. It
had served wealthy men well, allowing them a variety of sexual partners, and wives competing to provide them with their
domestic attentions. But I personally found that invariably
one wife was treated better than the rest—a situation bound
to create jealousy and two classes of family members.

To have an image of how my father's parents lived is to understand a great deal of what life was like in the dying days of an ancient, land-owning elite in a country still fighting against secession and tribalism. The luxuries they owned were unknown to the vast majority of Iranians. Their elegant mansion in Rezayeh was filled with family members, countless servants, several cooks, a nanny for each child and several drivers. My father, who often travelled back to those times in his memories, would describe them to me.

"Imagine, Sousan, how fabulous a scene. They took their meals sitting on the floor, with the plates served on a table-cloth placed over a magnificent Tabriz carpet. The table was always set for at least twenty people, even though Ashi and Salim were dining alone. After all, a host always had to be ready for an unexpected guest! Indeed, it was very common for people — say, ten or fifteen people — to drop by each evening. Try being that kind of a host nowadays."

Socializing, having a *shabnishini*, or evening party, was, and indeed still is, the main form of entertainment in Iran, and a good host, no matter how poor, must always be prepared. To entertain many people at a moment's notice—and make it seem effortless—was the true sign of a sophisticated, wealthy man.

Persian food consists of many small, varied dishes. Beef with whole ruby eggplants in its spicy juices. Chicken and the jewels from the pomegranate. Lamb with emerald spinach. On the side, always fresh mint to nibble on. And for dessert, a sumptuous presentation of the fruits of the season.

The base for the main meal is always rice, and the way it is prepared says a great deal about the effort, care and importance attached to dining. It takes several hours to make rice properly so that every grain is long, white, supple and separate. First, the very best long-grained rice is washed repeatedly and soaked overnight in salted water. Then the rice is boiled in a large pot and drained. In the bottom of another large pan covered lightly with oil, various ingredients are placed — a layer of Persian bread called *lavosh* or potato or a mixture of yoghurt, saffron and rice. The rice is then carefully placed on top of the first layer, in a pyramid shape; the grains cannot stick. The covered pan is placed over heat until it is very hot to the touch. At that point, a cup of a water and oil mixture is poured over the rice. The pan lid, wrapped in several linen cloths, is then placed over the rice, and the heat is reduced. The rice cooks for another two hours. The result: tender grains that can be picked out individually, and a delicious crusty bottom called the *tadiq*. Various meats, yoghurt and vegetable dishes, or *horesht*, are eaten with the rice.

My grandfather was famous for his hospitality. Once a complete stranger came to the door, invited himself in and stayed for three weeks. No one knew him or asked him where he had come from or what he was doing in Rezayeh. They accepted at face value the recommendation of a mutual friend that he had proffered on his arrival. It would have been in poor form to ask any details, and they never did find out who he was.

Salim was also popular because of his interest in the outside world. With the help of hard-to-find foreign books and the scratchy outpourings from afar that his radio — one of the few in the city—emitted, he managed to teach himself to read and write smatterings of English and French, along with his native languages, Persian and Arabic. Every night the house filled with friends wanting a glimpse of the world beyond the snow-capped mountains to the east that were the natural barrier to Turkey and Europe.

Late one night during the Second World War my grandfather Salim was killed. When, early in the war, Reza Khan had shown a worrisome sympathy for the Nazis, the British and Soviets invaded Iran. The British quickly dispatched the Shah to exile, and in September 1941, propped up his young son, Mohammad Reza, as the new ruler. At the same time, the Soviets made themselves comfortable in their occupation of Azerbaijan. A great nationalist who had long fought the secessionist forces in his province, Salim bristled at the Russian presence. One New Year's Day, the local Soviet representative paid a duty call on my grandfather as one of the leading political figures of the area.

"Happy New Year?" my grandfather scoffed at his polite greeting. "It will be a happy day only when you people finally leave our country."

A fearless, headstrong man right to the end, he had ignored everyone's warnings, including Ashi's, and one night insisted on taking his regular evening stroll despite the many armed men in the streets. He was shot at close range by a man who stepped out of the shadows for an instant and then disappeared.

"It was a public execution, right there in the street," Ashi would say. "He was too much of a nationalist for the Russians."

The Soviets did not leave Iranian soil until 1946, and then only after the threat of a showdown from U.S. President Harry Truman, whose country had also built up its presence in Iran during the war.

My grandfather's death brought to an end a whole way of life. Acting on family rumours that Salim had buried a treasure in jewels in his garden in Rezayeh, my father had the vast grounds torn up, but the cache, if it had ever existed, was never found. Shortly afterwards, my grandmother Ashi sold the mansion, discharged most of her servants and moved into a smaller house with a single, faithful servant. Persian life in the grand style was over.

Sometime during 1950, my father, Jahangir, was introduced to the younger sister of a Teheran socialite who was living in Rezayeh for a short time. A handsome, mustachioed young man who was used to being pursued as the most eligible man in town, my father suddenly stopped running away from emotional entanglements. He fell in love with an undeniably beautiful woman called Sima.

"Sousan, if you had only seen your mother in those days," he told me when I grew to womanhood. "She was only twenty-two. Black, black hair all curly . . . maybe a little too skinny. But she had dimples, a smile that could take in the world, and the largest, darkest eyes I had ever seen."

They dated in the Iranian way: they always saw each other in public and were carefully watched over by a chaperone. Even that contact would have been impossible if he had not stated his intentions to marry right at the start.

My mother, too, was enchanted.

"He was so different from other Persian men, Sousan. He was so romantic with women. He loved to paint. Whenever he wanted to make a point, he would do it in verse. And, you know, in his house there were at least four cooks, but he loved to make the special meals himself. He just had a talent for cuisine. Well, you can imagine how unusual it was for a *khan* to even step into the kitchen!"

Their marriage the following year was a social event in both Rezayeh and Teheran, with a large reception held in each city to accommodate hundreds of relatives and friends. My mother's dress came from Paris, a confection of white lace, feathers and pearls that I carefully kept in storage for years. As far as I know, it hangs, still, in a cupboard in our house in Teheran. We had another memory of those fabulous parties. Using a movie camera that he had brought back from France — the first one any of his friends had seen — my Uncle Kurosh filmed and kept alive happy moments that were to be all too brief. That film may still exist, but I have no way of knowing because the Komiteh has taken away most of my family photographs and films. Those precious mementos are still locked up inside Teheran's Monkerat prison.

After their marriage, my parents lived in Teheran. A first-class graduate in engineering from the new University of Teheran, Jahangir started up a construction company with two partners. Through stewards, he was able to take care of his lands. In the beginning, the villages did well under their local managers and my father was able to concentrate on his new company. But as the years went by and agriculture started to decline in importance and farm labourers left for the big cities, the villages started to have problems. While the Shah and his advisers became mesmerized by their schemes to industrialize the country, agricultural output slowly declined, the victim of neglect and outmoded farming methods. Our lands, once the source of our family's strength, eventually became a great drain on my father. He was forced to leave his work in Teheran more and more to make the twelve-hour journey to his properties. Finally he made the difficult decision to move back to Azerbaijan and abandon construction. The city held hope of the riches of the future, but he could never have turned his back on his heritage. In 1963, when the Shah launched his White Revolution, my father was stripped of much of his property—he was left outright ownership of one village and several tracts of land. He became a beleaguered landowner, powerful only in his memories. And then the revolution came and took away what he had left.

I was born in Teheran on September 17, 1954, and my arrival was remembered mostly because my mother's doctor could not be found when she went into labour. Sima's brothers finally came upon him, drunk and angry, in the middle of a poker game that he was losing badly. They had to pay off his large debts before they could persuade him to come with them to attend to my mother. My father was just then in the throes of deciding whether to move back into the countryside permanently, and my arrival only made it more difficult for him. My mother did join my father in our country home for a couple of years while I was still very young, but once I was ready to start attending school, they decided that she would have to live in Teheran with me. In those days — and it is not much different now — there was a world of contrast between life in the capital and life in a small village. What schools existed in the villages were primitive. There was no cultural life — at night the only entertainment was to visit friends or listen to the radio. In Teheran, I could attend a private girls' school run by Italian nuns, and my mother, surrounded by most of her family, could have an active social life.

My childhood was divided between the school-day order of winter in Teheran and the freedom and fun of summers in my father's village. My father poured his energies into his favourite, and later his only, village, Sabbalon, which was inhabited largely by Christian Assurians, who were known for their progressive attitudes. Over the years, many of the villagers had emigrated to the United States and they continued to send home money and the products of Western affluence, along with novel ideas about how a society should function. As a result, our villagers were better off and better educated than most, and they had a better awareness of the world outside.

Even now when I think back to those years in Sabbalon, its beauty comes back to me and I can smell the jasmine on the breeze. It was built on a hill overlooking Lake Rezayeh; its red mud-brick houses spilled down in a tangle of gardens. My father had built a large, sprawling house at the very top of the hill. He personally designed the eighteen-room home and the large garden that cascaded below it. An underground spring that emerged at the top of the garden filled a large swimming pool before it divided into two streams that wandered down the levels of the garden, keeping the air full of moisture and soft, gurgling sounds.

He also built several outdoor pavilions so that he could have his breakfast in a different part of the garden every morning, surrounded by tulips, azaleas and ornamental bushes, all timed so that the garden was in bloom throughout the growing season. Above all, he loved to be encircled by his roses. Apart from my mother and poetry, roses were my father's passion. At great expense, he developed his own hybrids and turned his garden into one of the most colourful and lush in Azerbaijan. A giant greenhouse permitted him to experiment with plants and to protect the more delicate ones imported from abroad. In the mornings, my mother and I often found him crouched over some new addition to his collection, one or two gardeners in attendance, examining the plant with care.

"With a little patience, this one may survive. All it takes is patience," he would say. He often had more of that quality to spare for his plants than for people.

I loved my life in the village. After the social constraints of Teheran where I had to behave like a well-bred young lady, the village gave me a chance to spend time with people that my parents would not otherwise have approved of as playmates. I spent the long summer days running off with the village children, stealing fruit from the trees (which, in any case, belonged to my father), being scolded by the old men guarding the trees (until they realized who I was) and, occasionally, with my mother's hesitant approval, going for lunch to the home of one of the villagers. No one ever forgot that I was the daughter of the *khan*. When I met them on the street, the men would tip their hats and the old women bent low to kiss my hand.

"Mama, why do they do that? I don't like it."

"Sousan, you are the *khan*'s daughter. It is a sign of respect."

In Sabbalon, the rigid code of conduct that was necessary in Teheran — to keep a proper distance between the family and the servants — was ignored. In fact, the highlight of my week was my lunch with all the servants of our house in the kitchen. It was a giant room presided over by the master cook and his assistant and dominated by an enormous stone fireplace that blazed at all hours. A giant pot of stew hung from an iron ring and burbled cheerfully.

"Come in and take a handful," the cook would say.

I was not a very big eater, but the smell of the small, freshly picked herbs, the tomatoes and the long-simmering stew enticed me as nothing else could. I joined the noisy crowd of servants around the giant kitchen table and, like them, I broke off a chunk of fresh-baked bread and dipped it into the communal pot. I was allowed that treat only once a week but every time I finished, I said: "That was the best-ever meal." And all the servants would laugh, the cook the loudest, knowing how I routinely turned away his best cooking, served properly with silver and decorum at the dining-room table. He would laugh now if I told him that even meals served in the best restaurants that I have visited in Europe and North America could not compare with those kitchen lunches.

Our retinue of servants included two cooks, several maids, a couple of drivers and a nanny. My father also had a manager who was responsible for hiring seasonal workers to do the farming. As a landowner, he expected to be cheated on the accounts by his manager because that was how things were done in Iran—and still are. Over the years, he poured a great deal of money into Sabbalon, and, as the agricultural sector became more and more chaotic, he had to sell off his father's valuable coin, jewellery and stamp collections just to keep the farms operating. Eventually, my mother also invested in his lands the money that she had inherited from her family.

I sometimes found them talking quietly in the garden, my mother with her arm around his big shoulders, her voice tranquil and encouraging.

"Don't worry. Everything will be fine. Next year we will have a better harvest. Let's go on. Let's try one more year."

But I rarely saw their worries. I only remember that the house was always full of laughter, games and guests from Teheran. We would dine at about six in the evening, and after dinner my father or some of his guests would read poetry out loud. Hafez, Saadi, Omar Khayyám, Malavi — all of our best-loved poets. To outsiders, this may seem unduly romantic and sentimental, but poetry is like bread and potatoes to Iranians—the stuff of every day, needed for sustenance. Iran has a great deal of violence in its history, but Iranians also have a continual yearning to pour out their feelings and hopes. Now that I am so far away from that close family life and that gregarious society, I often think back to those clear, starry nights. They seemed suspended in a fragrant air, as cut off from harsh reality as our lives were from the everyday turmoil that was besetting my country.

The crueller truth was that the 1950s, my youthful, bounding years, were also years of great upset and of attacks on the life of our Shah. Those years saw the rise of a fervent nationalist movement. Under the septegenarian prime minister, Mohammed Mossadegh, or "Old Mossy" as he was known, the country struggled to wrest the control of its oil fields from British hands and to loosen the foreign hold on domestic politics. After failing to negotiate a new oil deal, Mossadegh overthrew the Shah in 1953. For a few days it appeared that a prime minister with open links to the country's Soviet-backed Communist party was in charge. But in just days the Shah triumphantly returned from his brief exile abroad, thanks to a counter-coup engineered by the CIA and British intelligence. From then on, the Shah was determined to fight back, strengthen his power base within the country and ensure that no one could chase him out again. In Sabbalon we heard only the distant echoes of his opening shots.

My mother, Sima. For those who think that all Moslem women live, *chador*-clad, in the shadows of their husbands, my mother would have been a revelation. She was the light of our family. I realized very early on that she was a special woman by any standards. While my father had learned impatience and an autocratic manner by growing up as master of the village, my mother, although surrounded by wealth in

Teheran, was a gentle, moderate person who treated everyone well. She often blunted my father's anger towards the servants. I remember once when we had guests visiting the garden, my father asked a servant to bring a large basket of our very best grapes for them to try. He was very proud of his grapes, and his wine was renowned in Azerbaijan. When the servant came back, my father took one look at the grapes, saw that some were less than perfect and tossed the entire basket angrily on the grass.

"I have to do everything myself," he thundered, and promptly went off to cut his own grapes while the servant watched, mortified. It was my mother who smoothed over the hurt feelings of the servant, calmed my father down and helped the guests to ignore the incident.

My mother was the exact opposite of my father in some ways. In a society which jealously guarded its traditional ways, Sima was very modern. She helped my father manage his lands. At harvest time, when the grain was being threshed — manually in those days — she stood all day under the sun, wearing a straw hat for protection, and counted out the portion owing to the manager, to the villagers and to us. She often kept my father from quarrelling with his managers over their sloppy bookkeeping because she knew full well that no matter how dishonest they were, my father needed them. "Patience," she would say. "They need to eat, too. And, besides, that's how it is done."

I now realize how much my mother must have left unsaid, because she never once complained. She lived in Sabbalon with my father two years when I was not yet old enough to attend school and never once did she say that she missed her family and friends or the more cordial life of Teheran. The typical Iranian woman, the traditional matron, is by style a complainer, apparently believing that if she says that all is going well, something terrible will befall her family; someone might even put a curse on them. And so it has become a sort of cultural expression to be continually whining.

Sima was also much more independent of her husband than most Iranian women were. Because she had to live much of her married life separated from my father, she took many important family decisions. She had a quick mind and was fluent in French and English as well as Persian and Turkish. Never worried about public censure, she was a stylish dresser, and she bought most of her outfits in Europe on the many trips that she took abroad with my father. She was the most important person in my life apart from my grandmother Roghieh, and I wanted to grow up to be just like her. I did not realize that she was a special Moslem woman and that we were all privileged. I thought everyone was as open-minded as my family. It was not until I grew up that I understood how exceptional my mother was, that I knew how rare our kind of tolerance. Even when she was a young woman, there were signs of the growing gap between the Westernized, forward-looking elite and the mass of poorer, suspicious Iranians. But she and her friends could ignore the occasional public criticism of their behaviour by the country's *mullahs*. In her day, the Shah was winning most of his battles against the guardians of Islam.

In April 1960, my mother's entire family was gathered for the weekend—the Islamic weekend is Thursday and Friday—in my grandparents' summer house in Shemiran. In those days Shemiran was just a small but well-off summer community about one hour's drive north of downtown Teheran. There the city's wealthier families built their weekend retreats behind high walls that hid large gardens. They kept servants all year round but visited only during the spring, summer and fall because the drive was considered too long and the location too bleak in winter.

My uncles had built villas all around, but the Friday evening meal was always taken with my grandparents, Mahmoud and Roghieh. My brother Cyrus had been born just a few months before, a source of great joy because my mother had had such difficulty conceiving after I was born. We had spent most of the day in the garden. Then, at about 4:00 P.M., my grandmother went up to her room to say her prayers.

Apart from Roghieh, the Salmans were not very religious. We had very little contact with the turbaned *mullahs*, many of whom were no doubt powerful, but many of whom were also beggars who did little to keep themselves clean. Only Roghieh visited a mosque from time to time and we rarely invited a *mullah* into our home. In that, we were typical of our social group but very unlike the majority of Iranians, to whom religion is as much an expression of nationalism as a code of ethics. The Shi'a faith has distinguished Iran from many of its Moslem neighbours, and for decades it has fed the desire to rid the country of foreign influences.

That afternoon, we were twelve grandchildren waiting for Roghieh to finish her prayers so that we could all go for a walk to my uncle's garden next door and enjoy the end of the warm spring day. Grandmother had promised to point out on the way all the flowers that had bloomed since our last visit. Roghieh had inexhaustible patience for her grandchildren. Every night when I was staying with her in Teheran, she would wrap me in a blanket and tell me the fables of old Persia. Always, a little chocolate would be waiting for me under the pillow.

But that day she was long in coming down, so my cousin Lili and I ran upstairs to hurry her along. When we quietly entered her bedroom, we saw grandmother kneeling on a prayer mat, her body bent forward and her forehead resting on the floor. We called gently, but there was no reply. We called again. Still not a murmur. We ran downstairs to call our parents.

My grandmother had been suffering from a heart condition and the family guessed immediately what must have happened. One of my uncles drove to Teheran to get a doctor, but it was too late.

I was just a child, but even I remember the great outpouring of grief for Roghieh. The matriarch of our large family, she had run her household with firmness and tolerance. She had given each of her children a sense of ambition and she had had real power in the family, not the kind given by law or even by the Koran. She was sixty-three when she died. For the first week after her death, about fifty or sixty people came to visit her Teheran house each day. Lunch and dinner had to be provided. All the uncles and aunts sent their servants and drivers to help my mother. The closest friends returned every day. There were tables filled with special pastries made only for such occasions. Even the more liberated women friends wore their lacy *chadors* out of respect. My brother and I were considered too young to stay in the house during the two-week period of mourning so we went to stay at a friend's house until the most hectic time was over.

In its all-consuming sorrow and ritual my grandmother's funeral was typically Iranian. As a Westernized Iranian, I am aware that to outsiders there are several customs which seem to stand out as visible proof of our backwardness. A Moslem funeral is one. The death of a family member, within the close, self-sufficient unit that is the extended family in Iran, hits at the very core of a Moslem's life. Iranians, like Moslems in general, are very emotive. Funerals are occasions for loud mourning, weeping, even self-punishment. I have seen women pull their hair out, bang their heads against walls, shriek themselves to exhaustion. A funeral is also an important social occasion and a person of wealth is very careful to make certain that no expense is spared. In Iran, you could measure the extent to which a family had become Westernized simply by looking at how much commotion and wailing was present at its funerals. It is also true that most Iranians view those from the West as people with few emotions, who seem to care little when someone close to them dies.

The Friday night gathering of the Salmans changed after

my grandmother's death. The eight children and the numerous grandchildren no longer met at Roghieh's Teheran mansion or at the summer place in Shemiran. Instead, my uncles and aunts took turns hosting smaller groups. The family focus was gone. My grandfather, the founder of the big, money-making Salman construction firm, died about two years later, having never found another person on whom he could rely to see to his every need as Roghieh had done. That left my mother, my brother, my Uncle Fayegh and myself living alone in the big Teheran house with its high, decorated ceilings and wall murals, while my father continued to live in Sabbalon. Eventually, we sold the house and moved into a spacious apartment.

But there was worse to come. I was eleven years old when my world changed irrevocably. By then we were well established in the routine of alternating between Teheran and the village. I loved the school I attended; it was run by an order of Italian nuns, and the language of instruction for the mostly foreign students was English. As one of the few Iranian Moslem students in the Catholic school I escaped religious studies in any form. One day my mother came to pick me up at school in the chauffeured car. She seemed especially lighthearted. She hugged me and asked, "Sousan, did you have a wonderful day today?"

I happily launched into a story about one of the sterner nuns who taught me, but she was barely listening.

"Sousan, I've been to the doctor today. I probably didn't tell you, but I've been having some pain in my stomach. Anyway, the doctor says it's ulcers, not cancer at all. Here, all along, I've been thinking it might be cancer."

It was typical of my mother that she had said nothing of her troubles, not even to my father, it turned out. Only now, when she felt the danger had passed, did she mention her fears. But what she did not tell us was that she did not completely believe the ulcer diagnosis. The doctor she had consulted was the husband of her good friend, and to have gone for a second opinion would have been insulting. So she did nothing and said nothing.

Shortly afterwards, we set off to spend the summer in Sabbalon. After we had been there about two weeks, the house was again filled with friends and relatives — about thirty of them in all — also visiting for the season. But it was to be a difficult summer. My father's younger sister was killed in a gruesome car crash, and he fell into a deep depression. For a time we all became joyous again because my mother discovered that she was pregnant after years of trying; however, it soon became evident that all was not well with her. At first, her stomach pains, nausea, vomiting and loss of weight were attributed to her pregnancy. But when we went back to Teheran for the fall, my Aunt Tootie, the dentist, forced my mother to get another opinion, and the family received the terrible news: her disease was cancer after all.

I try never to think back to the months that followed. She was forced to undergo an abortion and even though the doctors attempted an operation, they found it was simply too late to do any good. My father and my Uncle Fayegh took her to Europe for tests and surgery, but there was little that even the more advanced Western medical technology could do for her. They stayed in Switzerland for two months, trying to find a cure, but in the end they had to come home without hope.

By the month of March it was evident that my mother was dying. In the last weeks, my father brought in two nurses to be with her night and day. The Teheran apartment started to fill up with friends who came to say their last goodbyes. Many times she could not see them, but they continued to come anyway.

April is such a beautiful month in Iran, full of delicate spring greens and a generous sun that does not yet overpower the land. I had just returned from a ballet class to my Aunt Tootie's

house, where my brother and I were staying. The chauffeur
was to come to pick us up and take us to see mother. When
he was late in arriving, I called the apartment. When someone
answered I could hear in the background the dolorous sound
of a *mullah* praying. I started to scream. I wanted the voice
to go away, because I knew what it meant. My brother, too
young to understand my rage, stared at me wide-eyed. When
my father's sister Ashraf came to get us, she was wearing black.
I wanted to hit her, pull those horrible clothes off. Somehow,
they managed to get me into the car and to the apartment. I
ran in, past my father and my uncles and aunts, and went
straight to my mother's bedroom. The bed was freshly made. I
buried my face in her cushion, then threw myself on her
favourite armchair. I was half-crazy, screaming and crying. I
just wanted to catch her scent on the things that she had always
used as if in some way I could touch her by touching the
things that were hers.

My father grabbed hold of me and shook me, but I only
sobbed.

"Why did she leave us? She loved us so much. How could
she leave us here?"

Later they gave me tranquillizers to help me sleep. In Iran,
children do not attend funerals. Iranians believe that they
will be marked for life by such sorrow. My mother just disappeared from my life in April 1966.

At my mother's death, my father was faced with a difficult
decision about my future and that of my brother, who was
then only six. In Iran, without a mother to care for young
children, a man often finds himself unable to cope. And in
my father's case there were logistical problems to overcome.
He had on his hands a young girl reaching puberty and a young
boy who hardly realized how much he had lost. Sabbalon
was not the right place to educate two young people. I made
it clear that I did not want to live with my Aunt Tootie, who

had offered to take us in. I found her cold compared to my own mother, and I was jealous of the love that she showed her own children. The only option was to send me away to school.

My father gave me a choice. I could go to a boarding school in France: on one of his recent trips there he had visited some schools and found one to his liking. Or I could go live with one of my three uncles who were living in North America at that time: Ardeshir, Amir or Darius. After my mother died they had held a family meeting and decided to invite me and my brother, when he was older, to live with one of them.

I felt terribly torn. I had anticipated going abroad to school some day because all my friends and cousins were already doing so. But I did not feel ready. North America did not appeal to me. It seemed so much farther away than France, which I had visited as a girl and of which I had vague memories. But there, at least, I could be with family. I decided to go to Ann Arbor, Michigan, where my Uncle Amir was a professor of dentistry at the university.

On the morning of July 15, 1966, my father, Uncle Fayegh, Aunt Tootie, my brother and I set off for the new Teheran airport. The night before, my father had come to my room carrying a little gift. It was a gold chain with a gold coin stamped with the Persian symbol for Allah.

"Here, take this with you," he said, putting it around my neck. "You are going to a foreign country, one that is very different from Iran. It is not a Moslem country, but Allah will always be with you. You will never stop being Iranian. If you are ever unhappy, you can always come home."

As I boarded the airplane, I was already dreaming of when I would come back. I had no thoughts for where I was going. America? What was that? That was where my uncles had disappeared to for years of study. That was where all the catalogues about the latest appliances and farm equipment came from, the latest cars, the latest gadgets, the latest *every-*

thing. The airplane was a sleek new jet proudly bearing the blue and white of Iran's own airline. It was a new gadget and it belonged to Iran. As I was flying off, America had already arrived in Iran, but I would not know it until I had come home.

Chapter Two

Growing Up American

The apple blushes
the quince goes yellow
with the sickness of desire
and thus the garden teaches us
the story of Love.

FARROKHĪ

 What I noticed first about Ann Arbor was that there were no walls around the houses. If you wanted to, you could look right into the living room of a neighbour and make out what program he was watching on television. People did not feel the need to hide their possessions or their women the way Persians did after centuries of conquering and being conquered. The early

Persians, the Achaemenians of the seventh century B.C. and their empire-building king, Cyrus the Great, had given way to the Macedonians under Alexander the Great around 330 B.C., and subsequent centuries had seen a parade of dynasties. We were conquered by Turks and overrun by the Mongol tribesmen of Genghis Khan. No wonder we built walls not just to protect our gardens from the wind on the desert, but to hide our belongings from those who might covet them. Here in Ann Arbor there were expanses of spongy-soft lawns and gardens exposed to the curious. Such gardens hid nothing and offered no mystery, not like the Persian garden which always surprised the visitor who penetrated the high stone walls surrounding a Persian house.

America was everything that we in Iran thought it might be. Two of my Salman uncles, Amir and Ardeshir, lived in Ann Arbor, and a third, Darius, lived in Los Angeles; they had all acquired a well-polished portion of the American dream. Amir, with whom I went to live, was a dentist who had made a fortune on the stock market and in real estate. He lived in a luxurious house, high on a hill. Every inch of floor space was covered with the most intricate Persian carpets made to measure and shipped directly from Iran; the walls showed off Iranian workmanship in paintings and sculptures. Heavily worked silver tables and decorations gave lustre to every corner. Full-time American servants kept everything tidy to suit my Aunt Soraya's very demanding standards. Their American friends called it the Persian castle.

But it was all the gadgets of my new life that kept me perpetually intrigued. Amazed, I pressed a button and found that music suddenly filled my room or that I could talk to my aunt in the kitchen even though I was in the bedroom. And I could take as many hot showers as I pleased without having to worry that the water might run out. No one seemed to bother about wasting electricity; even the rich in Teheran always went about the house turning off unneeded lamps. In winter, I discovered that no one thought to conserve fuel; every room was hot enough for summer clothing. In Teheran, the capital of an oil-exporting nation, the wealthy covered up with sweaters and the poor did without heat, except for their small cooking fires.

My favourite outings were to the supermarkets, gleaming wonders that contained all the food one could hope to find, all under one roof. There was no need to visit a dozen little shops as we did at home. Still, my uncles waited eagerly for friends and relatives coming from Iran to bring with them Persian sweets and caviar, the best of which comes from the Caspian Sea north of Teheran. Every six months they received a special shipment of long-grained Persian rice. To compromise on the quality of rice was unthinkable to a wealthy Iranian.

Despite such luxuries, I was a lonely child.

"You're here with us to get a good education," my Uncle Amir said to me shortly after I arrived, "and we are going to make certain that you get one. We're going to start by speaking to you only in English."

They stuck strictly to that rule. Their two sons, Andy and Alex, had been born in the States and spoke no Persian. Right from the start, I was isolated by my own inability to speak English and was unable to express how terribly homesick I was. The Americans I met all seemed so distant to me. In Iran, even complete strangers kissed on the cheek when introduced. Friends hugged freely in greeting. How could I become accustomed to a society that was sparing even with its handshakes?

When I received letters from home, I hid for hours in my room to read them over and over again, trying to keep my links with Iran strong, my memories fresh. No one had much sympathy for me. After all, many of my first cousins were in exactly the same situation. My Uncle Amir and Aunt Soraya always had at least two or three Iranian children other than

their own living with them. They regarded it as their duty—
something people from the West might find hard to understand—to make it possible for others in the extended family
to get the sort of first-class education that was still not available in Iran and to earn a place in a wealthier society.

The first thing my uncle and aunt arranged for me was a
visit to a doctor and dentist for a complete check-up. New
and more effective braces were immediately prescribed; I owe
my smile to my uncle and aunt. They also took me shopping
to buy a new wardrobe, making me feel like a Cinderella who
had found her fairy godmother. I should have been grateful,
but I cried myself to sleep every night. I wanted to be in Iran.

In the fall, I went off to the local junior high school and
was placed in grade seven, my English only slightly improved
after the summer's exertions. As the only foreign student in
the school, I became a notable oddity. In 1969, Vietnam was
the only foreign country students seemed to know about and
they saw that through the distorted images of war. Iran they
had never heard of, and even my teachers had no idea how
to locate it on the map. One student who bothered to speak
to me asked me if I came "from the place where people live
in tents in the desert." Americans were so unaware of the
country whose name would inspire fear and hatred just over
a decade later.

At home, I was a stranger in another way. My aunt, a tall
blonde with fine features, born in Iran of Russian parents, ran
the house with a precision that allowed little room for a moon-
ing, pining teenager. We were under orders to come home
straight after school; there was to be no television on week-
days; I was not to wear jeans outside the house, or curlers
and a bathrobe outside the bathroom; make-up was forbidden.
Dating was also prohibited until I reached fourteen, and then I
was not to see Iranian boys because the ones who lived near
us tended to be several years older than I and they might
distract me from my goal, which was to look and sound like

an American. For my first year, I visited a private tutor every day after school for extra English lessons. Several times a week, Andy and I also attended a finishing school where we learned to sit properly, use cutlery, dance and walk with good posture. My uncle and aunt were determined to give us the best of all things American. But not one of us forgot for one moment that we were imitating Americans only to become better Iranians.

After a year, my brother Cyrus was sent to the United States so that he could start his education. Only seven years old at the time, he was sent alone on a flight to England. My Uncle Kurosh was there on business and was to pick him up for the night before putting him on a connecting flight to Detroit the following morning. Because he spoke no English, Cyrus carried a large sheet of paper, tied around his neck with a cord, with useful questions written in both English and Persian (Where is the bathroom, please? May I have a drink of water, please?). Unfortunately, when he arrived in England, my uncle was a couple of hours late in meeting him at the airport, and the child sat alone, wondering if he had simply been abandoned.

After he made it safely to Ann Arbor and he could give in to sobs of fear, he told me, "Nobody came for such a long time. I thought they just wanted to get rid of me, so they sent me far away."

Poor little fellow. And now, instead of living with me in Ann Arbor as had been planned all along, he was being sent on to Los Angeles, where my Uncle Darius's children were closer to him in age than the three of us living with Uncle Amir. At the end of that summer, he went off, alone and frightened, with the same sheet of paper hanging from his neck, and we were separated once again. The shock of changing cultures so drastically so soon after losing my mother caused him terrible psychological problems later. The hardest part was that he went to live with a family where no Persian was spoken: my uncle's wife was American born. One morning, about six months after moving there, he woke up to find that he could neither speak nor understand Persian any longer. To this day, when Cyrus is at a family gathering, one of us has to translate for him when the conversation turns to Persian.

Somehow I grew up, a strange mixture of Iranian and American.

When I was sixteen, Uncle Amir announced at the dinner table: "It's time for you to go home for a short visit this summer. Your father would like to see you."

Home. The village. My father. I was finally being released. America had all the comforts, the consumer goods, the best in entertainment and education, but all I wanted was the dry, hot, summer air of Iran and the noisy, emotional embrace of my people. I wanted to go back then — and if only I could, I would go back even now.

That summer in Iran, spent mostly in Sabbalon, was magical. Relatives came to spend the summer with us, including several of my first cousins who had come home from schools all around the world. Even Seemin, a general's daughter and my best childhood friend, who had spent summers with me in Sabbalon, rushed from Teheran to be with me. Every day seemed to be a party. My father showed off his wine, the cooks turned out the delicacies I had missed for so long and the nights were filled with the sounds of musical instruments while my father recited selections from the writings of the great poets. It was as it had always been, with Seemin beside me ready to find a spot of innocent trouble, but there were signs of change, too. Now, when my father's drivers took Seemin, my cousins and me into Rezayeh, there were discotheques to visit and bars where women were permitted. My women relatives, much less strict than my Aunt Soraya, even encouraged me to dress up a little in my new American clothes. We could wander around freely, wearing our minis, bandanas and hot pants. People stared and occasionally scowled at us, but we were just back from abroad or from Teheran and we had picked up the latest trends; we felt as if we were at the vanguard of change, of fun, of modernization. To be free to walk down the street with my hair flowing, my legs proudly exposed in a Moslem country that just thirty years before had banned the *chador* — it was almost unbelievable.

But I was too young and too much in a hurry to take more than a blurred snapshot of the Iran that had been taking shape in my absence. Soon I was back in the United States under the disciplined rule of my uncle and struggling to fit into an alien culture that I both admired and rejected. Finally, when I was eighteen, I was sent to a private art college, Woodberry, in Los Angeles to study design, a field I had always been interested in. For the first time in my life in the United States, I felt what it was like to be free, to come and go as I pleased. My Uncle Darius's household was much more easy-going than Uncle Amir's, and I found myself making friends, especially from amongst the huge contingent of Iranian students in the city. Under the Shah, funds had been made available to lower- and middle-class students to study abroad and many had taken advantage of the opportunity to do so. They joined the hundreds of wealthy students who were sent by their parents to UCLA and Stanford to finish off their education.

I loved Los Angeles. The climate reminded me of home. I was old enough to enjoy the outdoor parties, the socializing by the swimming pool and the non-stop night life. The revolutionary drop-outs involved in local student politics were alien to me: I had nothing in common with students who wandered about barefoot, their hair tied back in braids whether they were male or female. I didn't drink alcohol and I had no interest in trying drugs. I was still more Iranian than American and my interests were those of a well-brought-up débutante: fashion, sports and young men.

One day a friend said to me, "Listen, Sousan. You have

to come with me to a lecture at UCLA. There's a prof there who gives great talks on Iran. He tells us about all kinds of things — things our parents don't tell us.''

I was ready to try anything new then, visit anywhere, talk to anyone. My curiosity was unleashed after years of having been shackled. Why not go to UCLA? Besides, I really liked the Iranian UCLA students that I had met. I found in their easy, friendly company some of the warmth that was lacking in my life.

That afternoon we attended a lecture on living conditions in Iran given by a professor who had recently visited the country. He spoke about the feudal farming system and the large private landowners such as my father, who, despite the reforms, still controlled much of the countryside and ruled their villages like mediaeval lords. Then he told us that up to 70 per cent of the people were illiterate, that most had only minimal hygiene, that Iran was ruled by two hundred power-ful families who in one way or another had managed to lock up all the nation's wealth. Both sides of my family could be counted in that two hundred.

It was the first time that I had heard anything critical about how my country was run. The lecturer showed slides of poor Iranians — their rustic, flowered clothing dirty and ragged — huddled in mud-brick houses. I was shocked to see such images. My father's own villagers were so well off by com-parison. I wanted to do something for them and yet I was well aware that my very ignorance proved how far removed I was from their lives. I became determined that when I went back I would follow the example set by my relatives. When-ever the Salmans signed a lucrative contract or the Azadis had a good crop, they pledged a portion to their preferred charities. My aunts were always careful to see that their servants and their relatives had all that they needed. Whenever there was a mishap in a servant's family, my uncles and aunts provided comfort and financial support until the trouble had passed.

But even as my eyes and heart opened to a new, harsher side of Iran, I did not question anything so basic as my right to be rich and have servants. And yet, that was just what the more radical students wanted me to do, I discovered. After the lecture, in the cafeteria, the students talked about the Shah.

"He is corrupt and he steals from his own people. He suppresses the freedom of the press," one young man said.

I was shocked to hear a student whose tuition was being paid for by the Shah talk so bitterly about him. Up to then, like all good students, I had learned to speak of the Shah in the same reverential tones used for God and Country. The three went together in an indestructible triangle of authority.

Another student told us, "We're on a list, you know. Every student who comes to these gatherings is on Savak's list."

Whenever the talk turned to the Shah's dreaded secret police, Savak, the students became nervous. Rumour had it that any student who had been involved in an anti-Shah demonstration while in the United States was immediately arrested when he stepped back onto Iranian soil. And sometimes the family did not see him again or even find out what had happened to him. Worse, the family was subjected to official harassment, either at work or through government services that were suddenly slow in coming. The stories were no doubt exaggerated, but they were prevalent enough to inspire fear in my family, especially the Salmans, who had extensive holdings in Iran and many government contracts.

The other students found me naïve. They wanted radical change in Iran. Although the lecturers themselves were not politically motivated, the Iranian student groups that promoted the talks hoped that by awakening people like me to the poverty and inequalities in Iran, we, too, would slowly become politicized. They wanted us to go home and demand reforms: freedom of the press, the abolition of Savak, a true political opposition and the curtailment of the Shah's mighty power. The Shah ruled under the 1906–1907 charter, which set up a constitutional monarch with vast authority. He could hire and fire the cabinet, top military officers and even public prosecutors. He could convene or dissolve Parliament at his whim and easily reject laws that did not suit him. I could not agree with the students that the Shah had too much power — my family were staunch monarchists — but I was fascinated by how differently they viewed our king. In their eyes he was a power-hungry puppet of foreign states, who was out of touch with his people. Although I attended only a few of the controversial lectures, my family found out soon enough about my involvement with radical Iranian students.

The way they found out says a great deal about Iranian men and Iranian society. Shortly after arriving in Los Angeles, I had met a close friend of my family, a thirty-year-old married man. He was very friendly in the Iranian way, but I soon began to notice that he tried to spend a lot of time near me, especially when he found me alone in the house. My experiences with men were limited to the attentions of just one Iranian teen-ager who swore love to me and then married someone else (he told me that he had been forced to marry because the woman said she was pregnant). It took me a long time to realize that this man's attention was unusual.

Finally, one day while we were alone in my uncle's house, he said very boldly, "Sousan, I love you and I want to have you."

I stared at him, shocked. "But you're like a brother to me. And what about your wife? You're married."

"She doesn't matter. I'll get a divorce. I want to marry you."

I managed to fight him off when he tried to kiss me, but before he left he told me to think about his proposal and that he would be back. I was too frightened to say anything to my uncle. I hoped that the man would simply go away. But he did not. He continued to press himself on me for several months and finally, when it was evident that I would not agree to become his mistress, he said, "I'm warning you, Sousan, I will have you. And, if not, I will tell your uncles the kinds of things that will make them take you away from here.''

At first, I did not take his threat seriously. What terrible things could he possibly say to my uncles? I did have one weak point. My Uncle Amir was already concerned that my grades were low that semester. If he heard that I was wasting my time, I would be ordered back to Ann Arbor. But I continued to resist my unwanted suitor and, in the Iranian female's way, I felt so embarrassed and guilty about being caught up in that sort of situation that I told no one about my predicament.

Soon afterwards, I received a call from my Uncle Amir.

"Sousan, I am disappointed in you. How could you let us down after all we have done for you? Your marks are terrible and now I hear that you spend your time hanging around with a bunch of radicals and getting into all sorts of trouble. If your marks are not in the A or B level this semester, you will be sent back to Iran. We have done as much as we can for you. This is no way to repay us.''

I could guess where my uncle had received his intelligence but by now it was too late to tell him about my aggressive suitor. He would never believe me. That second semester, I tried hard, but after missing so many classes I could not bring my marks up, even though by now, for the first time in my life, I was not looking forward to being sent home. The United States seemed to offer the best of everything in education. Where would I be able to study design in Iran? And, then, where could I live in Iran? In my father's village in winter there would be nothing to do after sundown. Suddenly I began to fear losing all the things that I had come to take for granted in America.

When my semester grades came in, many were in the Cs. Without further discussion, arrangements were made for me to fly back to Ann Arbor to pack up my belongings. Just before I left Los Angeles, my persistent suitor came to see me.

"All you have to do is say you'll marry me and you can stay

here," he said. "I told you I could make things happen and I've proven it to you."

I ran from the room.

I stayed in Ann Arbor for just one week. Although little was said, I could sense the disappointment that my aunt and uncle felt: I was the single failure after many years of rearing other people's children. My father had not even been consulted. This was a decision made strictly by the Salman uncles who were paying for my support.

At one point I tried to tell them about my would-be lover, but, just as I expected, they did not believe me. Or perhaps by that time they were just so disappointed that they did not even listen. If my marks had been high, perhaps other things would have been forgiven. But the Iranian elite believes in high achievers. Its members see education as an investment in the future strength of the family, even for women whom they expect to marry and be supported by men. Education is part of the dowry that makes a woman more attractive to a prospective husband.

I did not know then that what my uncle and aunt had in mind was to send me home for just a short time to chasten me and then to bring me back again, presumably less recalcitrant. But their plan never materialized because, once back in Iran, I became caught up in the excitement and the headlines of a new, oil-rich country, an Iran that sparkled with its own pride, an Iran that was swept up in its own rush to have the very best, faster than anybody else on earth.

Chapter Three

The False Jewel

*O take me, take me, heart-fondling hope,
to the city where verses and passions bloom.*

FORUGH FARROKHZAD

 When I landed in Teheran, it was a bright, hot, dry day in July. I was eighteen years old and feeling very much a woman returning to a country that I had known only as a child. As we drove from the airport I noticed, at the northern entrance to the city, a tall, elegant tower rising just ahead of us. Its delicate arches were intricately tiled.

"What's that?" I asked my father, who had come, along with some of my closest relatives, to welcome me.

"Ah, that's the Shahyad, the king's tribute to Persian monarchy," he said. "I guess the country can afford such monuments now."

That year, 1973, the image of the rich Persian was born. Iran had already been growing steadily, fed by the gushing oil of the desolate desert regions of Khuzestan, its progress lit by flaring gas. But the brief, intense, Arab-Israeli war later that year, in October, made us rich overnight. To bolster Egypt's attack on Israel, the Shah and Iran joined with Arab countries in using the oil cartel OPEC, the Organization of Petroleum Exporting Countries, as a weapon against Israeli allies. The cartel applied an embargo on Israel's friends and the price of crude oil rose dramatically. Overnight, Iran's revenues for the sale of that precious commodity went from $5 billion annually to $20 billion. So much instant wealth for a country that had been poor for centuries and where the ownership of the oil fields had been entirely in foreign hands until the 1950s. It was the beginning of heady times both for my country and for me. The future, like the desert, had an ever-receding horizon.

But the truth was that I had been kicked out of the United States by the Salman side of my family. I had not measured up to the family ideal. I had done badly at school and I had disgraced the family by mixing with the wrong type of Iranian student. My own relatives in the United States had rejected me in a very public way by ordering me back to Iran. I was full of foreboding that on my return to Iran I would be disowned. I was not far wrong. Gossip about my presumed drug habit and my probable pregnancy had preceded me even though nothing could have been further from the truth. But in Iran, gossip alone was enough to condemn me. After all, I was a woman, fully expected to be so blameless that not even gossip should attach itself to me. Men did not have to live with the same sort of strictures. But I have to confess that in those days even I accepted that double standard quite readily. I believed that if gossip trailed a woman, there had to be some hidden indiscretion, even though my own case proved to me how wrong that assumption could be.

Although my father was as warm and loving as ever, my other relatives were careful to see little of me. The very issue of where I should live was fraught with embarrassment. No one on my mother's side of the family was interested in providing me with a home in Teheran, and both my father and I thought that living in the village would be a heavy punishment. According to the social rules, it would not be proper for me to live alone in Teheran, even if a full-time servant stayed with me. In the end, my father struck a deal with his sister Ashraf, a retired school principal and a widow, who was grateful for a little rent money.

The following three months were among the most miserable of my life. Although she meant well, my aunt had an authoritarian manner. A sophisticated, chestnut-haired woman who had travelled widely, Ashraf was the family's female intellectual. She always teased her daughters and nieces because they wasted their trips to Europe on buying clothes.

"What about the museums, the art galleries? All you know about is shopping," she complained, not always good-naturedly.

I soon found that I could not live with her. After enrolling at a private English language college and overcoming my father's concerns about my leaving my aunt, I moved into a nearby boarding house filled with students and workers from out of town who needed a temporary residence in the city. Once again I was living under an ultimatum: improve my marks or move to the village.

What were the options for an upper-class girl of my age in Iran in 1973, the year of the great economic liberation? We were not permitted to work if working meant taking just any job. It was becoming permissible to work as a professional, like my Aunt Tootie, the dentist, or several of my cousins who had become physicians. Otherwise, should we not be so talented, our fathers, our brothers, our uncles and our husbands supported us. It was unheard of for us to live alone, so if I did not do well at school and my father wanted me to return to the village, I would have to go.

There was one other choice, and it soon became evident that both sides of the family saw it as the best way of taking care of a problem member. That was to be married off, as quickly as possible, to the first eligible man who came along.

Almost obsessively aware of all these pressures, I was sensitive to every snub, every sign of coldness from my relatives, such as those who out of pity invited me to their homes, then took great care to ignore me while I was with them. It was a matter of great shame that a family member of the Salmans, some of the richest builders in the city, was forced to live in a boarding house because no one would take her in. No outsiders, and few even within the family, ever knew where I had gone to live. I kept even more quiet about it when one of the few cousins to know said to me: "You know that boarding house you're in? Watch it. I hear it's full of prostitutes. Oh, sure, they say they're students or secretaries. But everybody knows better. Otherwise why would they be living on their own in Teheran?"

Despite the depression I felt about my status, I slowly began to know the exciting city that Teheran had become in my absence. A metropolis of more than four and a half million people, it descended on the north from the foothills of the Alborz Mountains, sloping gently but surely down into the flat desert. With new hotels, highrises, housing projects and roads in various stages of completion, the city could claim construction as probably its biggest business. The poplar seedlings that Reza Khan had forced his soldiers to plant in the 1930s when the city had only 35,000 inhabitants had matured to give leafy shade to the boulevards, and the water that was channelled from the mountains and swept down the gutters on either side of every street kept up a soothing chatter all day and all night.

The rich lived high in the foothills in large mansions surrounded by massive walls that hid scented gardens, orchards and swimming pools. The middle class were lower down and the very poor lived in the hot, dusty, southern part of the city, below the railway line that acted as a divider, right near the massive Behesht Zahra cemetery where rich, poor and middle class alike went when they died. When it rained, the fresh shower that bathed the northern gardens turned into a debris-filled torrent as it rushed down the gutters and finally became a flood in the poorest quarters. The bazaar with its winding, covered alleyways was in the centre of the city, but I never went there until I was in my twenties, nor did I have any cause to venture south of the busy shopping streets to see the Teheran of the poor, where the sheep, chickens and small entrepreneurs shared space on the crowded streets.

Together with my old girlfriends Seemin and Yossi, I started to visit the new discos, nightclubs and restaurants that seemed to be opening at the rate of one a week to cater to the growing number of young people with money to spend and acquired Western habits and tastes. The most popular gathering spots that season were two private, flashy discos called the Key Club and the Cheminee Club. But the most exclusive and most sought after was the Royal Club, a private sports, dining and gambling complex in the heart of the city. Along with tennis courts, stables for horses, fine trails, and golf and other sports, the club offered one of the best dining rooms in the city, an outdoor restaurant spread around the large swimming pool. At night, candle and flower arrangements floated on the pool's surface. Several times a year, when the French couturiers were bringing out their latest designs, the club flew in models and clothes from Paris for an intimate showing at the poolside.

The main clubhouse had several dining rooms with any number of superfluous waiters in black tie and white gloves. The large reception area was modelled after what was assumed to be a typical English club, complete with deep leather chairs, hunting prints displaying the greenest of pastures and even a moose head over a massive stone fireplace. Surrounded with the trappings of another culture, it was hard to remember that the desert stretched flat and uncompromising just south of the city.

In the afternoons, the wealthy, the well known and the merely beautiful would arrive for cocktails as a prelude to dinner. Having spent most of their days having manicures, pedicures and facials, the women would appear in their latest Diors and Chanels—their husbands, fathers or lovers having paid for a shopping trip to Paris. As for the men—industrialists, builders, import-exporters and politicians—they somehow always found the time to lounge around discussing which was the best of the new crop of restaurants. These beautiful people owed much of their ease to the Shah who, while I was studying in the United States, had led the country through a period of growth and modernization. In my absence, the rich had indeed become richer.

On all our outings I never had to worry about money. Although I was receiving an allowance from my father, I never actually had to pay for the expensive meals or for membership in the clubs. No one, especially the men, expected a woman to pay for herself. Instead, men in our group took turns picking up the rather hefty restaurant and bar bill.

I saw other aspects of the new Iran, too, and if I had not been so young and careless I might have realized that they were portents of future trouble. Everywhere I turned, in every government building, bank and factory, the proud Shah, his third wife, the Shahbanou Farah Diba, and their children stared down at me from posters, a constant reminder that God, King and Country were one in Iran. I was surprised to hear complaints even in our strongly royalist circles about the pervasive power of the royal family. Where once there had been almost obsequious respect, now there was contempt. The young who had just returned from studies abroad deplored the lack of freedom to express their opinion or to read a newspaper that was not heavily censored.

Businessmen complained even more vociferously about the corruption of the royal relatives: dozens of brothers, sisters, cousins, aunts and uncles of the Shah who made good use of their names and titles to make profits without really working for them. Most of my uncles' friends and business associates had bowed to pressure and had brought onto their boards of directors or into their companies relatives of the king, as silent partners; those royal leeches collected a good portion of the company earnings merely for making the right introductions to those government officers who were in charge of giving out contracts or purchasing for the state. My uncles, the Salmans, always refused to play by those rules, and even though, as the first major contractors in the country, they continued to receive large building projects such as hospitals, bridges and roads, after the oil boom of that year they saw many of their less principled competitors surge ahead of them.

When people complained, I noticed that they did so only privately or to their most trusted friends. No one knew where a spy of Savak, the Shah's secret police, might be listening. The wealthy had a great deal to lose by complaining too loudly.

One evening, a week before I was to help host a birthday party for Yossi at the Key Club (which she had rented for the night), my Aunt Ashraf called me.

"Sousan, some friends of the family have invited you out to the engineers' ball at the Hilton for next Tuesday night," she said. "You'll have to prepare your best outfit."

"But that's the night of Yossi's party," I complained. "Besides, I don't want to go to a boring party with people I don't even know."

But she insisted, and family life is such in Iran that you do not disobey an older member. After a while, I realized that the invitation was probably just a ruse to introduce me to some eligible bachelor. And, frankly, the idea was not completely unwelcome. I realized how vulnerable I was with no mother, my father far away in Azerbaijan, my brother too young and too distant to offer support and my uncles still angry with me. I knew I could not live comfortably in Iran without the help of a man. Although I had met a young man a few weeks before and he had joined my group of friends in our outings several evenings, I was open to being introduced to other men. I had grown up in the States, but I had not given up making a practical assessment of what I would need in a husband in Iran. He would have to be from a good family, because both sides of mine were in the top rank socially, and he would have to be wealthy to give me the life I was accustomed to.

The engineers' ball, held at the Hilton, was as dull as I imagined it might be, and I inwardly lamented having missed Yossi's party. As for eligible men, most of those I saw were old and had wives well anchored on their arms. The only man worth noticing was a handsome playboy, in his late thirties I imagined, who seemed to be escorting an attractive woman, but who kept flirting with all the others. He paid no attention to me and I soon ruled him out as well.

After deciding that I had been wrong about my aunt's motives, I simply forgot about the whole thing until about a week later when Aunt Ashraf called again.

"By the way, the night of the engineers' ball, there was a man there who met you and would like to meet you again. He wants to see if he is interested enough to pursue a relationship with you," she said, sounding very pleased with herself. "But I warn you, you don't stand much of a chance of catching this man, so don't be disappointed if he decides that after all he doesn't want to see you again. He's using the same couple who took you to the ball as the go-between."

After going on about how eligible he was, how he was the head of a large construction company, had never been married before and had no encumbrances, how so many women had already tried to snare him but had failed, she repeated again that I was not to get my hopes up.

"He wants to settle down and has been looking for a wife for the last four or five years. He's already been shown photographs of your cousin Samineh, but he wasn't interested.

Then we introduced him to your cousin Shideh — after all, she's ten years older than you and needs to get married a little more urgently. But, there, he just wasn't interested. So now we'll see what happens with you. It would be a shame to let such a good fish get away.''

She said little more, and I, unused to seeing formal match-making in action, treated the matter as a joke, trying hard to imagine which of the many uninteresting men I had seen that evening had suddenly taken a fancy to me.

The meeting took place several days later at the home of the go-between couple. I was accompanied by my Aunt Ashraf and my grandmother Ashi, who happened to be on a visit to Teheran. The invitation was for a late afternoon tea and we arrived promptly at 5:00 P.M. When we walked into the formal sitting room of their home I saw a tall, well-tanned, wavy-haired man, who stood up at our entrance, and I had to work hard to keep my shock from showing. My admirer was the playboy who had kept so many women entertained that night and who had said barely a word to me. All I could think was, ''But he's so old!''

Throughout our encounter, he almost never looked at me directly, but spoke freely with my aunt and grandmother. Even when he did ask me a question (''When did you come back from the States? Are you glad to be back?''), he seemed to be looking at a spot somewhere behind me, as if he must not inspect me too closely. But I was aware of his careful scrutiny. Because I treated the process as an odd, anachronistic custom, I was much more comfortable than he was, and I took time to notice that the grey at his temples was becoming, that his body was obviously firm as well as slim, that his clothes were expensive and well chosen and that he was, for an older man, rather handsome. His name was Bijan Amini and his age, I learned later, was thirty-nine.

After about an hour and a half of polite and inconsequential chat, the three of us got up and left. On the way home in the car I asked my aunt: ''What do you think, then? Isn't he old?''

Looking back on it, I realize that my aunt played a very crafty game, one that I suppose many Iranians have played. She carefully refrained from putting any pressure on me.

"I certainly liked him," she said judiciously. "He is very respectable, obviously. A very serious prospect. I am not sure how he reacted to you. He may not even propose to see you again. He's had so many women offering themselves to him. Who knows? The only drawback, I agree, is his age. You are only eighteen. But, then, even that could be an advantage. A younger man won't have his stature or his wealth. And with you being so much younger, he is likely to be very protective of you and more caring. Men like him, when they reach a certain age and they have everything they want, get pretty demanding with women, especially those of their own age, but with a younger woman it may be different."

My grandmother, the Qajar princess who had seen many suitors come and go in her large family, nodded and added: "Yes, he's a good one."

Although she was careful to say little more about Bijan, my aunt did mention that he owned his own construction firm, one of the largest in the city, which was then building a hospital, along with other projects; he was said to be in the process of building a sumptuous mansion in Shemiran, not far from the king's palace, Niavaran; and he was wealthy even by my uncles' standards.

Because she seemed not to be pushing me, I became more intrigued by the game and soon I came to see it as a challenge: would he reject me like all the others? And who did he think he was if he did? Wouldn't I be mortified if he did? We would see; maybe I would succeed where others had failed. I was not mature enough to realize that, from the moment I met Bijan, I began to measure myself by how he felt about me. I was caught by the age-old art of matchmaking. What had been a joke had turned into a test of whether I was attractive enough, interesting and exciting enough to ensnare this man who had come to look me over twice. It didn't strike me at the time that I had been paraded like a prize animal before a prospective buyer.

A few days later my aunt received another call from the go-betweens: Bijan wanted to see me again and was asking my aunt permission to take me out to dinner in the company of chaperones. Because we did not want him to find out that an Azadi and Salman was living in a boarding house, I rushed back to my aunt's to be ready the night that he and the chaperones came to pick me up. It proved to be an excruciating evening. We went to the Bistro Pop, a popular new restaurant, and Bijan was clearly nervous — much more so than I was. In between awkward pauses, he made attempts to start up a casual conversation with me, but he found it easier to talk business to the other man while his wife and I tried vainly to find something to say to each other. The go-betweens, who had now become our chaperones, were an older couple, about my father's age, and only Bijan seemed to find anything of interest to say to them. But he was at all times considerate to me and I liked his quiet manner.

After that, he asked me out several more times, always in the company of our chaperones, and each time we tried one of the new restaurants. Still reserved, he asked me mainly about my studies in the United States (he himself had graduated with first class honours in engineering from the University of Teheran). He rarely asked me anything truly personal. I asked him even fewer questions, partly because I was already well briefed and partly because I had been advised not to appear too curious.

After about a month of formal meetings, during which time it was understood that, if all went well, the dates would lead to marriage, I finally suggested, again through a third party, that the next time we should try going out alone together so that we could get to know each other better. It turned out that he found the notion perfect and had hesitated to suggest such a thing himself out of respect for my family, whose disapproval he feared.

Finally, after knowing him only in contrived settings, we went off together for an evening of dining and dancing, alone. Soon we were dating every second night, then every night. By then I had moved back into my aunt's house, not wanting to risk any gossip. I could tell that she regretted having been too strict with me and causing me to leave her home now that I was on the verge of marrying a wealthy man. Emotionally, I felt myself getting more and more involved with him—with his charm, his determined character and with the power that comes from being very wealthy. Bijan made my younger boyfriend seem uninteresting by comparison, and I soon stopped seeing him altogether, much to his disappointment.

I regard it as a weakness now that I found only men with that kind of wealth and personal power attractive. I liked to walk into a room with Bijan and see the immediate respect that he commanded, or go to a restaurant and see how the staff treated him with the courtesy reserved for favoured customers. I never thought then that I should strive for my own sense of worth. Iranian women derived their power, their status in society from their husbands, fathers or boyfriends. To make a good catch was to marry someone who gave you the best security and the greatest comfort in your life.

Everything about Bijan promised an exciting and luxurious life. I had heard that, as well as his mansion in Shemiran, he was building a villa on the Caspian Sea not far from where the king had his own compound. He also kept some of the best Arabian horses at the Royal Club, where he was a member, and he was always flying off to Europe for the fun of it.

He would say to me: "Sousan, when we are married I want you to have a suitcase packed and ready to go all the time in case I want us to leave immediately for London or Paris. We will be doing a lot of travelling."

Or: "When the house in Shemiran is finished I want you to pick out whatever furniture you want. We'll go shopping together and you can have anything at all."

More than anyone else I had ever met he had a clear sense of what he wanted out of life and he seemed to have such control over it — in sharp contrast to my casting about for some security, some safety. And those were the qualities I sought in a husband.

"I know exactly what I want to do after we are married," he said one day. "I can more or less retire from work. I have made a lot of money and I don't need any more. I want to stop now and have a family and spend time with my wife and children. I want to putter in the garden and do nothing very much but enjoy what I have earned. I have all the money I want."

When I met Bijan he had just come back from a two-year trip around the world with one of his partners. In Paris, where he often went to buy designer clothes, he had actually worked briefly as a model at the request of one of the large houses, because his features were so classically handsome. With him, I would never again have to worry about living in boarding houses.

Then, as we spent more and more time together, I realized that I was becoming fond of him. I began to feel that even if he did not have so much money, I would love and admire him. In the end, I knew I was not primarily interested in his wealth. I suppose I was lucky. In my vulnerable situation, and with the pressure I felt from my family, I probably would have ended up marrying someone at that time and it could just as easily have been someone less rich and much less fine and caring.

On a clear night in December 1973, two months after the Arab-Israeli war and the raising of oil prices, and three months after he had met me, Bijan drove with me up the winding road leading to the Alborz Mountains and parked at a lookout high above the city. We had enjoyed a long, romantic dinner and many glasses of Pouilly Fuisse and we looked down happily at the glittering city. From up there, Teheran could have been any Western city twinkling in neon splendour. The vast desert below the city, the mud-brick hovels of the poor, the smoke that rose from the brick kilns on the outskirts—all of that was hidden in the darkness. Nor would we have seen the poor even by day, mostly because we almost never ventured to southern Teheran, but in truth because it was easier not see them. The glitter was from a false jewel that lay at our feet.

That night Bijan kissed me and proposed marriage. My aunt had warned me: "If he asks you to marry, don't be foolish and tell him that you'll think about it the way young girls sometimes do. Because I warn you he won't come back if you do. He's a proud man."

But I didn't have to think about it. I was intoxicated that night. I was finally home and safe.

We were to marry in March, and shortly after formally asking for my hand from my father and my uncles in Iran and in the United States, Bijan went off to Paris for a couple of weeks. When he came back he brought me a suitcase full of gifts, including a complete riding outfit and saddle from England so that I would be appropriately dressed at the Royal Club.

One day he said, "Sousan, it's time for you to meet my family."

It may seem strange that I had agreed to marry him without knowing his family, but once my relatives had approved of him as socially suitable, I never gave his family a second thought, assuming that they would be like us: Westernized, well travelled and religiously liberal. He was very concerned that I might be nervous on the first meeting.

"If you feel at all uncomfortable during dinner, just give me a sign and I'll make an excuse and we'll leave right away," he assured me.

But the dinner went off well enough and I saw very little evidence of the fanatical religiosity that would cause me so many grave troubles later on. Members of my family, better versed in the ways of the country, probably had some hint of how different they were from us, but they said nothing, not wanting to endanger the proposed marriage to a wealthy and powerful man.

The Aminis lived in a large, three-storey house in the Usefabad section. Bijan's mother, Sarje, and two unmarried older sisters, Parvaneh and Fatimeh, lived on one floor, his brother, Ali, a doctor, with his wife and two children on another, and his younger sister, Nasrine, and her husband, Parviz, a psychologist, on another. The house itself was modest, but, as in many middle-class Iranian homes, there was a wealth of Persian carpets on the floor, in some rooms, one piled on top of another. Amongst the rather ordinary furniture were some notable antiques which I later learned Bijan had bought for them. The mother and sisters were well dressed in European silk dresses and I thought little of the fact that they wore long sleeves and used very little make-up, or that the mother kept a scarf on indoors.

Throughout the dinner, they watched my every move, but they gave no hint of anything other than pleasure at meeting me. I remember that I wore a mini-skirt, the leggy look being in vogue that season, and black patterned nylons, my long, blonde hair loose down my back — all affronts to religious Moslems. I was used to moving in circles that took their inspiration from the West and I really had no idea that I was marrying into a family that, like the vast majority of Iranians, not only disapproved of our habits, but hated us for them. They saw anything that came from outside the country as evidence of selling out to a corrupt foreign culture. I suppose the Aminis did not dare show their displeasure because Bijan wanted me. I was, after all, an upper-class woman and a good match. As for my family, Bijan's worth was in his personal drive and they did not care about his family origins.

In Iran, the engagement is a very formal matter, and at one point Bijan's entire family came at a prearranged time to my Aunt Ashraf's house to propose marriage. Before arriving, Bijan sent a huge basket of orchids by his chauffeur. In attendance from my side of the family were my father, who had travelled down from Rezayeh, my Uncle Kurosh and his family, and my dear Uncle Fayegh, with whom I had lived as a child.

After chatting casually for about half an hour, Bijan said to my father: "We have come because I want to ask you all for permission to marry Sousan."

My father replied: "We agree to the marriage. My only concern is that Sousan is young and I would like to be sure that she will be able to continue her studies."

"Of course," said Bijan. "I would also very much like her to do so."

After everyone toasted us, Bijan presented me with a gold band, and I was officially engaged to be married. What a difference that simple promise made. Suddenly, I was no longer a social outcast but a woman worth knowing. Invitations to teas, dinners and outings started to arrive from friends and relatives I had not heard from since my return to Iran. It had taken the approval of a man in a very man-controlled world to give me back some respectability.

We were married on March 12, 1974, and the ceremony, held in the large mansion of the family patriarch, Uncle Kamel, was lavish with flowers, fruit and pastries. As is the custom, Bijan paid for the wedding, including a $5,000 Dior wedding dress. Together with my aunt, he saw to every detail with the help of an army of waiters, drivers, florists, pastry makers and chefs, all under the guidance of a chief caterer. I had nothing to do but go for fittings for my dress, accompanied by Bijan, and choose a wedding ring. In that matter, my Aunt

Tootie demonstrated her better knowledge of the Iranian way of doing things.

When she came with me to select the ring, she admonished me: "Don't choose the most expensive ring you see; otherwise you might be embarrassed if he decides he doesn't want to spend that much. Instead, choose one of the most inexpensive ones and that will give him an opportunity to buy you a much nicer one if he wants to."

As a result, I chose a diamond that I did not like at all, and when Bijan came to pay for it, he tossed it on the jewellery counter, saying, "Let's get a decent ring. What is this cheap thing?"

My wedding ring was a 4-carat diamond of the finest quality, and years later it helped me to obtain my release from Iran. I sold it for $50,000, and every penny of it went to buy my freedom.

My family was instructive about another Persian custom. Bijan and I had decided to dispense with the traditional woman's dowry and the man's promise of a *mehrieh* — a legal undertaking that in case of divorce, or upon the death of the husband, the wife would be given a stipulated amount of money as a kind of protection against being badly used by her spouse. When the husband dies, before taxes are taken from the estate by government and before other family members get their share, the *mehrieh* is supposed to be set aside for the wife. But when my Aunt Ashraf heard our plan, she said, "You are young and you need protection should anything happen. You must have the *mehrieh*."

And so we did. Bijan set the amount at about $170,000. In the later chaos I never did get the *mehrieh* and it proved useless to me. As it is, when an Iranian man wants to be rid of his wife without paying the *mehrieh*, he simply makes life so miserable for her that the woman leaves without it. The practice is not infrequent. So much for the vaunted protection of Moslem women dictated by the Koran. Instead of a dowry, my father gave us as a wedding present two gorgeous carpets from Tabriz, all peaches and minty greens, but those, too, I lost in the end.

For the wedding day itself, Bijan and I sat on low chairs on an antique pearl-encrusted *termeh* (a small floor covering) that belonged to my Uncle Kamel's wife. The *mullah* sat in front of us, and we could see our reflection in the mirror that was bought especially for the occasion. By custom, it was placed behind the *mullah*. All the elements of a Moslem wedding were present: the antique Koran, the *nabot* (the little sculptures made of sugar to represent the sweet life) and the long, Persian bread decorated with sayings from the Koran. I could scarcely believe that in less than a year I had gone from being an American teenager dreaming of dating boys to being the wife of a handsome Iranian businessman with a comfortable niche in the increasingly wealthy circles of Teheran.

Chapter Four

Flowers in the Desert

*In the land of poetry, nightingales, and roses
living is a blessing, yes, indeed.*

FORUGH FARROKHZAD

 Upon my marriage to Bijan, I entered a jewelled world. Even I, raised to take deference and comfort for granted, could not help but be awed. All around me society was undergoing an economic revolution. The new oil revenues were gilding our lives. One day you would see a friend with a new car. A month later he would have a better car, and the month after that he would have two cars. And then maybe after another month he would buy a larger house. His wife would suddenly start wearing a lot more jewellery. Parties would sparkle from the light of new diamonds bought and paraded. The middle class was getting richer, too. The Royal Club and the expensive restaurants had always been the haunts of the very rich, but now there were new faces there, those who could suddenly afford what had once been a drop-in centre for the elite. Everyone was buying, buying, buying, rushing to spend all the money that just seemed to pour in. It seemed that Teheran itself was being rebuilt. Everywhere you looked, new highrises were going up; new luxurious condominiums and villas reached higher on the slopes of the Alborz.

If there were mutterings against the Shah, they came only from people who were not too busy making money from the oil boom. As if from a long way away, I saw the early signs of trouble: word-of-mouth reports about intellectuals who suddenly disappeared into prisons for months or years; the laments of the religious leaders, the *mullahs* and the *ayatollahs*, that the Western habits of the Shah and his entourage were an insult in an Islamic country. Trouble could even be foreseen in the more muted complaints of the *bazaaris*, the powerful merchants of the bazaar, who were frustrated by the inefficiencies of the bureaucracies, the long waiting periods before goods could be brought in and the incredible overloading at the docks. Iran was choking on its wealth. We could not get enough consumer goods fast enough. It was as if the whole country was being force-fed a diet that was too rich.

In our circles, when complaints were voiced, they were about the corruption of the Shah and his numerous relatives. My husband's company was also one of the few that refused to buy a royal connection for the firm, although there was so much work to do that it mattered little. But none of my friends and acquaintances thought that the enchanted life we were leading would ever come to an end. God, Shah and Country — it would always be that way. And then, of course, there was the four-hundred-thousand-strong army to back up that triangle of power. There had always been an elite in Iran. There had been a king for 2,500 years. Now there was even a rising middle class. If you did not speak out against the Shah, you would be left alone. The price was a little bit of personal freedom, but, then, look at what we had: a beautiful country where family relationships were warm, strong and binding; the kind of personal power that most Western industrialists cannot even buy because their cultures don't permit that sort of omnipotence; the easy availability of cheap labour for servants, workers and gardeners. And now we even had a growing sophistication as the West moved in with all its technology, its goods and services, hungry for some of our oil money. To be wealthy in Iran was to live the life of a minor potentate. To be poor, well . . . we never had to think about it, I now regret to say.

When I look back to how my husband and I lived, I am amazed, in the light of later events, at how we got away with it in what was really a Third World country still largely blighted by poverty. Our lives were flower-sweet and we just forgot that the flowers were growing in the desert.

The night of our wedding, Bijan and I moved into the Royal Suite of the Hilton Hotel for a month.

"The house still needs a few bits of furniture," he said. "I don't want to move until everything is perfect. Let's try out some of the best hotels and do a little shopping."

That's just what we did. After the Hilton we spent a month at the Intercontinental and another month at the Sheraton. Every morning Bijan would get rid of his work in a couple of hours and we would spend the rest of the day prowling around the shops buying furniture, fixtures, clothes. If I ever mentioned that I might like something, he bought it without further discussion. It seemed as if there were absolutely no limits to our whims, our desires. In the evening, friends would come to see us and we would either have dinner catered in our rooms or take our visitors to the best restaurants. On weekends, we drove through the stream-filled Alborz Mountains to the Caspian. I remember seeing the villa for the first time, nestled in a leafy compound in a narrow, flat belt between forested mountains and the sea. An airy, window-filled, modern villa with a magnificent view of the beach below, it was set in a 25,000-square-metre garden. The complex included a swimming pool, tennis courts, windsurfing boards, motor boats, a giant man-sized kite and an indoor games room. A husband and wife lived in separate accommodations on the compound and looked after the house and cooked and cleaned for us whenever we visited.

Most of the villas in the area had been newly built. Like our own, they were one of the most visible signs of oil money. But most of the people who owned the villas were too busy making more money to come up to the Caspian to enjoy them, and these giant mansions by the sea were empty most of the time.

Bijan was everything I had dreamed of in a husband. I went to him as a sexually inexperienced bride. Indeed, he had made it clear that he wanted to marry a virgin. And in an arranged marriage such as ours, it was perfectly acceptable to set out the desired qualities of a prospective spouse. Not that he ever had to state explicitly what his wishes were in that regard. He merely had to say that he wanted a young woman who was "innocent."

Attitudes to sex in upper-class Iran in the early 1970s were much as I imagine they were in the American middle class of the 1950s. Sexuality had its place — generally in the privacy of the marital room. Young women wanting to know about its mysteries could ask older, more experienced female family members. Men preferred to marry virgins, although young, attractive widows with good inheritances had little trouble remarrying. Adultery was frowned upon, although that did little to stop it. But a woman of good breeding would never stoop to have an affair with a married man.

Even such a conservative approach to sex was worlds removed from that of the average, religious Iranian. Many an Iranian man saw the face of his bride only on the wedding night, when the veil was removed for the first time in his presence. Men and women rarely showed affection in public, and certainly never caressed. They walked separately, rarely touching hands. Sexual education was at a minimum, even within the family. A woman was most often seen as the temptress, the cause of a man's downfall. For this reason, the Koran admonished women to dress modestly and the religious establishment insisted on the wearing of the *chador* or the *hejab*.

In sex, as in many other matters, we, the elite, went our own way, living by our own standards, as if the mass of fundamentalist Iranians did not exist. I think now that we should have had more respect for their feelings. I remember how our servants occasionally walked in on Bijan and me in our family room as we hugged and kissed. They were mortified. I began to take care that they should not find me sitting on Bijan's lap too often.

Bijan was a sensitive and patient lover. He needed to be. I had looked forward to having sex and had even been willing to make love to him before marriage, but he had refrained.

"Let's wait," he said. "It will be better after marriage."

Years before he met me, Bijan had decided to marry another well-bred, innocent young woman who had never dated. The families had celebrated the formal engagement and invitations had gone out. Just before the marriage, the woman felt confident enough to tell him that she had had a lover and was not so inexperienced as she had pretended. Immediately, Bijan cancelled the marriage. He was a perfectionist, with high standards in all matters.

"It was the lie as much as anything else that bothered me," he said. "A lie is a terrible thing to base a marriage on."

On the night of our marriage, I was frightened. I knew so

little of what was expected of me. It took a long time for me to be comfortable sexually. Through it all, Bijan was thoughtful, putting my feelings before his needs. I felt lucky to have married such a perfect husband.

Every day Bijan would surprise me. One day we were standing by the hotel window and he pointed to a new luxury highrise that was being built and asked, "Do you like that building?"

"It looks impressive," I said.

"We own a large apartment in it."

Or we would be driving by a vast tract of land in an expensive part of Teheran and he would suddenly say, "We own all this."

I slowly came to realize that I knew very little about my husband. Like most Iranian men, he was very secretive about his business life. In my world, many wives often had no idea what their husbands were worth. Nor did they have immediate access to any money of their own. Bijan never told me exactly what he owned or what provisions he had made for me. Right to the end, he kept all his business to himself, and this had severe repercussions on me. Iranian men also rarely bothered to discuss the details of their many projects with women. Often I would hear someone remark on a beautiful building or the engineering marvel of a giant bridge and not know that my husband or my uncles had built it. Frankly, my kind of women were not much interested in how the money was earned. We lived comfortable lives and that seemed to be all that mattered to us. There was a price to be paid for being "kept" by our husbands — but I found that out only later.

In the beginning, nothing could have been more perfect than my life with Bijan. We made plans to go on long trips to Europe and Africa. In June, we moved into our house in Shemiran. The gently sloping Shemiran is one of the greenest, most beautiful northern suburbs of Teheran and our house was among the largest and most impressive. One of my husband's work crews had taken three years to build it, and Bijan and the architect had spent lavish amounts on it, experimenting with design, and tearing down walls when the result was not the one desired. The house had every modern convenience: four bathrooms, five bedrooms, a playroom, a gambling room, an office, a sitting room, a darkroom with an adjoining photo library and projection room, a separate apartment in the basement for the servants, and two large balconies that wrapped around the second-floor bedrooms and gave magnificent views of the garden. The house was set in twenty thousand square metres of beautifully landscaped garden and orchard (the work had been done by the Shah's own private Swiss gardener), which flowered with the best fruit trees of Iran and with exotic imported plants and shrubs. Three gardeners kept the growth lush, never sparing water no matter how hot the weather was. The full-time gardener and his wife lived in a small house at the end of the garden. For the main house there were four servants and a driver.

Bijan had seen to every detail personally. The master bedroom was separated from the rest of the house in its own suite of rooms, which included a large room that was merely a walk-in closet; a bathroom with imported black ceramic fixtures, gold-plated faucets from Italy and hand-painted burgundy and gold tiles on the ceiling; a small bar complete with refrigerator; a stereo system, small stove and library. The couches in the living room had been brought in from Italy. The huge, round, dining-room table had been made from rosewood that had been sitting, at Bijan's instructions, in a special oil for ten years until he was ready for it. The table sat twenty-four people comfortably.

Because the house was situated just south of the Shah's Niavaran Palace, the air was constantly filled with the thwacking sound of helicopters. The king and his family travelled by air, rarely attempting to tackle the Teheran traffic that had become famous for its intractability. Because of that, Bijan had insisted on special soundproofing for the entire house: special glazed windows and foam insulation that were unavailable in Iran and had to be imported at great cost. In fact, inside the house, it was impossible to hear any noise from the outside.

Other details included an elaborate video monitoring system to check on visitors at the door, and a forced-air system, activated by pushing one of the doorbells, that wiped dirt from the visitor's shoes as he stood waiting at the door. There were perpetually heated towel racks that kept the towels warm and toasty. All of this luxury was enclosed in typically Iranian fashion by a high wall, even though the property was so large that it was bounded by three different streets. There were three major entrances, all of them with gates. Despite all these urban accoutrements, early each morning we were awakened by cocks crowing. In one corner of the garden, Bijan had set up a little farm, complete with goats, chickens and other small animals. And every day, we had fresh milk and eggs.

When we got up in the morning, the servants served us a large breakfast with fresh bread, toasted for caviar, fresh fruit, coffee, tea—all of it beautifully arranged on one of the many outdoor tables in the garden, either by the pool or under one of the rose arbours, or up on the balcony off our bedroom. We would spend an hour having a leisurely meal and then Bijan would set out at about ten o'clock to go to the office. Sometimes if I asked him to stay home and keep me company, he would do his work on the phone and then we would swim or go horseback riding. He spent hours photographing the flowers in the garden while I painted watercolours of the roses. He had done as he had planned: he had more or less retired, even though his firm was doing more business than ever building the trappings of the great industrial power that the Shah was determined to acquire overnight.

In the late afternoon we visited friends, cousins or uncles and aunts and finished the evening off in whatever happened to be the popular restaurant of the moment. We went regularly to the Royal Club and rode the beautiful Arabians.

At the end of July, we staged our actual wedding celebration (always held sometime after the religious ceremony), having waited for my brother, uncles and aunts to come from the States to join us. It was a marvellous night at the Hilton. The ballroom was decorated with large branches of trees with vines and grapes hanging from them. Flowers filled every part of the room and the centrepiece of the lavish dinner was a four-foot-long ice sculpture of a swan, filled with twenty-five pounds of the finest caviar the Caspian could produce.

In November we were to go to Europe and then to Africa, but just before we left I discovered that I was pregnant. Although I was somewhat apprehensive about having a child so soon in our marriage, when we had yet to embark on the travels that Bijan had promised me, he was overjoyed and rushed out to buy me a giant sapphire and diamond ring. In England I visited a doctor who counselled me not to proceed with our travel plans to Africa, so instead we stayed in London for a month. While we were there, Bijan suggested that we go to see a friend of his.

His friend lived in a highrise, but when we arrived at the apartment on the twelfth floor, we found only workmen who were going in and out, putting the finishing touches on what was very evidently a brand-new building.

"I guess my friend's not here," Bijan said, but while I hung back, he wandered about freely inspecting the fabulous furniture in the rooms. Everything was modern, with glinting glass and chrome. The living room consisted of highly polished lacquer pieces and hand-printed suede couches.

"Do you like it?" he asked finally.

"Of course. It's superb."

"Good — because it's ours."

When we went on to Paris for a month, he pulled a similar trick. On some other excuse he took to me to see a lovely apartment in a new highrise overlooking the Seine, not far from the Eiffel Tower, and waited to see how charmed I was before announcing that it, too, belonged to us. Months later, over a coffee at the Royal Club, he casually bought an apartment in Valencia, Spain, that a friend happened to show him in a catalogue. Bijan took delight in pulling out these little properties, like little trophies, to impress me. And I *was* impressed. But he never stopped being secretive and I never inquired about any details of his business or his ownership. On subsequent trips we stayed in our apartments rather than in hotels, but on that first foray into Europe, because everything was not exactly perfect, he preferred hotels.

After staying in Europe for three months, we returned to Iran. On July 17, Farhad, my son, was born. With the birth of a male child in a country that still valued men above all else, our lives were complete. Bijan turned out to be a wonderful father. I was so young that I tended to treat Farhad like a little doll. I would dress and undress him in the most exquisite European baby clothes. Bijan would laugh. "Leave that poor child alone. You've already changed him four times today." He was the more patient parent. He spent hours playing with our son, teaching him his first words, encouraging him to take his first step. We were never closer as husband and wife than during that first year and a half of marriage.

Around us, neighbours and friends were buying properties in the United States and Europe, sending their children to the best boarding schools abroad, opening and fattening up Swiss bank accounts. In Paris, the shops had signs that read, "We speak Persian," for those quickly rich Iranians who had not yet had the time to acquire other Western trappings, such as a second and third language. Whenever I went to Paris, I returned with an average of eight new suitcases full of clothes. But we really did not have to go to Paris anymore. The shops along the Shah-Abbas Boulevard now offered the best from around the world. If you were prepared to pay, you could bring almost anything into the country. All the parties we attended required very formal wear — long dresses for the women, for which we regularly paid up to $5,000 each. It was not unusual to see the wife of a rich man wearing $100,000 worth of jewellery on a regular evening out. When our friends really wanted to throw a bash, they flew in flowers from Holland and brought food, waiters and chefs from Paris for the night.

The Shah and his family set the pace in lavish spending. Every winter, he and his entourage moved to his estate in Switzerland, where he ruled the country from the ski slopes. At his coronation in 1967, he placed on his head a crown of red velvet, white egret feathers and 3,380 diamonds. He marked 2,500 years of monarchy in Iran with a sit-down dinner for thousands in tents at Persepolis, the city that the great Darius built to celebrate the New Year and where the ruins still testify to the splendour of old Persia. Maxim's of Paris catered the caviar-stuffed quail and lobster mousse, while the refreshments consisted of twenty-five thousand bottles of Château-Lafite Rothschild at $100 a bottle. One year, Queen Farah returned from a holiday in Paris aboard her own jet, followed by an Iranian Boeing 707 carrying three tons of French marble for her new swimming pool. In Niavaran Palace the gold-leaf spigots in the royal bathrooms were shaped like dolphins, which had precious stones — jade and amethyst — for eyes.

Our friends were not the most flamboyant spenders. One businessman, a former truck driver who had helped the Shah when he was in brief exile in Rome in 1953, had made a fortune as the importer of Pepsi-Cola; he built for himself in Teheran a $15 million replica of the Petit Trianon at Versailles.

Somehow I knew that this fantasy life could not go on forever. And I was right. By the mid-seventies, the strain of the oil glut was showing: rapid growth caused terrible short-

ages of skilled labour and raw materials. Construction of a
hospital would stop midway because there was no cement.
The contractors might build a badly needed school on time,
but then there might not be teachers to staff it. People were
earning more, true, but the cost of living was rising even
faster. Everyone knew that to get anything done in the chaotic
government bureaucracy you had to bribe people all along
the way. We called it tea money. Because attempts to modernize agriculture had largely failed and because so many
villagers had moved to the big cities looking for better-paying
jobs, Iran went from being an exporter of food to an importer
in just a couple of decades.

Underneath the wealth, the patina of Westernization, was
a country that had not really progressed and a people that in
many ways reacted against the changes that were taking place.
There had always been rich and poor in Iran, but we had all
been Iranians, bound by a long history. We understood each
other, shared the same notion of the hierarchy, accepted the
rule of the king, respected each other's place in society. In
my father's village the class structure had been the same for
centuries. The people largely accepted his dominance and
looked to him to settle their family disputes or post bail for
them, as well as to provide the water and tractors they needed
to grow their crops. Rich and poor were tied together with
strong cultural bonds. But now the members of the elite were
looking and sounding different—like foreigners almost. The
rich had so much more money than they had ever had, it
seemed. We had moved right out of the local hierarchy. We
were just copies of Westerners in the eyes of most Iranians.
We paid lip service to Islam, never visited the mosques except
when a family member died, flaunted our sexual freedom.
As far as many were concerned, we were not even Iranians
anymore. There was a roiling resentment of all things foreign.
And that resentment existed even among the very Iranians
who were most eager to copy the West.

Even in my personal life, the bloom was fading — and for many of the same cultural reasons. I had married a man who said that he loved to see me dance and would take me out to the best clubs. He told me that he respected my freedom. But over time I realized that I was a prisoner behind golden bars and that his protestations of liberalization were empty. The realization came only slowly. At first I didn't mind being a guest in my own home, never having to do any work, leaving everything to the servants. And I didn't mind Bijan being with me every minute of the day, helping me to select anything I might need. He even came with me to the doctor or sent one of his sisters with me if he could not be there.

Bijan took care of everything related to the running of the house — paying the servants, dealing with the gardeners, bringing in repairmen. My only responsibility was to make sure the freezer was properly stocked. But he would come with me to the supermarket and test me.

"How many chickens do we have in the freezer, Sousan?"

"Two, I think."

"No. You are wrong. We have three."

He said he didn't trust me to buy the fruit, a major staple of every Iranian household.

"You can't tell when the fruit is ripe and they will cheat you on the quality."

I had no credit cards, no bank accounts. I never paid any bills and I only carried a little cash which Bijan parcelled out to me in case I needed to pay the hairdresser or make some other minor expense. I was literally never out of the house alone because a driver took me everywhere.

"I know you had your driver's licence in the U.S., but Teheran traffic is something else," he told me when I wanted to drive by myself. "You'll just have a nervous breakdown so don't bother to get your licence here."

It was convenient to have the driver, so I never worried about the fact that my freedom was slowly being eroded.

Then another side of Bijan started to emerge—his over-whelming attachment and sense of responsibility towards his family: his two brothers, three sisters and widowed mother. His two older, unmarried sisters consulted him on every move, every dress they bought, every decision. He often went to visit them after work or over the lunch hour, while I waited at home starving, and they stuffed him with his favourite dishes. Sometimes he came home at about three and would be completely uninterested in the meal that our cook had prepared for him.

He also began to avoid going out to the parties given by members of my family. Although we did not frequent the Shah's parties, my first cousins were very close to his sister Shams, and our gatherings tended to be formal. But more and more I found that Bijan preferred to visit his family instead, where it was more relaxed, but also much less fun. Nor was I free to accept an invitation on our behalf without consulting him, while he continually made plans and told me about them only at the last minute.

After a while he began to refuse to go to any discos or do any dancing. He had once said to me, "I love to watch you dance. I want to film you dancing. When we are married, I will join the best disco clubs so you can dance."

Now he said: "Why do you, a married woman, want to go to the discos? Only women who want to be picked up go to the discos."

I could not believe I was listening to the man I thought I had married.

My beautiful house began to seem like a prison. I saw that whenever he told me not to bother to join my cousins for lunch at a restaurant but to have them to the house instead, he was not being hospitable. He was trying to keep me at home. Whenever his sisters accompanied me to the tailor or the doctor, they were not doing it to be nice. They were my guards. And what better spy to see where I went during the day than the chauffeur who took me everywhere?

Bijan used to say that he preferred my cooking to that of our full-time chef and he encouraged me to make jams from the many fruits growing in the garden. But it was not my cooking he was truly interested in; he was just trying to find ways to keep me occupied at home.

In particular, he disapproved of my going to the Royal Club without him. He had turned our house into a kind of private club for me, complete with swimming pool, tennis courts and gambling room. But I began to want to go out, just to walk freely without concern.

Once, just before he left for a brief work trip to Tabriz, he said, "While I'm gone I'd rather you didn't go out with your cousins. Have your friends in instead."

I was surprised, but I didn't take it as a complete ban on going out. When his younger brother and some of my female cousins asked me to go to the Royal Club for lunch, I went. I had not been expecting Bijan home until the following day, and I intended not to tell him about the outing. But when we all came back to the house for coffee after lunch, a servant came up to me and said, "Mr. Amini is at home. He asked us where you were and when we said you had gone out, he went up to the bedroom and said he had a headache."

Suddenly I felt a terrible dread about confronting him. I realized that I was actually afraid of my own husband. I hadn't done anything wrong — even his own brother was with me—but still I felt fear about what he might say to me. When I went up to the bedroom, I found him lying on the bed staring up at the ceiling.

"Where did you go?" he asked.

"We all went to the Royal Club—with your brother, too."

"I thought I told you that I didn't like you going there without me."

For the first time in our marriage we argued and I answered back.

"Do you think you own me or something?" I asked, enraged. "Do you think you bought me? Because if you do, think again. That's not the way it works. You can't just order me around.''

He was furious: ''You can do whatever you want and go wherever you want when I'm around and that's the way it works. But I don't want you going out to lunch with a bunch of girls anywhere — and especially not the Royal Club.''

What he feared was the cozy atmosphere at the club. Everyone knew everyone else, and it was not unusual for a male friend to join you at a table and laugh and chat with you for a while. But what could be wrong with doing that? Bijan obviously thought that when a married woman talked to a man, even if she was in the company of friends, she was committing some sort of sin. I could not believe this was the Westernized man I had married. I loved him and had no desire to cheat on him, but he did not trust the people I might meet when I was away from him. Suddenly, the man whom I had treated very much like a minor god seemed just a man, after all, and with a lot less confidence in himself than I had imagined.

Finally, I said, ''If that's the sort of traditional Iranian wife you wanted, you shouldn't have married someone raised in the States with a different mentality. You should have married a nice little Iranian girl who wants to stay home and make jams for you.''

What he had wanted was a veneer of Westernization. He had been intrigued by my American upbringing. He liked marrying into what was known to be a liberalized and Westernized upper-class family. But deep down he was traditional — as was most of Iran. His character should have helped me to understand the basic underlying conservatism of the country as a whole. But I was living in too small a circle to understand that Bijan was just displaying, in very moderate form, what so many Iranians felt: a deep ambivalence towards the West and its values.

After that argument, I rarely went out on my own, and Bijan made it clear that he had no intention of changing his mind on the subject. The incident that finally crystallized the issues between us involved the young man whom I had dated briefly before meeting Bijan. A few months after Farhad was born, my former boyfriend started to send messages to me through friends that he was still in love with me and that, should I divorce Bijan, he would marry me and take care of my child as well. I sent back discouraging replies but I was touched by his care and I wanted to meet him just once, in a very public setting, to tell him that I was happily married and wanted to stay that way and that he should try to meet someone else. I arranged with my cousin Firouzeh, my Aunt Ashraf's youngest daughter, to invite him to a very large party that she was having, where I would try to get a few minutes alone with him. When we were dating, I had told Bijan about the young man and he had said there was no reason why we should not be friends. He pretended to be very tolerant about the whole thing. But now I doubted that he would be so pleased about a planned meeting, and as a result I said nothing to him.

That night, my former suitor was very complimentary to me. But when I got a chance to meet him quietly, I told him that there was no hope for a relationship. I even introduced him to Bijan, to whom he extended an invitation to a party being given that night by one of the Shah's nephews — which my husband declined. I thought nothing more of the meeting until several weeks later when I was speaking to Firouzeh on the telephone. Suddenly we heard two voices speaking on the same line. We were about to ring off, because such interruptions occurred regularly in Iran, when we realized with horror that the two voices we were hearing were our own. As we listened, we recognized a previous conversation we had had, something innocuous about one of the servants. It came to me that my husband must have been taping my conversations and that, somehow, through some technological fault, we were accidentally hearing the tape. And I realized that he knew all about my meeting with my former boyfriend.

When Bijan came home that afternoon, I confronted him.

"You have been taping my conversations," I forced myself to say through my fear. "How could you? I am so insulted."

At first he tried to laugh the whole matter off. So what if he had eavesdropped on my chit-chat? It was just for fun. But when he saw how angry I was, he, too, hardened. Indeed, he insisted that he had every right to keep a watch on his wife and that, in my case, the electronic surveillance was well merited. As the fight progressed, I began to fear for our marriage.

In Iran, it is customary in times of family trouble for a husband and wife to go to close relatives to try to sort out the problem. That night we visited my Uncle Ardeshir and Aunt Guity. They had moved back to Iran from Ann Arbor in the early 1970s to open one of the city's best French restaurants, *La Réserve*. When we had laid out the problem for them, my uncle took a very liberal position. He, like the others in my family, was highly respectful of my forceful husband.

"Mr. Amini, if every little thought that a woman had were written on her forehead, most marriages would end in divorce," he said. "You have to look at what she actually does about those thoughts. I don't think you can count a woman guilty until she actually does something wrong."

My husband was unmoved. "For a married woman to even be thinking of meeting, even casually, with a former boyfriend is wrong. She is guilty. And I tell you, if she continues to hang around with her cousins who are a bad influence on her, this marriage will end in divorce for sure. If I hear that she ever sees that boyfriend again, it will be over."

By the time that Bijan and I celebrated the second anniversary of our marriage, there were serious disagreements between us. I had come to realize by seeing others in the same situation that many Iranian men liked to marry a younger woman so that they could shape her into the kind of woman they wanted, turn her into their own image of the perfect spouse. In my case, my husband wanted me to be outwardly modern, progressive and chic, and inwardly conservative, traditional and modest.

In order to relieve some of the strains on our marriage we decided, in December 1976, to make one of our many trips to Europe together, only this time without Farhad. He was to stay with my husband's mother and sisters. As we usually did on our trips, we made our first stop in Switzerland, where Bijan was to receive a check-up in Geneva for a recurring problem of stomach acidity. Most Iranians who could afford it went to Europe for their health care because, despite the best intentions and the great progress of the previous few years, there was still no comparison between Western medicine and that practised in Iran. We were expecting a two-day stay at most, and then we were going on to Paris. But after Bijan's regular check-up, doctors were perplexed by his continual stomach upsets and decided that a stomach operation was needed.

The prospect terrified me. In all my life I had never stayed alone in a hotel room, nor had I ever been anywhere without my husband or family to accompany me. While Bijan recuperated, I would have to stay in a hotel for days — alone. Just the idea of having to visit the hospital and be responsible for a very sick person overwhelmed me. There had always been someone to take care of me, and now for the first time in my life I had to be strong for someone else.

We had been staying at the Hotel Président by the lake, and we booked a $700-a-night room on the top floor of the Hôpital Cantonal. The top floor seemed to house mainly foreign patients, and many of them were wealthy Iranians. This was where the Shah's own relatives came when they needed operations. The king could import Western technology with oil money but Western know-how and professionalism could not be fostered overnight.

On the eve of the operation I stayed with Bijan until midnight, when the brother of Jamshid, one of my husband's
two partners, who had been visiting us, offered to drive me
back to my hotel. Jamshid's brother was a doctor and owned
a private clinic in the city. It was a rainy night not long before
Christmas, and as he drove hurriedly to get home, he went
through a stop sign and crashed into an oncoming car. Our
car careened and finally ploughed into a ditch. I was in shock
but somehow managed to get out of the car. Shards of glass
from the broken windshield covered every part of me. The
doctor also managed to get out of his side of the car and
immediately asked me if I were all right. In the dark and rain
he inspected me as best he could to see if I had suffered any
major injuries.

"Just a little cut over the right eye," he said. "I'll take you
back to my house. My wife will help you undress and the
clinic is right next door if you need stitches."

After calling the police, he insisted on waiting for the officers to arrive and then made a patient and detailed report of
the accident. During that unreal half-hour, his professional
calm was the only thing that kept me from screaming out in
delayed terror as blood trickled from over my right eye and
my legs felt weak beneath me. Later, at his house, his wife, a
nurse, helped me to remove my clothes. As I lifted off my
blouse, I could feel tiny pricks from the invisible pieces of
glass rubbing against my skin. When I took a shower and
washed out my hair I could hear the tinkling of glass hitting
the ceramic tiles. As I rubbed my skin with a washcloth, fine
little lines of blood appeared and turned the water red. Even
my eyebrows were filled with glass, and as I ran my fingertips
through them, trickles of blood appeared on my face. When I
looked at myself in the mirror and saw my bruised and puffy
right eye and the traces of blood on my face I shivered with
an uneasy presentiment.

The following morning, after a sleepless night worrying
about Bijan and whether I would lose sight in my damaged

eye or be left with permanent scars on my face, I arrived at the hospital to find that my husband was still in surgery at the time that he should have been in the recovery room. As the hours slipped away, I became more and more nervous. What could be taking so long? Eventually, after five hours of surgery, the doctor came out and took me aside.

"I am sorry," he began, "your husband has cancer of the stomach. We have had to take out most of his stomach, but we think we have caught all the cancer. In these severe cases we don't really know for ten days whether the patient will recover because we have to see if the stitches take properly. If he starts to bleed internally, there is little we can do."

I felt myself slipping to the floor in a faint but the doctor caught hold of me and helped me to a chair. The one thing I will never get used to in the West is the way that doctors give patients and their families bad news without preparing them for it in any way. They discuss impending death as if it were nothing worse than a forecast of bad weather ahead and they treat reactions of grief as if they were out of place.

I started to cry and to plead with the surgeon to give my husband the best possible care. I came from a country where connections and the right kind of pressure could get me anything, and I suppose I thought that if he really felt like saving my husband, if it meant enough to him, then somehow he would. I even suggested to him that my uncles in the United States had good medical connections and that perhaps an American doctor should be flown in, but he was clearly offended.

"I assure you that if anything can be done, we will do it," he said stiffly and left me alone to cope with the terrible news he had just delivered.

I was twenty-two years old; I had a small child, I lived a life of almost unbelievable luxury and I loved my husband of three years, no matter what our problems were. Now it seemed as if my dreams were about to vanish. Whenever there were crises in my life, I called in my family, and that morning while Bijan was in the recovery room still oblivious to the threat to his life, I called my uncles in Teheran and my father in Sabbalon. All of them wanted to fly immediately to Geneva, but I urged them not to. The doctor had left it to me to decide whether Bijan would be told about the cancer immediately or after the ten-day critical period was over. I had opted for the latter and I didn't want Bijan to be tipped off to the gravity of the situation by the arrival of relatives from Iran.

As it turned out, one of my uncles called Bijan's family to inform them of the operation, and Ali, his brother, who was a doctor, came to Geneva. During the ten-day waiting period I spent every night on a cot by my husband's bedside, keeping a worried vigil and watching for every sign of a worsening condition. At the end of it, the doctor pronounced that the immediate danger was over and informed my husband for the first time that he had cancer. With typical self-assurance and strength, Bijan accepted the news with calm — unlike his brother who broke down at the word even though he had already known the nature of the illness.

Because the doctor said that Bijan would need regular check-ups for three months and then another visit at six months after the operation, the three of us moved back into the Hotel Président, where the chef was asked to prepare special puréed meals for my husband. After three months of living in the hotel, during which time we took only occasional walks around the city when Bijan was better, the doctor told us that he was well enough to go home. The entire stay, including the hospital and surgery, cost us $300,000 which my husband drew from a Swiss bank account that I had known nothing about.

When we had been back in Iran for two months, Bijan again started to complain about pain, only this time it was centred near his appendix. I was terrified by that new sign of illness: with his life under threat, I realized more each day how much I loved Bijan and how I dreaded the prospect of life without him. I wanted to do everything possible to hold on to him. I was intent on taking advantage of a special medical service that had been set up in Geneva to cater to wealthy Iranians: on a few hours' notice, a jet, complete with doctors, nurses and emergency services, could fly into Teheran, pick up the patient and fly out again. If necessary, emergency operations could be performed on board. The service made hotel reservations for family members and saw to every detail of an emergency.

At the insistence of our relatives, Bijan first went to see a local doctor, a friend of my family. Ali and I accompanied him, and as soon as the doctor examined him he said: "This man has severe appendicitis and I would not recommend delaying surgery for even a few hours. He doesn't have time to fly to Geneva."

During all the time we were at the doctor's office neither Bijan nor his brother told the doctor about the nature of his previous operation, and, as a wife now more accustomed to Iranian ways, I, too, kept quiet for fear of speaking out of turn. When the doctor began the operation, he had no idea that Bijan had suffered from cancer and when he found a large tumour he took out what he could and then waited for the results of the biopsy. In a country that could afford villas and palaces, hospital and laboratory facilities for performing biopsies were so primitive that it took ten days to get any results. It was cancer again. By now, Bijan was so wasted away and so weak that we had to give up the notion of going back to Geneva.

When he was well enough to travel, we took a long, leisurely trip to the United States, where he booked into the Mayo Clinic. At that point, the doctors told him that he had no more cancer in his body. More cheerful than we had been in some months, we set off to visit my uncles in Ann Arbor and Los Angeles.

I remember how Bijan looked out over the Pacific, listened to the waves pounding the shore and said: "If Allah gives me more time, we'll move and spend the rest of our lives here."

We had been back in Iran only a short time when Bijan's regular doctor's appointment in Geneva came up. Perhaps we were just ignoring all the signs of a terminal disease, but we brought Farhad with us and intended to continue travelling afterwards. Instead, Bijan was immediately hospitalized while doctors decided whether to operate on him or wait until he was a little stronger. The final decision was to proceed, and this time the prognosis was completely bleak.

"Your husband has only a short time to live," the same surgeon told me. "I would advise you to take him home."

Bijan and I had never talked about the possibility that he might die. He had made no preparations, nor had he become less secretive about his affairs. In the few months that remained to us, we were never again able to have a private moment because, with death imminent, a culture that was Iranian and yet almost totally foreign to me took over our lives. His sister Parvaneh and Ali joined us in Geneva, and we moved into a furnished apartment near the hotel. His family immediately took over the running of our little household and the dealings with the hospital. I was not permitted to go anywhere without being closely questioned about it or watched. Fortunately, my father happened to be visiting his nephew Dara in Berne at the time, and he made repeated train trips to visit me, giving me the few breaks from the depressing life that Bijan's family was intent on forcing on me.

Their attitude seemed to be that you could not be feeling grief if you were not making a great public show of it. Because I had a sick husband, I was not to take any pleasure out of life. Even walking out in the park for a breath of fresh air was not permitted because I might, for a few seconds, forget the agony that my husband was going through. The family displayed that strain that runs through Iran's religious fanaticism, that revelling in pain and martyrdom, that pride in self-punishment. They wanted me to behave like a traditional Moslem woman whose husband was dying.

All the time, the doctor was advising us to go home, to leave Switzerland, and I began to feel that he did not want us there, although why that should be, considering the amounts of money we were spending there, I don't know. Bijan wanted to be where his doctor was, where the best medical help could be bought. Perhaps the doctor realized more than we did our need to be in our own culture at such a crucial time.

After two months, we finally went home and I became even more a prisoner of the Aminis. His mother and two sisters moved in permanently, and the rest of the family visited all day long. I was not allowed to sleep in the same room with him and I never again had so much as five minutes of privacy with him, when he might have told me that he loved me or given me advice about the future. In fact they never allowed me to give him so much as one glass of water those months that he lay dying. They took over the running of the house and I was not even permitted to go out and do the shopping or to cut fruit from the trees. When I dared to cut down a few cherries from a tree heavy with ripe fruit to send to my Uncle Ardeshir, they treated me like a thief.

In the following six months I left the house perhaps three times, each time because of a family emergency. Friends and relatives came to keep me company, and they always left horrified at the atmosphere in my house. What we were seeing was the deeply fanatical side of Iran — the conservative face of the country. The Aminis were behaving no differently from any other fundamentalist Islamic family. I had married a rich man and, according to them, I had no right to enjoy my life while he was dying, and not even afterwards. My life should be over with his.

Because they knew a little more about fundamentalist Moslems and realized how much the Aminis hated me under their guise of family love, my father and uncles told me to call them immediately when it looked as if Bijan was taking a turn for the worse. They feared what his relatives might do to me if I were alone in the house with them the moment he died. It so happened that my father was visiting from Azerbaijan and in our house the morning that Bijan slipped into a coma. It was June 25, 1977, three weeks before my son's second birthday, when my father woke me around 5:00 A.M. to tell me that I had better say my last farewell to Bijan. I rushed into his room, oblivious of his mother and sisters who sat glowering at his bedside, and held his hand for the last time.

That day will always remain a horrible memory for me, and not only because I became a widow at an early age and lost a man who had a lasting impact on me. During the 1979 revolution, Westerners became accustomed to seeing thousands of Islamic mourners beating themselves, screaming out in pain; they saw the passion unleashed by the death of demonstrators who had risen up against the Shah. But until my husband died, I had not yet experienced that dark and violent form of mourning.

When it became apparent that Bijan would soon die, my father telephoned my Uncle Ardeshir and he and Aunt Guity arrived immediately. We all sat in my matrimonial bedroom, watching and waiting for death to end Bijan's pain. Along with his mother and sisters, Bijan's brother Ali and his younger sister's husband, Parviz, the psychologist, were also present. Their hostility towards us was such that they could not even bear to look at us.

At one point, the psychologist turned on my father and shouted: "Why don't you do something? Get a doctor. Get some oxygen. Do something."

The fact that a doctor was present, Bijan's own brother in fact, and that my husband was beyond anyone's help seemed to be lost on him. My relatives just bowed their heads and said nothing. I cried uncontrollably as I held Bijan's long, emaciated hand, trying to will strength back into him.

At around 8:00 A.M. life just left Bijan, quietly and with almost no sign of having done so. When it became apparent that Bijan had died, his mother and sisters started to wail terribly. Parviz jumped up and confronted us.

"You people killed him. You wouldn't get a doctor. You wouldn't do a thing for him."

My father refused to answer him and instead grabbed me by the shoulders as I stood trying to kiss Bijan's hand and said quietly: "It's not safe for you in here. Let's all go downstairs."

I was terrified that the Aminis would start to beat me up, and even though I was grieving terribly now that Bijan had died, I was aware of the danger I was in and grateful that family reinforcements were there to protect me.

Within a half-hour of Bijan's death, the house was full of our relatives, friends and business associates. Two of the first to arrive were Bijan's partners, Jamshid and Abdullah Taslimi, who went immediately upstairs to talk to the Aminis. After a while one of them came down and asked my father and me to join them upstairs. I was afraid to go back up there for fear of what the Aminis might do, but flanked by my relatives I took courage. Upstairs the Aminis were in an even fouler mood. They had opened my husband's briefcase, which had sat next to his bed and which contained legal documents, including the will. But in it there should also have been a large wallet with about $30,000 in foreign currency that he always kept in case he had to make a quick, unplanned trip abroad, as well as about $50,000 worth of tumans — the Iranian currency.

"Where is the money? What have you done with it?" Ali asked.

I stared at him in disbelief and then looked around at the rest of the Aminis. That wallet had been there the night before. I looked in the briefcase and noticed that a bag containing some of our best jewellery was also missing.

"Admit it," said Parviz. "You and your father stole it."

Until Bijan had become wealthy, the Aminis had been middle-class people who had never travelled abroad, had never seen the inside of a Shemiran mansion and had never looked beyond their own suburb for inspiration. For years they had gratefully taken whatever gifts Bijan had chosen to give them and I have no doubt that they loved him, but now that he was dead, there was no way they were going to allow a young widow to enjoy what he had earned.

My father and uncle were too embarrassed to reply to their accusations and the lost wallet and jewellery were never seen again.

Somehow, despite the seemingly uncontrolled nature of their grief, the four Amini women found time, between screaming loudly and pulling their hair, to change into black suits and heavy *chadors*. I was so disoriented that I had to be reminded to change into black, and I sent a cousin of mine up to the bedroom to pick out something appropriate to wear. After a few minutes she returned, embarrassed to tell me that she had failed.

"I am sorry, Sousan," she said, "but they said things were being robbed and that they were not going to allow anything to be removed, not even your own clothes, unless you went up personally."

Overcoming my revulsion, I went upstairs, accompanied by some of my friends, and managed to grab a black skirt, blouse, scarf and shoes. I ran hurriedly back down. After a while, a *mullah* the Aminis had invited to the house began to call out a mournful prayer. By ten o'clock so many people had arrived that it would have been the right time to wrap the body, according to custom, in a Persian carpet and take it to the cemetery for the ritual burial. But Bijan's mother insisted that we wait until even more mourners had had time to come, even though that meant holding the funeral during the hottest time of the day. It was almost noon before we set off for what would be a four-hour burial preparation.

During the ceremony at Behesht Zahra cemetery, while Bijan's body was being washed and wrapped in a white shroud and his grave was being dug, my in-laws continued to mutter insults about my family, and several times my friends and relatives had to ask them to lower their voices.

Ali was heard to say, "She killed him. Her mother had a cancer and she gave it to him." This was from a medical doctor trained in Iran.

At one point, my father overheard Ali tell his uncle to put the silk carpet that the body had been wrapped in, in his own car and not to bring it back to the house. My father waited a few moments and then confronted the uncle.

"There have been enough malicious things said and done today," he said, losing his temper for the first time. "We have ignored them all. But if that carpet is not brought back to the house there will be a scene that your family will regret."

The uncle quietly transferred the carpet back into one of our cars, but several other carpets, including two my father had given us as a wedding gift, which Bijan and I had stored at his mother's house for safekeeping while we were in Europe for his operations, were never seen again.

When the service was over, the entire Amini family moved back into my house for the official mourning period. Iranian funerals and the later mourning period are very elaborate and lengthy. For the first week after a burial, the house is always filled with people who drop in to pay their respects and often stay to lunch or dinner. Every bereaved family, rich or poor, makes available the best in food and non-alcoholic drink that they can afford. Often people go well beyond their means to put on a proper funeral. With his eye for detail, Bijan had set aside $40,000 just for the funeral, but my own family also contributed heavily. My Uncle Ardeshir sent chefs and waiters from *La Réserve* and enough cooked food to serve dinner to about fifty people a day. On the seventh day, a special day of mourning, we served dinner to over two hundred people.

Because the Aminis were still in the house, I always had about five or six relatives staying with me. During that entire period of mourning the Aminis showed nothing but hatred for me and my family. They hated me for having survived my husband and having time to enjoy his money, and simply because I was different from them.

One day, Bijan's relatives from the countryside came to visit for the first time. They were simpler people, mostly small businessmen from Arak, a city southwest of Teheran. All the women wore *chadors* and I could see that they were watching me carefully to see if I, a Western-educated widow, would display grief in the traditional way. I could see them staring at the luxuries in our house. The men actually paced the garden, measuring how wide and long it was and counting the trees, admiration and envy mixed in their shrewd eyes.

If I had ever needed a lesson in the great contrasts within my country, that funeral provided it starkly. My family, on one side, were dressed in Western-style mourning clothes, the women made up a little more simply than usual, the men talking about trivial things to keep our spirits up. In Bijan's family, on the other hand, the women were cloaked in *chadors*, devoid of all make-up; they screamed loudly for hours on end, taking time out only to eat rather large lunches and dinners, and talking as if the whole world had come to an end, even for those who had not seen Bijan in years. I began to suspect that behind their torrent of grief was as much artifice as true sorrow. After the *mullah* left, the Aminis made sure the awful wail would still fill the air; they brought in tapes of prayer and played them from morning till night.

I knew the customs of the vast majority of Iranians so little that during the mourning period, after taking a shower, I automatically sprayed a little perfume on my neck. The first person I greeted was the American-born wife of an Iranian cousin who said quietly to me so that the Aminis might not hear, "Sousan, for heaven's sake, you must not wear perfume right now."

"Why?" I asked, genuinely perplexed.

"Because for a Moslem that is a sign of being happy."

"But the days are so hot. I just didn't want to stink."

"For a Moslem, it's better to stink than to wear perfume at a funeral."

One day, Bijan's sister-in-law, Ali's wife, went into the kitchen to serve sherbet to some guests. Suddenly we heard a scream and a great crash. We all ran to find her sprawled on the kitchen floor in the throes of some kind of fit. Her husband promptly started yelling in panic but fortunately my cousin Chloe had the presence of mind to give her mouth-to-mouth resuscitation, and after a few moments the woman regained consciousness. After a doctor had come to examine her and give her an injection (for what purpose I never knew), Chloe and I happened to find ourselves alone with her momentarily. Despite the difficulty she had in talking, she forced herself to tell us a rather strange story.

"I saw Bijan," she said. "He came to me. He thanked me for helping to serve the guests." Then she grabbed hold of me and stared into my eyes. "Watch them. Watch them all. They're devils. They're after your husband's money. I'm a religious person, a good Moslem. I can't bear to see my children eating food that belongs rightfully to another child. God will punish me if that happens. Watch Bijan's family."

When she heard someone approaching, she became silent and after that never made reference again to what she had said. In those days when everything seemed sinister, her fear and her story seemed perfectly fitting. It is only now that I am years and miles away that I can see how nearly fantastical those events were.

A few days after the funeral, my husband's will was read to my father and my uncles. When they recounted to me the terms of my husband's last wishes I was humiliated and shocked. My husband had left all his shares in the construction firm to his brothers and sisters. He had left his mother and two unmarried sisters a healthy sum of money and land, because, after all, they had no man to take care of them when the wealthiest son died. To my son, he left all his property, his house, the villa, the apartments abroad, tracts of land throughout the city and in the countryside—millions of dollars' worth, if only everything had not changed with the revolution. To me, his wife, the woman he had treated like a defenceless child incapable of buying her own fruit, he left almost nothing. He left me a small amount of money — about $150,000 in bonds — a pittance for a man who counted his money in the tens of millions. It was the equivalent of throwing two pennies at a servant who had done poor work.

But perhaps the most insulting aspect of the will was that my husband had not seen fit to include me among those named to be my son's official guardians. Under Islamic law, a widow can easily lose custody of her children to her husband's male relatives, although under the Shah women had gained some limited rights. But I had thought that my husband would have been more liberal, more respectful of me as a person. Instead he had been a traditional Iranian man to the end. He had given full control of Farhad's life and his fortune to his two partners and his brother Ali. I was to be a mere babysitter. He had also made it certain that I, a young attractive widow, would not have much of his money to enjoy with another man.

It was the final betrayal. I had married one man and watched another one die. As long as I did not remarry, I could live in the house with my son and drive my husband's cars and have a modest allowance which would barely cover the monthly expenses on the Shemiran property. If I married, I would lose everything, quite possibly even my right to keep Farhad with me. At any time they chose, the Aminis, by pressuring the two partners with whom they were now linked in the company, could threaten to take Farhad away. They would have to be able to prove that I was an unfit mother, but in Iran it is not difficult to stack the weight of evidence against a woman. At eighteen, my son would be a wealthy man with holdings in Iran and Europe that I still knew little about.

But while my husband lay dying, the Iran that he knew was also disappearing. Every day there were anti-Shah demonstrations on the streets. Every day news reports told us that the army had scattered a gathering of students or leftist agitators. Bijan thought that he was passing on the empire that he had built and that it would continue to grow under the indestructible rule of the Shah. But the time would come when to be rich and to have land would count as a liability, and much of what he gave his son, Farhad would never be able to claim.

Chapter Five

The Gilded Cocoon

You were made king to keep your folk from harm,
To treat their wounds with vivifying balm.

NIZAMI GANJEVI

 By mid-1977 when my husband died, it was impossible, even in our protected enclave, to ignore the evidence of a serious assault on the monarchy and the political regime. In May of that year, fifty-three lawyers addressed an open letter to the imperial court to demand an independent judiciary. Ours was notoriously susceptible to pressure from on high. Leading authors and intellectuals began to write openly to the prime minister demanding the end of censorship and the restoration of the freedom of the press. Just two years before, they would not have dared to speak so publicly. But although there was widespread dissatisfaction with the Shah, no one that I had afternoon tea with, or shopped with, or met at cocktail parties wanted to see a change of leadership. My relatives, friends and I simply could not see any likely alternative. The opposition seemed to be composed mostly of leftist students, some of the more radical *mullahs*, various disunited factions in the country and remnants of the old National Front, the party that under Mossadegh had been involved in the brief overthrow of the Shah in 1953.

"It will be 1953 all over again," one of the older men in my group often said. "Wait and see. The CIA will step in again and then there's the army to think about. Do these kids really think they can take on the army?"

We had built up a myth about our army. The Shah had spent lavishly on the armed forces. Between 1972 and 1976 he had bought $10 billion worth of American-made arms. He had bought F-14 Grumman-Tomcat jet fighters armed with Phoenix missiles, an $850 million electronic surveillance system from Rockwell International, Spruance class destroyers and countless tanks in a buying spree that had drained both money and manpower from the rest of the economy. There were an estimated 140,000 men in active duty and another 400,000 on reserve. But all of us underestimated the forces at work within the country and if we saw a threat at all, we thought it might come from the army, which might move in to stamp out the student unrest. Nobody talked yet of the power of Ayatollah Ruhollah Khomeini. The fiery religious leader was then living in Iraq, having been forced into exile by the Shah in 1964 after Khomeini had led a bloody revolt against the Shah's land-reform program. Khomeini had been scathing about the Shah's attack on the mosques' land-owning power base.

In my own private world I was busy trying to grow up quickly. After staying in my house for the ten-day mourning

period, the Aminis finally left, but only after my father called
a meeting with the company partners and the doctor and
politely told them they had to go. Grudgingly, they moved
out, leaving me mistress of my household for the first time in
my life. With the severe cutback in income, I immediately
discharged the chauffeur and one gardener, as well as a couple
of other servants. I retained only one servant and one full-
time and one part-time gardener. When Bijan was alive, the
monthly expenses of the house had been about $12,000, but
I stopped entertaining in the lavish style we had adopted and
managed to bring down my expenses to about $3,000 a
month, which my family helped me to cover. Hardly poverty,
but not that limitless luxury that I had known.

Iran and I were belt-tightening at about the same time. By
1977 it had become evident that the Shah's great dream of
turning Iran into an industrialized world power overnight had
turned into a nightmare. All that oil money was not enough
to cover the nation's bills, and the Shah found himself scrap-
ping purchases, even for his beloved armed forces.

I remember receiving my first household bill — for water
and electricity. In a panic I telephoned my Uncle Ardeshir to
find out what I should do with it, and he patiently explained
that I was to take it to the bank to pay it. I managed to pay the
servants for the first time, keeping the receipts as I had ob-
served my husband do. I had always been terrified of having
any direct dealings with the gardener, because my husband
had never given me an opportunity to handle anything so
complicated as the management of the garden. But now I
found that I was quite able to choose the flowers and shrubs
that had to be ordered and planted and was not embarrassed
by the result. When something went wrong with the swimming pool or the air conditioning, I found out whom to call
and then stood watching as the repairmen did their job,
determined to learn something of what they were doing.

Such simple things — but for me, a well-kept toy whose
only job had been to look pretty and select new outfits, it

was like starting a new life. Through connections, I even managed to get an international driver's licence without having to take another driving test. I simply used my expired American licence as proof of proficiency. The dreadful Teheran traffic proved to be not so bad after all. Over time I slowly began to gain confidence in myself and even a little self-respect. I hadn't realized how little I had come to think of myself.

My greatest new responsibility was Farhad. During his last months of life, Bijan had made every effort to spend as much time as possible with his son. It was only in the last few weeks, when he feared that his emaciated face and bloated stomach would create a lasting nightmare for Farhad, that he asked us to keep his son away from him. During the mourning period, Farhad stayed at the home of a friend, but when he returned home later he sensed how much had changed. He knew by my swollen eyes and the downcast looks of our relatives that something was wrong, but even then, Farhad was an introverted child, never asking questions when things were obviously bleak. I knew how dreadfully he would miss his favourite playmate and, wanting to break the news to him gradually, at first I told him that his father had gone to Switzerland. For months afterwards, every time we saw a man speeding past in a silver Mercedes, the kind of car his father drove, he would jump up and down excitedly: "Look, Mummy, it's dad. Look. Look." Even in crowds, he would run up to men who resembled his father, only to turn away quietly when it was not the one he was searching for. Finally, I told him that his father would never be coming back. "He has gone to heaven and joined my mother. I was also very young when I lost her." Long after that, he seemed to be always waiting for someone. But, like his father, he said little and rarely showed his pain.

Having, by my own account, been a flighty mother until then, I was determined to do my best for Farhad, find the best school for him, teach him discipline as his father would have done and try to be as loving as any two parents could be. Raising Farhad without Bijan to guide me was my greatest challenge.

At first, I still lived in my husband's shadow and would rush home at lunchtime half expecting him to be there scolding me for having been out too long. It took me a while to realize that no one was monitoring me. For weeks, I refused all invitations to dinner and family gatherings. But about ten months after Bijan's death, I went to the Caspian villa for a weekend with Farhad, my cousin Firouzeh and her two children. Her husband, another construction czar, was often away on business and we had begun to spend much more time together.

After we had settled the children down for the night, we took a taxi to the Hyatt hotel, about an hour's drive away, to have a "grown-up" dinner. In Iran, even in the upper class, it was unusual to see two women dining out alone. As a result, we drew quite a lot of attention: Firouzeh, a striking, lean beauty with long, blonde hair and large green eyes, and I, still in my widow's black. Several of Firouzeh's friends who happened to be there quickly joined us. It was then that I met the man who would come in and out of my life for the next three years like a careless, fun-loving imp, and the man I will always associate with those last days of pleasure, those rather willful, wild days as we all danced to a more and more reckless tune, knowing that soon the dance would be over.

Hamid was the playboy bachelor son of an important industrialist. His mother was a flamboyant socialite, known in Teheran for her wild parties of five hundred or more people. Once she asked her guests to show up dressed in pyjamas; another time they were to come dressed only in black and white. At one gathering, mules walked about the stately rooms of her Teheran mansion laden with baskets full of fresh fruit. Hamid himself had the franchise to import a well-known automobile and was best friends with the Shah's sister, Fatimah. A charmer and a wit with an easy-going manner, he was often found at royal parties or on the jets bound for Paris, which he regularly visited on a whim for a weekend of frivolity. Determined not to be trapped by a woman, Hamid, at forty-one, took pleasure in all women and had never married. After we met that night at the Hyatt he called me several times and eventually we formed a strong relationship.

Once, when I was still at the stage of trying to impress him, I hosted a very expensive little dinner party, hiring the French chef and waiters that my uncle had brought to Iran for the opening of his second French restaurant. But when I called to invite him, at the last minute to make it look like an impromptu affair, I was told by a servant that he had just left to spend the weekend in Sardinia. In the end, it was I who was impressed.

In many ways, Hamid represented illicit fun to me, especially after the months of sadness I had lived through. We saw each other casually for some time before I became intimate with him and, even then, I tried to keep the relationship as discreet as possible—it wasn't seemly for such a new widow to be sharing a bed with a man. It was companionship and a social escort that I wanted from him more than sex. As far as I was concerned, sex was still just a woman's duty to her husband. But for Hamid, a good sexual relationship was an essential part of any dating, and I realized that if I wanted to hold on to him, I would have to learn to enjoy making love. I was finding out that even in Iran there were plenty of women, married or not, who would be only too pleased to make love to an eligible man. I had considered myself a fairly liberated woman, but suddenly I found myself in much more risqué company—and I liked it. There was something exciting about having sex that was not sanctioned by society. And Hamid represented a challenge to me as a woman. I had to be a good sexual partner, and I became determined to be better than any of his other lovers.

By early 1978, while I was making my name in the younger crowd as someone who could be counted on to provide sparkling entertainment, the mood of the country was darkening day by day. In January of that year seminary students in the holy city of Qom demonstrated against an article published in the government-controlled newspaper *Ettelaat*, which insulted the good name of Ayatollah Khomeini, by now the most revered of the Shah's enemies. Now the Shah's nemesis was fulminating against the Pahlavis from Najef, Iraq. Tapes of the Ayatollah's sermons were smuggled into the country and his voice thundered invective against what he called the Westernized, satanic regime of the Shah.

It was a cold day that January when soldiers confronted the students and shot many of them to death. In Iran it was never possible to know the exact number of casualties. We read censored accounts and then heard uncensored gossip, and the violence seemed to belong to another country—not the one I knew. But the atrocity was such that forty days later, according to Islamic custom, mourning ceremonies were held for the dead and in several major centres violence again broke out, creating a cycle of protest that the army could not break.

Even in my gilded cocoon I could feel the hatred of the mass of Iranians for the sort of Iran that I and my kind stood for. We dressed in Western clothes, enjoyed Western films and night life, music, alcohol and gambling — all expressly forbidden in the Koran. We thought nothing of women working or travelling alone. The growing conservatism of the country — a reaction against the too-rapid change of the previous decade and the influence of the West — began to frighten us. Then, in August, we received horrible news. A fire that had been deliberately set in a packed cinema in Abadan had killed 477 people. The protestors blamed the government for setting the fire, while the government blamed dissidents. No one knew whom to believe, but the nation was so incensed that the Shah began to make concessions to his adversaries.

It became clear that the Shah feared the conservative forces in the country as much as we were beginning to. After the fire, he dismissed his prime minister, shut down gambling casinos, nightclubs and cinemas, abolished the post of minister of state for women's affairs that he had created in spite of the *mullahs*' anger and instead set up a ministry of religious affairs. He also permitted greater freedom of the press.

But in September, 100,000 people crowded into Shahyad Square to offer a mass prayer for the nation, and after three days of demonstrations, people in the streets began to call for an Islamic state led by Khomeini. The night of September 7, after that call went up, the government declared martial law. The very next day, people took to the streets again and this time, in Jaleh Square in a working-class suburb of Teheran, the soldiers fired on them, creating many more martyrs for Khomeini's cause. By October, the first of the many strikes in the public sector took place. It seemed that no one had control over Iran anymore — unless it was Khomeini. That autumn, the Shah asked Iraqi president Saddam Hussein to kick Khomeini out of his country, but that proved to be an enormous tactical error, because the religious leader went to France and in Neauphle-le-Château just outside Paris he was surrounded by the world's press. Now his fulminations against the Shah could be heard worldwide.

While these events unfolded, my uncles and older relatives, fearing the worst, began to lead more conservative lives: they avoided large parties, drove less expensive cars and attempted to mute the more conspicuous signs of their wealth. But we younger Iranians seemed intent on enjoying every last minute of our privileged lives.

My new boyfriend Hamid would complain, "So what do you think will happen to us if there is a revolution? Aren't all these demonstrations crazy? What do these people think they are going to gain? They're just going to destroy this beautiful country of ours."

A friend of ours countered, "What can they do? Take away our land? Our money? We might as well enjoy it now."

But as the demonstrations gathered momentum and violence became a daily occurrence, Hamid started to warn us, even as we drank our imported scotch and listened to American music and made plans to go shopping in Europe, "We'll be lucky to get away with just losing our wealth. What we're talking about now is losing our lives."

Perhaps the strongest signal that our days of freedom would soon end came in November 1978, when the Shah took to the airwaves to assure the people who were calling for his overthrow that he understood them.

"I have heard your revolutionary message," he told the nation. "There will be changes, I promise."

Was this our Shah talking? The King of Kings, the Light of the Aryans, the man who had claimed an ancestry going back to King Cyrus 2,500 years before?

All around me I began to see the signs that the upper class was pulling out, protecting itself, making contingency plans. Many of the wealthy had already built up extensive holdings abroad; until now it had been easy to send money out of the country. Even during the troubled year of 1978 people had little difficulty smuggling out carpets, jewellery and other moveable valuables. All it took was a few bribes.

No one declared publicly that he was leaving the country. Instead, acquaintances, friends, leading political and business figures just quietly packed up and left for a "holiday." One day when I went to visit a friend I found that her father was selling off his very fine collection of antique furniture.

"Oh, it's nothing," she said when I asked about it. "We just have too many things around."

Two months later, she and her parents had left. They now live in Geneva.

In August, my cousin Firouzeh and her husband left for a holiday in Europe, taking with them only enough clothes for the summer season.

"I'll be back, don't worry," Firouzeh said as I kissed her goodbye tearfully.

But they never came back, and shortly after the revolution, the new government confiscated her husband's company, their magnificent antique-filled mansion right next to the Niavaran Palace, and all their lands.

People left in waves: first the Shah's closest relatives, then their friends, then people closely identified with the regime and finally the leading industrialists, bankers and landowners who simply abandoned their companies, factories and villages, placing them in the hands of subordinates.

Hamid's family wisely left in the second wave of emigrés, but he stayed in an attempt to protect the family property and to keep his own business going. One of my female cousins, Nono, who had been trained as a physician in Austria and who was the personal doctor of one of the royal princesses, received a call one morning from the royal household. A member of the Shah's court had just called and given the princess and all the other relatives one day to leave the country. After packing what they could in a few hours, the royal household evacuated — and my cousin went with them, for she knew she would certainly not survive under a new regime should the Shah fall.

For those of us who remained — either because we mistakenly believed that the revolution would not come or because, like me, we naïvely assumed that, having done nothing wrong, we would not face reprisals — life became increasingly difficult. We could not talk, even amongst ourselves, about the impending revolution without becoming involved in emotional outbursts and terrible fights. Although the troubles became our national obsession, we tried to ban political discussion at our family gatherings. Too often, worried questionings about the nation's future would turn into feverish debate, with one or more stomping out in anger or in tears.

The Salmans had given so much to Iran. My Uncle Fayegh, who had never married because he wanted to put the needs of our extended family before his own, spent all his free time helping nonprofit organizations raise funds for the disabled.

He also gave much of his private wealth to groups offering social services to the poor. A gentle, erudite man, he was one of the closest to me of all my uncles and he retained a deep love for my mother. My Uncle Kurosh, the patriarch of the Salmans and the most famous, had undertaken many difficult engineering jobs for the state. A cigar firmly planted between his teeth and immaculately dressed even when visiting a job site, he was proud to be part of the country's development.

Of all my relatives, only my Uncle Ardeshir and Aunt Guity believed that the country would be better off without the Shah.

"Aren't you afraid of losing everything?" I asked them once.

Guity replied, "You can't be selfish. You have to think of the country as a whole. A revolution would be the best thing for the people. There are so many poor, so many uneducated people. We have to help them. It's not only our society, but everybody's. As long as the Shah stays, nothing will change."

I suppose my aunt and uncle represented the side of the family with the most conscience. Educated in the United States, my aunt was a volunteer worker with handicapped children, and her family, the leading distributor of home fuel in the country, was known to be religious. A big, softly round-ed blonde, Guity was generous with her hugs and guidance, and had become my surrogate mother since her return to Iran in the early 1970s. My uncle, the most handsome of the Salmans, who owned *La Réserve*, had always made a point of driving a very inexpensive car, although he could afford much better.

"This is a poor country," he would say. "Why aggravate people by a conspicuous display?"

I had to admit that my friends and I had become so wrapped up in our own lives that it was difficult for us to understand the needs of others whom we almost never encountered. Perhaps we did not want to understand. But also, we could not. Our lives were too different.

Once that fall I went with my Aunt Guity and her husband
to see a mass demonstration that had been called for the late
afternoon on Shemiran Boulevard. I had become adept at
avoiding the street demonstrations that seemed to break out
regularly around the city. But that afternoon, as I watched
hundreds of thousands of people flowing down the wide
boulevard, their fists raised in anger, I saw the faces of the
revolution for the first time. There were the poor, the middle class and even occasionally the well off. There were older
women, young men, girls proudly wearing the *chador*. They
yelled "Death to the Shah. Death to Satan, U.S.A." They prayed
for the early return of Khomeini.

So many expectations were written on their faces. The
intellectuals thought that with the Shah gone, they would be
free to create as they wished, Savak would be disbanded, the
press would print without fear. The poor put their hope in
Khomeini's promises that the homeless would be housed and
the hungry would have food. The peasants dreamed of rid-
ding themselves of their landlords. The merchants would no
longer have to deal with a corrupt court. The nationalists
would finally see the country escape the dominance of the
United States and no more would Iran buy billions of dollars'
worth of arms from the Great Satan. All of the Shah's disparate
critics had come together in an historic moment of unity.

In the winter of 1978, when strikes were stopping all necessary functions in the country and demonstrations were the
main daily activity of many Iranians, I decided to take my
son to Europe. In December, the Shah, in a last effort to hold
onto power, named National Front leader Shapour Bakhtiar
his new prime minister. It was only a matter of time before
that government, too, would collapse. With such a future,
where would be the best place to raise my son? Was it fair to
disrupt his life, take him from his family and friends and start
all over again in a strange country? If he stayed in Iran he

would be a rich man. But in exile, how would we survive? And yet, was it fair to try to raise him in a country which would soon be thrown into chaos?

The Aminis made it very clear that they would oppose any effort I made to take Farhad out of the country permanently. For them no other place existed on earth. Nor were they swayed by our arguments that Farhad might be safer abroad. My husband's brother Ali said to my Uncle Fayegh, ''If children die in Iran, his blood is no redder, no better than that of others. He should die with the rest.''

The fact is that they did not want him out of their grasp because they did not want to lose any control over his money. They used their power over the two partners and Farhad's trust fund to keep money from us so that we could not travel freely without their consent. Before I set off for Europe, my Uncle Fayegh had to sign an undertaking that he would be responsible for making certain that I would return to Iran and he had to pledge a sizeable amount of money.

When I left in December that year, I really had no idea who would be in power when I got back. The trip, ultimately financed by my uncles, was a contrast to my usual forays to Europe when my husband's money had eased the way. We stayed at our apartments in Valencia, Paris and London and lived simply, mostly visiting relatives. All the while, I heard on the news that Khomeini was calling on Iranians to force the Shah out and that he himself was making plans to return home.

By that time, Khomeini had come to be seen as the inevitable new father figure for the country, and a cousin in Paris said to me, ''Why don't you go down to Neauphle-le-Château and see him? All the Iranians are going down there to pay homage. He is a great man, a great patriot.''

But I did not share her confidence in the man and refused to go.

One day — it was January 16, 1979 — I was visiting my cousin Firouzeh and her husband, Manouchehr, in their

English manor house in Wimbledon when he came rushing into the sitting room where we were having tea.

"Come quickly," he yelled. "Come to the television. The Shah is leaving. He's leaving."

There on the screen was the pitiful sight of the King of Kings, a handful of Iranian soil in his pocket, getting ready to board a blue and white Boeing 727. Firouzeh and I started to weep. Although we would never have defended the Shah's unlimited corruption, we could not help but be sad that the monarchy itself had been reduced to running scared from the country.

Manouchehr said, "Well, thank God that's over. Now maybe the country can go back to normal. His leaving is the best thing that could have happened."

"How can you say that?" his wife asked. "Everything that you own is because of the Shah. It was under his regime that you became rich."

Firouzeh and I were emotional and we screamed at him that he was stupid, that he did not realize that he was about to lose everything.

"Who the hell is Khomeini?" she shouted. "How can he run the country? He's just a *mullah*."

I looked around at all that Firouzeh and Manouchehr had managed to amass. The manor house was renovated and decorated in chintz, its magnificent carved fireplace warmed by a blazing fire. In the driveway stood their Rolls and their Mercedes. In London, they owned a highrise that was being renovated and that they eventually sold at double their investment. Did he think he would be able to thrive in the same way under new masters?

But then, in times of such great change, you do not really know what will happen and you just keep hoping for the best, never really believing that you will be caught up in the great events of history. I am sure that at that moment there were many future victims of Khomeini's revenge who were blessing the Shah's departure. Even the most pessimistic did not predict that Khomeini would toss the country backwards several centuries.

Two weeks later I was in our Paris apartment packing our bags and getting ready to go home. I had no choice but to go. There was Uncle Fayegh's written promise to consider and the fact that I was ill-prepared financially to think of cutting myself off from Iran for good. After closing down the airports for days to keep Khomeini from flying back home, Bakhtiar had finally bowed to pressure and reopened them. I was scheduled to take the midnight Air France flight back to Teheran and I was idly listening to the television set when I heard the announcer say that Khomeini was finally going home — and on the same flight as mine. A delirious nation was making plans to greet him on his return.

Panicked at the thought of being on the same flight as a man I was beginning to hate, I called Air France to have my booking changed, but, as it turned out, I had already been bumped off the flight by Khomeini's entourage. All the passengers scheduled to leave on that flight had been booked on one leaving about two hours later. Khomeini's flight was to be only half full so that the plane would have enough fuel to make the five-hour trip home if it was turned back at the last moment. The Ayatollah took with him only his closest advisers and some press, leaving the women in his party behind for fear that the plane might be sabotaged.

When we reached the airport, I found that police were nervously patrolling the waiting rooms and departure lounges, which were crowded with turbaned *mullahs* and women hidden under their *chadors*. These were the Ayatollah's people who had not made it on his flight and were evidently going to be on mine. I had never seen so many *mullahs*, their black or brown robes sweeping the floor, or so many women in *chadors*. The sickeningly sweet scent of rosewater, the only perfume worn by devout Moslems, filled the air. Although they must have lived in France for at least a few months and must have acquired some Western habits, they chose to eat their food while sitting on the floor and left their garbage strewn everywhere. As the hours went by, the police became more and more surly with the passengers. Apart from me, there was only one other Iranian woman dressed in Western clothes. Even Farhad, clinging to me, was unusually subdued. Instead of asking his endless chirpy childish questions, he only whispered every now and then and looked around wide-eyed. How different from the other flights I had taken back from Paris, filled with Iranians sporting the latest designs. A new order was very visibly taking control of my country and I was flying back with those who would be in power, an unwanted passenger on the wings of change.

Chapter Six

The Ayatollah's Revenge

*We suffer enough at the mullahs' hands, without all this as
  well:*
*Yet follow them once more, but what fools we — not to break
  away.*

KASSUM-BEK ZAKIR

 "Welcome back to the best country on earth." The
porter beamed with the afterglow of Khomeini's
joyous return as he took my bags and propelled
me towards my waiting relatives at Mehrabad Airport. Airport workers were singing a song that one of the
nation's composers had written especially for the great home-
coming. The portraits of the Shah had already disappeared
and been replaced by those of the grim-faced Ayatollah. Along

the boulevards leading into the city, trampled flowers, ban-
ners and heaped garbage testified to the arrival, just three
hours before, of the Imam, the holy father of the country, a
seventy-seven-year-old man with a long memory for grudges.
Some streets were literally clogged with carnations and chry-
santhemums that had been strewn in front of his cavalcade.

"You should have seen the crowds," my father said, still
in shock. "I've never seen such euphoria. How long will it
last?"

It did not take long, really — just a few months — for that
early bounding national joy to turn into fear and suspicion.
Iranians were so happy to have chased out the Shah that they
did not realize he had not taken the problems of the country
with him. Khomeini's first act the day he arrived was to visit
the cemetery and stand by the unmarked graves of the many
demonstrators killed in the struggle against the Shah. Later,
he ordered that a fountain of blood be built, using red dyed
water, to remind pilgrims of those who had sacrificed themselves for the revolution. Many more were to be sacrificed—
only this time Khomeini himself would be responsible for
their deaths.

The *taghouti*. The devil's followers. That is how Khomeini
branded all of us who had not supported the revolution, who
had been close to the royal family or had run major enterprises, who wore Western clothing or had gone to schools
abroad, who were rich or lived in the upper reaches of the
city, those of us who went to cinemas or still had alcohol in
our homes — all of us who did not follow the "Imam's line."
In speeches he exhorted his followers to hunt us out. He
whipped up such hatred and paranoia about us that it became
dangerous to walk out in the middle of the day. We might be
recognized as *taghouti* merely because of the way we dressed
or the kind of cars we drove.

I remember seeing an interview with him on Iranian television the day he arrived. Iranian and foreign journalists
crowded around him as he stepped out of the airplane.

"What do you feel coming back into your own country after so many years?" one journalist shouted.

Khomeini's face was impassive. "Nothing," is what he replied.

Soon the persecution began. Just before he left, in a last desperate attempt to hold on to power, the Shah had allowed the arrest of 132 government leaders, including the former long-time prime minister, Amir Abbas Hoveyda, and the former head of Savak, General Ne'matollah Nasiri, as if the human offering would appease the Islamic fundamentalists. With Khomeini's return on February 1, 1979, there was little hope for them. On February 11, Bakhtiar's government fell and Khomeini proclaimed the creation of an Islamic state. No *taghouti* could hope for a fair trial.

The first to be executed by firing squad were armed forces generals, the head of Savak and Hoveyda. I remember how we huddled in the home of Firouzeh's older sister, Azi, and watched the imprisoned men being "interviewed" on television. It was obvious that some of them had been tortured. Some could barely speak. But in a brutal fashion, in a parody of justice, they were being forced to recant their loyalty to the Shah. After the terrible spectacle that all Iranians had been ordered to watch, they were shot and their mutilated bodies displayed on the screen. I was speechless with fear.

"I never thought they would kill Hoveyda," Uncle Kurosh said. "The fool. He thought that because he said he had done nothing wrong he would be able to put his case to the public and be saved. How can anybody be safe in this madness? Now that they've shown they can kill that kind of man, where will they stop?"

We were to ask ourselves that over and over again in the following weeks as the *mullahs* and *ayatollahs* began to take control of the country. Over five hundred people were executed in the first year of the revolution. We stayed indoors for some time after those early executions because it was becoming increasingly dangerous for us to be seen at all. Any day we expected the new rulers to come and arrest us, simply because we were wealthy. Even without that threat, we were in danger of being killed by accident by the dozens of armed men who now patrolled the streets. With the army effectively disarmed and the regular police force powerless, the *mullahs* set up their own armed security forces — the revolutionary committees known as the Komiteh. With automatic rifles taken from ammunition dumps, the new rulers confiscated Range Rovers and Mercedes — once the almost official vehicles of the rich and now almost exclusively the sign of the new regime — and rode shotgun through the streets firing on anything that seemed suspicious. The prisons were opened up and inmates released, the tortured intellectuals of the Shah's regime and common criminals alike.

Even more than Khomeini, the man who most typified the vengeful side of the revolutionary government was Hojjat ol-Eslam Sadeq Khalkhali, nicknamed the Executioner, a middle-level cleric who had been his long-time supporter. Those first few months he toured the country looking for victims — those guilty of being too rich, too hated by their neighbours or of having connections with the previous regime. He seemed to find them with ease: landlords, land-owners, industrialists, former politicians. It was Khalkhali who once ordered seven alleged drug offenders shot by firing squad in public in a Teheran street. He also defended an Islamic judge who had brought back a horrible mediaeval form of killing: the judge had ordered that four sex offenders, two men and two women, be buried up to the neck and then stoned to death.

One large land-owning family I was related to were the Sanandajis, who controlled vast parts of the Sanandaj province. One day, Khalkhali showed up at a village owned by the patriarch of the family, the oldest of many brothers and sisters. Despite the fact that the man was bedridden and very ill, Khalkhali ordered him to be brought on a stretcher to the centre of the village, where he put him on trial in front of the villagers for having plundered the region's wealth and mistreated his workers.

Khalkhali asked him, "Why do you have an American Standard toilet in your house? Why don't you have a Persian one like everybody else? And look at your swimming pool. Do you ever invite the villagers to come in for a swim?"

The Executioner commanded that the landowner be shot right then and there for all to see, and then he put out an order that all the man's brothers appear before him. Because to do so was certain death, most of the family disappeared, leaving all their belongings behind. Some managed to slip out of the country, while others found friends to hide them. One of them, my cousin Chloe, eventually came to live with me in Teheran where she hid for months until she, too, left the country.

It soon became dangerous just to be a foreigner in Iran. Not long after Khomeini's return, towards the end of February, the daily demonstrations in front of the American Embassy on Takhtejamshid Avenue took a violent turn. A group of leftists attacked the embassy, overpowered the marines, killed an Iranian embassy employee and took seventy people hostage, including the U.S. ambassador, William Sullivan. After a few nervous hours the Ayatollah's forces managed to free the hostages and reclaim the embassy, but word had spread throughout the city, and panic quickly set in amongst the many foreigners still living there. Several Western countries, including Canada, Britain and the United States, began to evacuate their nationals on special flights.

But the full-scale assault on the "foreign devils" did not come until November 4 of that year. I awoke one morning to the news that a group of students had once again stormed the U.S. Embassy. Thinking that the attack would again be short-lived, I went to visit a friend, Ladan, who lived near me. I had been at her house just a few moments when there was a knock at the front door. When she answered, she was surprised to find her next-door neighbours standing there. The two were Americans who worked for a U.S. engineering company. She and her husband had become quite friendly with them during the two years they had been neighbours. When she invited them in, we noticed that the visitors were pale and agitated.

Once they were safely inside, the tall, bronzed, fair one called Carl whispered, "They're after us. All the Americans have been told to go into hiding. Would you please let us stay here for a few hours? We're supposed to be meeting at a helicopter pad for an airlift, but it isn't safe for us to stay in our own house. Everybody in the area knows that Americans live there — and you know how quickly our landlord would sell us out just to get an in with the *mullahs*."

Ladan immediately assured them they could stay. We had nothing against Americans. In fact, most of us had relatives in the States or had studied there, and we had a lot of sympathy for their plight. Relieved, the two men went back next door to collect some things that they needed. They were back in minutes, with a couple of large bottles of whisky and vodka, and this time they were carrying guns in holsters strapped to their shoulders. Ladan and I looked at each other uneasily. We were two women with two small children alone in the house.

As we watched with growing nervousness, the two men started to consume the alcohol even though it was only about 10:00 A.M.; they paced up and down the living room, incapable of sitting still for even a moment. Ladan had never seen her neighbours act like that before. Those were hunted, frightening strangers, not the friendly easy-going Americans she had known, who had often invited them over for a barbecue. Ladan became so frightened that she grabbed hold of her two children and started to cry.

Patrick, the second American, quickly reassured us: "Don't be scared. We're not going to harm you. We just need to hide out. We're a little rattled, that's all. Some of our friends were arrested today and we don't know what's happening to them."

"Look, we have a freezer full of food," said Carl to calm us down. "Why don't we go and empty it. It will just go to waste otherwise."

The two of us went over and brought back a load of TV dinners and frozen meat, and we started to prepare lunch. Throughout the day, they were constantly on the telephone trying to find out what had happened to their friends. Whenever one of us received a call and we spoke in Persian, they looked at us suspiciously and finally told us to stay off the phone. After a while, the alcohol must have taken effect because they began to slow down and we became a little less scared.

In the afternoon, the two Americans suggested that we go over to their house and take anything that we wanted.

"We have to leave everything behind and the U.S. government pays for everything we lose anyway," said Carl. "I'd just as soon not leave anything for that miserable landlord of ours."

The offer was a generous one: Americans in Teheran tended to be very well stocked. "We've got two cars in the driveway too," said Patrick. "A Range Rover and a Firebird. You might as well take those, too."

"We can't just take all these things from you," I said. "But I'll see if I can get a few people to buy some of your things and we'll pay in tumans if that is of any use to you."

That is how I found myself, in the midst of the takeover of the U.S. Embassy, acting as a sort of estate agent for a couple of frightened Americans. That afternoon, we managed to sell most of their furniture — I myself bought enough rattan furniture to fill a bedroom — at low prices. But still, as the two men said, it was more than what they had expected to get. Later that afternoon, some friends of mine who had bought the bulk of the furniture hired a truck to take the pieces away and they took my things, too.

While we were in the midst of all that activity, Ladan's husband called, and when he heard what we were up to, he exploded.

"Have you any idea what danger you've exposed yourselves to? Haven't you heard that they've taken over the embassy? They're arresting foreigners on sight. Get them out of the house."

Fortunately, by late afternoon, the two men left, and I went with the truck driver to deliver the last load to my house. Later when I told my family about my acquisitions, they thought I must have been mad to take such chances. It would have been so easy for the Komiteh to stop that truck — they stopped any large vehicle — and if they had found that I had had contacts with Americans, I would have been treated as a traitor.

As the days went by and the Ayatollah did not send in his guards to rescue the Americans, it became evident that the country had entered a dangerous new phase of the revolution. For the first time, the government seemed to be condoning the seizure of foreign hostages for political ransom. Apart from our sympathy for the Americans—which we dared not express to anyone but our close friends—we were shaken by this new development. Would the Americans invade Iran now that the *mullahs* had given them a perfect excuse to do so? If they chose to retaliate, the Americans could destroy Iran. Were the *mullahs* trying to precipitate a Third World War?

Every one of the 444 days that those 52 hostages were held, we thought of those captured Americans and hoped for their release. One day, one of my cousins, who had applied for a visa at the Canadian Embassy, received a call from an embassy worker. She was told to go to the embassy the following morning to pick up her visa—even though she had originally been told she was to get it the following week. She did as she was asked and noted the hurried, hushed activities in the embassy. The next day, when she went back to ask a few questions, the embassy was closed up. That day we began to hear the first reports that six American embassy workers, who had been missed by the students when they attacked, had been spirited out of the country under false passports provided by the Canadian Embassy. Canadian Embassy personnel had risked their own lives to keep the Americans hidden for months until they could arrange to have them slip out.

As for the two frightened Americans who had sold me their furniture, they did not leave Iran swiftly as they had said they would do. Just before the hostage crisis was resolved through negotiations between the United States and Iran, a friend spotted them in the lobby of the Hilton Hotel. I suspect now that they were not simple businessmen as they claimed, but CIA agents. Otherwise, why would they have remained in the country long after most other sensible Americans had left the craziness of Iran?

Slowly, it became evident what kind of society the Ayatollah had in mind for us. For the many intellectuals and middle-class professionals who had hoped for a fairer, freer society, the realization that the Ayatollah was merely another dictator caused massive disillusionment and a sense of betrayal. In the process, I was given a fast and brutal education on life in Iran outside my own social group. Before the revolution, I could afford to ignore what was happening politically and socially to the country at large. But now I found myself listening avidly to the men as they discussed the chaos of their businesses and to my career women friends who complained that the *mullahs* were pressuring them to give up their jobs. Every rumour, every bulletin on legislative changes mesmerized me: never before had I followed the debates in the Parliament so carefully.

Hatred for the *taghouti* found victims every day. The Komiteh regularly confiscated the property of those who had left the country in a hurry and of people they disliked. But, often, instead of saving the antiques and other valuables and selling them for the state, the Komiteh destroyed them all. Often the homes of *taghouti* were, themselves, destroyed.

We took to dressing much more simply and avoided getting out of the car if we were driving from one part of the city to another. To be forced to stop in the middle of a street because of traffic or a breakdown was a nightmare. Sullen mobs would quickly surround the car asking questions. "So who is this person driving this big car? Why does he deserve to drive such an expensive car? This car belongs to the people." A *taghouti* — identified by Khomeini as the vilest person on earth — would be lucky to escape with a mere beating and the loss of his car.

The regime was determined to change any custom or service that had symbolized the life of the *taghouti*. The radio, now fully controlled by the *mullahs*, announced one day that full service for cars at gas stations was outlawed. From now on drivers would have to get out of the car and put in their own gas as in self-service stations, instead of waiting for the attendant to do it.

As the announcer said, "Why should anybody serve you? People are capable of taking care of themselves. Only the rich need this kind of service."

Radio announcers also continually exhorted us to start to live in the proper Moslem way and to follow the Imam on all matters. One of the first items Khomeini turned his attention to — while the economy continued to unravel and no one knew who was in charge of the streets — was the important matter of what women were wearing. By the early 1970s, Western dress had become almost standard in the educated urban classes. But in the late 1970s, as many Iranians turned away from what they saw as the corruption of the West, the *chador* became a symbol of the return to the purity of the Islamic tradition and a rejection of the Shah's enforced modernization drive.

After Khomeini took over, he began to order women, through radio broadcasts, to wear the *hejab*. At first, middle-class women resisted, but as each day went by, more and more of them began to cover themselves. Khomeini had often said that women were important to Iranian society, and he praised them for fighting for the revolution, but now, under the Ayatollah's direction, the *mullahs* were putting strong pressure on them to quit their jobs. In government, the new directors and bosses continually criticized the work of women employees and forced them to wear the *hejab*. Many women simply quit, rather than face daily abuse on the job. In private businesses, employers who still hired women suddenly found that they had difficulties with the authorities over minor but time-consuming matters. Throughout the country, women saw their salaries cut arbitrarily and they never knew when they might be walking down the street one day and be arrested by one of the new flying morality squads, who were connected with the Komiteh, because they were not properly dressed.

The job of the morality squads — the Monkerat — was to enforce the new social rules of the revolution. Women picked up at random because they were not wearing a *hejab*, and later a *chador*, or because they were walking with or talking to a man who was not an immediate relative, would be taken to one of the many new prisons where they were berated for hours about the need to be good Moslems. Often, their frantic families would be searching the city for them, calling every *mullah* they knew in an effort to have them released.

When the regime saw that women were too frightened to demonstrate — the few times they did, many were beaten or arrested and never seen again — they began to bring in even more restrictive laws, eventually ordering the wearing of the *chador*. What happened to my cousin Mani was typical. In ten years she had risen to be a top manager in a computer company, but when the *mullahs* took over, her salary was cut without explanation. Then she was given an ultimatum: either she resigned or they would make life so difficult that she would be glad to leave in the end. By forcing women to resign, companies and the government avoided having to pay expensive compensation. Mani ended up working as one of the managers of my uncle's restaurant, *La Réserve*.

Another, even sadder, story is that of the niece of Shery, the woman who eventually escaped with me. Shery and her family had always been involved in helping the disadvantaged. Shery herself had started up a string of schools for the disabled that the Salmans, among many others, supported both financially and through volunteer work. With her limitless generosity, she had always been an idol of mine. Shery's niece, the daughter of her sister, had also been an activist, but on the political side. After being involved in some demonstrations, the twenty-five-year-old woman was arrested and charged, although never formally in the judicial chaos of the new Iran, for being a *fedayeen*, a Marxist. The *fedayeens* had joined in the coalition with conservative *mullahs* to help bring down the Shah, but Khomeini was now systematically killing them off to remove any threat to his authority. The poor girl stayed in prison for three years — and her husband for four years — while her mother and aunt were told nothing about her condition or when she would be released. The silence was all the worse because both mother and aunt heard daily from other families that their daughters had been repeatedly raped while in prison. When she finally got out, that young woman refused to talk to anyone about what had happened to her while in prison, even though her mother once saw marks on her body when she was undressing. Even now, she and her husband are under continual surveillance and have found it impossible to get jobs. The horrible reality is that Khomeini can now afford to free such people because Iran itself has merely become a larger prison.

Khomeini was quick to remove those few precious rights for women that the Shah had fought to enshrine. One of the most ignored tragedies of the revolution is the violence that is every day done to women's rights in Iran. Within months of seizing power, Khomeini revoked the family protection act passed in 1967 that for the first time protected women from summary divorce, allowed them to claim custody of their children and outlawed bigamy. In the Iran of today only a man can seek divorce—and he can get one merely by asking for one — and girls only twelve years old can be forced to marry. Men can marry up to four permanent wives, as set out in the Koran, and as many as four hundred concubines, in a legal, temporary marriage called *siqeh*. In the event of divorce, men have full custody of their children.

The list of things women are not permitted to do is a long one. A woman cannot obtain a passport, nor can she leave the country, without her husband's approval. She cannot wear make-up or spend any time under any circumstances with a man who is not her father or her brother. Even uncles are suspect. She cannot join the legal profession. The only right left to us was one that we gained only in 1962—the right to vote. To be a woman in Iran is to be a hostage. The worst part is that all around me I saw people just accept that reality, as if nothing could be done about it.

The schools were another of Khomeini's initial targets. Educated in the traditional Islamic fashion through schools associated with the mosque, he had always resented the move away from religious studies and the new importance given to secular subjects such as mathematics and engineering—areas in which the West tended to excel. Private schools (Farhad had been attending a private kindergarten) were immediately abolished; most of the teachers were fired or sent to poor areas of the city if they had taught in the wealthy suburbs, while the militant *taghouti*-hating teachers were brought into our neighbourhoods. Even the children were bussed around so that poorer children could attend the schools that had once been the preserve of the rich.

I had no choice but to send Farhad to his usual school in Shemiran, which by the autumn of 1980 had become unrecognizable. It had been turned into a public school, and all the teachers were different from the ones he had known the previous year. Right from the start his teachers displayed their resentment of the rich children in their care. The *mullahs* were using the schools for propaganda purposes, and most of the studies now centred on the Koran; foreign languages, such as English and French, which most of our children had been learning, were banned, except for Arabic, the language of the Koran, which became mandatory.

The teachers' main job seemed to be to trick the children into spying on their parents. At my son's school, a teacher brought in several bottles of scotch and vodka and displayed them in front of the class.

"Whoever can tell me if he has seen these bottles at home gets a reward," the teacher promised with a big smile.

Having or drinking liquor had become illegal, along with listening to Western music, gambling and going to the cinema. The poor child who put up his hand to say that he had seen a bottle in his house would very soon lose his parents for a while. Within hours, the Komiteh would knock on the door and arrest his parents, taking them to prison for varying lengths of time, depending on the mood of the *mullah* presiding at the prison.

I always warned my son not to tell the teachers anything about what was going on in our home and that if they asked if I had a certain something or other in the house, he was always to say no.

One day, he came home from school and reported proudly, "Mom, I did something good today. The teacher showed me a Koran and asked me if we had one at home and I said NO."

He was just beaming, and it broke my heart to take my little child and show him where my marriage Koran was kept and to admonish him sternly never to say that we did not have the holy book in the house.

"You have to tell people that we pray every day even if we don't," I told him, hating myself for teaching him at such an early age to lie for survival.

I pitied the mothers of little girls. From the time the girls reached the age of six they had to wear the *hejab*, and the teachers did not accept their excuses if they lost or dislodged the cumbersome headcoverings while playing outside. As a result, the mothers devised an elastic band to keep the *hejab* on tight. And even in the heat of summer, the girls had to wear long-sleeved clothing to school.

My son was in that school system for two years, until he was seven, and I was never sure if I would end up losing him for good to another, frighteningly regressive mentality. Their brainwashing was that good.

Frankly, I was afraid of his teachers. On a couple of occasions I was horrified to find out from Farhad that a teacher had struck him on the head with a ruler because he had spoken out of turn. But when I went to see the principal to tell him how furious I was that my son had been punished physically, I received a berating instead.

"So what is wrong with what the teacher did?" the principal asked. The teacher, a *hejab*-covered woman known to be strongly pro-Khomeini, stood beside him silently and glowered at me. "You are protective and ridiculous. You are the one with the problem."

There was one other time when I had to face the censure of that teacher. Because almost every form of entertainment had come to an end under the new regime, most of the middle class and wealthy were relying on skiing as one of the few ways of relaxing. Women were forbidden to play tennis because their arms and legs would show. The main building of the Royal Club had burned down mysteriously one night, but in any case, apart from the remaining restaurant around the pool, only men could now use what was left of the athletic facilities. For those who loved sports, the regime's new rules had led to some ludicrous spectacles. When waterskiing, women were forced to wear *hejabs* and full-body wet suits. With that rule in effect, there was an immediate shortage of wet suits and those women unlucky enough to be able to get only short-legged wet suits had to wear long trousers over them. Even in our fear, we had to laugh at the sight of a woman flying over the water, covered from head to toe, the *hejab* flapping in the wind. When she had the misfortune to fall in the water, she did not know what to retrieve first: her skis or her *hejab*.

On the ski slopes it was no better. The *mullahs* segregated the hills — so that men and women could not accidentally bump into each other while skiing, I presume—and that meant that father and sons had to go in one direction and mother and daughters in another. Instead of having a family outing, they could meet only at the end of the day when they went home.

Women were also ordered to cover up their ski outfits because the *mullahs* felt that tight ski pants revealed too much. Many just stopped skiing altogether, but the really determined ones took to wearing huge capes and looked like Draculas as they came charging down the hills, their capes ballooning all around them.

The *mullahs* frowned on skiing more than on any other sports. One of the Shah's extravagant habits which had infuriated the conservatives in the country was his lengthy, annual skiing vacation in Switzerland. In making it difficult for us to enjoy sports, the regime was attempting simultaneously to punish the *taghouti* (because sports were seen as a pastime of the rich) and to make it impossible for women to lead what we considered normal lives.

I remember the remark of one woman friend, who was outfitting herself in a long, black cape on top of her usual ski clothes, her *hejab* and her sunglasses: "I'll be damned," she said, "but they are not going to make me give up skiing." Only women with that kind of attitude are still skiing in Iran today.

During our second winter under Khomeini I kept Farhad away from school on a Wednesday one time so that we could make an early start on a weekend trip to the Alborz, where a couple of nice resort hotels were still operating. By now, with the hotels not permitted to sell alcohol, people brought up their own bottles in their cars — at great risk, because the Komiteh regularly stopped cars on those roads — and drank quietly in their own rooms, avoiding the lobby crowd that might include any number of spies.

When I brought Farhad home again, his teacher managed to worm out of him where he had been for the weekend, even though I had coached him to say that he had had a cold. The principal called me in and this time it was the teacher who administered a lecture on the proper morals of a good Moslem.

"So, we hear that you have been skiing," she began. "Where do you get the money to buy that much gasoline? Why are you using up such precious fuel when there is a shortage, to do something frivolous like going skiing? You don't give a damn for what this country is going through, do you? Or that other people can't afford any gas? And then teaching your son to lie. What kind of Moslem are you?"

That question, and the accusation implicit in it, still haunts me, as it did during those years under the Ayatollah's stare, because I have never been able to answer it. I am a Moslem, but not an observant one. I am much like a lapsed Catholic who does not go to church or accept many of the tenets of the religion, but still retains an inner link with the faith. I have been in a mosque only on a few occasions, when a friend or relative has died. I have always been uncomfortable with *mul-lahs*, and I received very little religious education, so that I am not even familiar with the proper form of saying the daily prayers.

That day I sat silent in the face of that woman's abuse: the hatred flowing from her was so great that mere explanations would have been too flimsy a defence. She, a middle-class Teheran woman who had taught in the poorer areas of the city, who was permitted to keep her job by this anti-woman regime only because she was low-paid and because there was a shortage of teachers, could never understand my reasons for wanting to escape the oppressive, joyless quality of her revolution and for being horrified at what she was doing to my son. And I would never understand the reasons for her contempt of me. I was not an individual mother for her; I was a *taghouti*.

During all the time that I lived under Khomeini's rule, I, and most of the people I knew, were continually breaking the law because it had become impossible not to do so if you were determined not to be thrown back to a darker age. Every time we bought alcohol from the black market (the price of a single bottle of whisky went as high as $200), every time we rented a video under the counter (official films were censored so much that even women's bare arms were cut out), every time we bought illegal gas coupons (it would cost me about $50 to fill up my Firebird), every time we stepped out of the house without a *hejab* or had lunch with a male friend, we were actively engaged in breaking the law. Dancing, even just listening to music or the reading of poetry was suspect. We could do nothing to enjoy ourselves, to forget for one moment that the great Imam was leading us on the right path.

The mosque became a powerful weapon to keep us under the control of the *mullahs*. Because the revolution brought with it shortages of all kinds of foods and consumer goods, the government instituted rationing. You had to go to the

mosque with identity papers in order to get coupons to buy
necessities at reasonable prices. You would still have to line
up for hours with hundreds of others, in the hopes of getting
into the store before the supplies ran out. If you were rich
like me, you just bought on the black market and paid many
times more for the same item. A chicken, bought through
the mosque, might cost $4. On the black market, the same
chicken would fetch $15 or more. Coupons for gasoline,
which was strictly rationed, were also available through the
mosque. But I always bought mine illegally. In Iran, there are
two kinds of taxis: the public ones that you can flag down on
the street and share with other passengers and the orange
taxis that come directly to your home. I had used the same
orange taxi company for years and had come to know many
of the drivers well. On the side, they did a brisk trade in illegal
gas coupons.

Every now and then I had personal reminders of how
dangerous it was to break the law. One of my cousins owned
a giant video and record store in downtown Teheran. As with
many store owners, most of his business was under the counter, selling banned Western records and video movies. I was
a regular customer and often dropped in to pick up the latest
film smuggled in from the West. One day when I arrived at
the store I saw the front glass shattered. Inside, thousands of
dollars' worth of films, tapes, video-recording and video-
playing equipment lay in a mangled, charred heap on the floor.
Workmen were busy putting up boards across the window
and front door. As he began a lengthy prison term that morning, my cousin had become another victim of the morality
squads.

My older relatives, heavily involved in the business world,
reacted to the social and legal pressures by simply retiring
from active life. They avoided parties, dressed down when
they stepped out of the house, drove in small cars — any-

thing to avoid being noticed by a Komiteh man who was in an ill humour and looking for a scapegoat.

But we in the younger crowd seemed to be spurred on to even more wildness by the strictures that were placed on us. We sensed that we were losing everything and were determined to have our last bit of fun.

For the first few weeks after Khomeini returned I took refuge in my house, along with several other girlfriends who had chosen to stay behind when their frightened parents had left the country. Together, we created our own world and tried to shut out the chaos around us. As the months went by and we became used to the reality that the *mullahs* were running the country and were prepared to kill anybody to hold onto their power, I started to entertain lavishly again. Almost every week, I had a party of fifty people or more, complete with French chef and waiters from *La Réserve* and plenty of black-market alcohol.

Relations with my in-laws, the Aminis, were relatively quiet, and Farhad generally spent the weekends over at his grandmother's house. He had strict instructions not to tell them about my parties, and I taught him to treat Hamid as a friend of the family. It was only on weekends that I went to spend the night at Hamid's. I was lucky because Hamid doted on Farhad and for one of his birthdays bought him an expensive electric train set that must have been difficult to find in Teheran then. In turn, my son, who longed for a father, adored Hamid. Only a few of my family members knew about my closeness to Hamid. It seemed wise to keep the relationship secret from all but my immediate friends and the more understanding of my relatives.

Over the summer months, I took a huge group of friends up to the Caspian villa almost every weekend. The family of servants who lived on the compound cleaned and did some basic cooking, but I usually brought most of our needed food and drinks from Teheran so that we never had to leave the villa area. Inside, it was as if the revolution had never taken place. Girls in bikinis rode motorcycles on the beach or swam in the heated pool. In the evenings while the alcohol flowed, we watched uncensored videos, and at night unmarried men and women could be caught sleeping together.

I sometimes used to wonder how the servants dealt with the contrast: every day they heard on the radio that women had to be covered up and that Western behaviour was contrary to the Koran, but every weekend they served us alcohol and saw us gambolling half-nude in the garden. Hamid usually accompanied me on those weekends and he always gave the servants at least a $200 tip for two days' work.

I once said to him, "That's a ridiculously high tip. What are you doing?"

"Sousan," he answered, "a happy servant does not spy on you."

On an average weekend the servants were tipped about $600 by the guests, well above their month's wages. But he was right: servants had become the most dangerous spies of all because they were in our own homes. Many of them believed that if their employers were arrested they would be entitled to get some of their property. Apart from children, who were unwitting spies, servants were the greatest cause of arrest of people charged with drinking alcohol or having illicit sex. Most people were desperately trying to get rid of their live-in servants, but they did not dare fire them outright because that would be tantamount to calling in the Komiteh. Whenever a servant left his employment willingly it was a cause for celebration because those families that had no live-in servants were the only ones that anyone felt safe to visit.

I suspect that it was a disgruntled servant who caused two good friends of ours to suffer terribly at the hands of the Komiteh that summer. One Thursday afternoon in the second summer of the revolution, a group of us had just finished settling in for a quiet weekend at the villa when we received

a disturbing call from Teheran. A distraught friend was calling
to ask us for help. His brother, Reza, who owned a villa not
far from us, and a man and two women visiting him had just
been arrested by the Komiteh. He had no idea where they
had been taken or exactly why they had been arrested. We
could guess: the men and women were not married and they
no doubt had alcohol, cards and other forbidden items in
the villa. We had been expecting Reza and his friends to join
us the next day, and the call chilled us.

"I'm going to track them down," said Hamid, and he left.
He travelled along the coast, visiting local Komiteh headquarters asking if they were holding our friends. It was a brave
thing to do. The Komiteh could just as easily have arrested
him for asking—it was the sort of thing they were known to
do. But after a few hours, Hamid came back dejected. There
was no sign of them.

Not long afterwards, there was a knock at our door. When
I opened the door, Reza stumbled in, followed by his ashen-
faced friend. We could tell immediately that both were in
pain.

"We've been whipped," Reza said, wincing as he tried to
remove his jacket.

We helped them to remove their shirts, and for the first
time I saw what a whipping, a prescribed punishment in the
Koran, could do to a man's back. They had deep, raw welts
criss-crossing their backs. In some places the whip had bit-
ten so deeply that the flesh was exposed. They could not
bear to have even the weight of their shirts on them, and as
we tried to apply ointment to the wounds, the two men cried
out in pain.

The women in our group wept openly and Hamid and the
rest of the men hardly knew how to contain their anger.
Slowly, Reza told us what had happened.

"We had just come up from Teheran. We had our girlfriends
with us. We'd just finished unpacking. We had some booze

and a little hashish. Before we knew it, there was the Komiteh at the door. They searched the house and arrested us on the spot. Thank God they let the women go after just a scolding. Somebody turned us in, I'm sure of it. But who knew we were coming? The servants, sure. But they've been with the family for years. Would they do such a terrible thing to us?''

Afterwards, I spent hours walking along the beach with Hamid. I cried and wailed against the government. It was just as well that my words were carried off on the wind for all the good they would have done.

Invidious servants did occasionally end up inheriting their employers' wealth: many Iranians just abandoned their homes and villas and those residences that were not confiscated and used or sold by the authorities are still homes to the household servants. My second gardener was of that acquisitive type. After the revolution he felt that he had a right to a portion of the garden, and even though he refused to do his work most days, I had no option but to keep paying his salary and hope that he would not denounce me to the authorities on some pretext or other.

Landowners were also the victims of the envy unleashed by the revolution. At first, people such as my father were able to continue farming their land, even though their labourers often failed to show up for work and the Komiteh occasionally swooped down without warning to ask for their financial records. But in the second year of the revolution, Khomeini's people, having subdued the opposition and women, began to pay closer attention to landowners. One day, the local Komiteh drove onto my father's land near Sabbalon and in a few hours of official violence tore up the fine, new apple orchards that he had planted at great expense, in the hope that a more versatile crop would give better returns. He was about to reap the rewards and start to pay back the bank loan that he had taken out to buy the saplings when the Komiteh arrived. They forced his workers to pull out every tree by the roots.

I still remember my father's shattered face when he told me. "They said apples were a luxury. Unnecessary! 'Our people need wheat,' one of the Komiteh yelled at me. 'Only the *taghouti* can afford to eat apples.' My men came back afterwards and asked if they could take some trees and plant them in their gardens. I said, 'Sure, sure.' I didn't have the heart to save even one for myself. It was a sight: dozens of trees just drying up in the sun. And after all those years of work."

After that, my father's life was no longer secure. The banks, to whom he owed many thousands of dollars for the planting of the orchard, foreclosed and the Komiteh came and confiscated most of his property. One night, when my father was at grandmother Ashi's house in Rezayeh, some Sabbalon villagers, with the help of some Kurds living in the surrounding villages, ransacked my childhood home, the beautiful country house he had built more than forty years ago and that my mother had loved so much. They stole the carpets and other valuables, ripped up the upholstery, cushions and paintings, broke tables and chairs and gutted some rooms.

Why would the people my father had lived among for so many years suddenly turn on him? Why would they feel so much resentment against a man who had bailed them out of jail, given them cheap loans and resolved their family disputes? There is no easy answer. I suppose no one really wants a boss, and with Khomeini's arrival, workers began to enjoy a sense of power that they had never known before. Perhaps for the first time in their lives they were revelling in the kind of freedom from the strictures of class that anarchy brings for a time. Even now my father stays in the house in Rezayeh, hardly ever returning to Sabbalon except to run in and out in daylight to check on the land.

No one is doing much with the new freedom. Most of the fields are untilled. One *ayatollah* and one Komiteh head-

quarters have given my father a paper saying that he has the
right to farm his land, but another *ayatollah* from another
village disputes that right, and so he continues not to grow
the food that Iran desperately needs. Some of the villagers
have actually gone down on their knees and begged him to
be their lord again as in the old days, crying that their beautiful, wealthy village is now poor and ragged. But there are
still many others who dream of farming my father's land and
wait while the regime resolves its ambivalence towards private
ownership.

I never told my father or my aunts and uncles about the reckless sort of life I was leading under the *ayatollahs*. They had
so many urgent problems of their own and they would have
been shocked at the many chances I was taking. As for the
Aminis, they would have caused me endless grief if they had
had any inkling. Bland and blameless is how I wanted them
to see my life, and I was sure that I was succeeding.

The revolution had put the Salman construction firm under
severe financial strain. Even during the last months before
the Shah's departure, the company, caught in the middle of
several large projects for the government, had been stuck with
huge debts to the banks when the administration, under siege
politically and economically, refused to meet its installment
payments. The new regime put pressure on the company to
complete its projects but refused to pay for them. Foreign
companies which had happily extended credit during the
boom years were suddenly withdrawing it, and with the drop
in the value of the tuman against the American dollar, my
uncles were forced to pay much more for foreign materials
that had been ordered during more stable days. Even if my
uncles had contemplated quitting the country as so many of
their friends did, leaving their companies toppling under debt,
they could not do so because by now they owed, not only the
banks but also many of their closest friends, millions of dollars

that they had borrowed to stave off bankruptcy. Eventually, they received some payment for their work, but it was a pittance compared to what it cost them to finish the projects.

Many contractors were caught in the same sort of squeeze. They had taken on a government project and based their estimates on being able to buy the bulk of their materials abroad with the American dollar at seven tumans. Now, after the revolution, the dollar was worth fourteen tumans (it was worth seventy tumans when I left in 1982), and yet the government would not allow them to renegotiate deals or simply to drop out of the projects undertaken in better days.

Over the months Iran simply stopped working, and all around me I saw the effects. At first, striking oil workers and government employees had returned to work happy that they had contributed to the overthrow of the Shah. But soon there were purges of women, teachers, army officers and left-wing intellectuals. Thousands of civil servants either were fired or quit. In the foreign ministry alone, where I had a number of friends, just under half the workers lost their jobs. With an economic breakdown threatening on all sides, the Ayatollah started to order the faithful to go back to their jobs and to improve productivity. But it soon became evident that the chaos could not be bottled up as easily as it had been freed. In the private sector, where employees had been told that they no longer had to be subservient to the *taghouti*, workers showed up late for work if they bothered to show up at all, and no manager dared to reprimand them for fear that the Komiteh would be called in. Productivity plummeted. My uncles Kurosh and Fayegh had a long-time worker, one of whose responsibilities was to fetch tea for guests, the tea-break being a well-established business custom in Iran. The man became so insolent that he would take an hour to bring the tea and often simply refused to do his job. Still, my uncles did not dare fire him. That inability to manage started at the top and went right down to the bottom ranks of a company.

No one could interpret the government's attitude to private ownership of land and capital or to the functioning of the free market. Every day we heard *ayatollahs* spouting contradictory messages — either praising the right of ownership as being protected in the Koran or denouncing ownership as a blight on the nation. As far as I know, to this day there are conflicting signals from the government. Some workers still believe that they will take over and own the factories, some peasants still believe that they will own their landlords' land. But at the same time the government is trying to make the economy work with the remnants of the upper and middle classes who have stayed.

The Salmans' first brush with the revolutionary masters came three months after Khomeini's return. My Uncle Kurosh, who with the death of Kamel in 1977 had become the family patriarch, was attending a meeting of engineers at the profession's headquarters when a group of armed Komiteh entered noisily and arrested the six top engineers in the country, including him.

I was at home with Farhad that morning when I received a call from Uncle Fayegh. He was an emotional man, and he felt any family trouble very deeply.

"They've taken your Uncle Kurosh," he said in a nervous rush. "We don't know where he is and we don't know why but we'll call you as soon as we know."

"What can I do?" I asked, shivering.

"Nothing so far. The whole family is working on it. If you can think of anybody to call for help, do it."

The pitiful fact was that the Salmans had few connections in the new regime and no connections with the *mullahs*. When the Komiteh struck, every single member of a family became involved and that morning there were about one hundred relatives — all the Salmans and the various families that they had married into, including the Seppehris, who did have strong religious contacts — calling around town trying to find where my uncle had been whisked off to and why. Could anybody be bribed to get him out? If so, who and how much would it take? Work stopped completely in several head offices of industries, several restaurants and many homes until late that night when my uncle and the other engineers were finally released.

I saw him at a family gathering just two days later, and even though he had had time to recover, he was still visibly shaken.

"They came without warning," he recounted, "a few Komiteh, carrying those big rifles. They ordered us to go with them. They didn't tell us why and we didn't dare ask. They pushed us towards a bus and one of them said, 'I bet none of you has ever been on a bus before, you with all your chauffeurs. Well, now you're going to see how the poor people of Iran travel every day.' And they all laughed. You know me, I have trouble with my blood pressure and my knees aren't very good. I had a hard time getting up the high step, and they just jeered. The other engineers were in no better shape than I was, some even older and sicker. Anyway, at one point this young Komiteh comes up, takes hold of my suit jacket and says, 'Oh, fancy. Where did you get the money to buy such expensive clothes while the people were starving?' Well, I thought, this doesn't look too good for us.

"They took us to some building in town that I didn't recognize and they blindfolded us. Then they led us through some long passageways and kept telling us to bend down because the ceilings were low. We had to get down and crawl on our hands and knees. It took us ages to get to where we were going, most of the time bent over like that. Finally they interrogated us about contracts we had with the government. They said, 'You got those contracts because you were friends of the Shah. You are thieves and you've stolen from the government.'

"We said very little and after a few hours we were all thirsty, but when they offered us water, I thought, 'My God, this is it.' In the Koran it says that you have to offer a dying man water. I drank the water with my blindfold still on and then I was expecting to hear the sound of a gun blast. Instead they took off the blindfold and led us out of the building and, you know, I never saw the low ceilings that we were supposed to have passed through. The bastards. They put us back on the bus and dropped us off in the middle of the city.''

Uncle Kurosh was arrested at least four more times — on various vague pretexts—and once he stayed in prison for up to five months. The last time he was arrested was in 1986 when he answered a government summons asking anyone who owned dynamite to present himself to the local Komiteh. As a builder, my uncle rightly had blasting dynamite, but when he dutifully reported in, he was put in prison for two months — no explanations given.

In the new Iran, disappearances were common. About two and a half years into the new regime I was touched very personally by a dramatic abduction. One of my husband's partners, Abdollah Taslimi, was a leading Baha'i, a member of a sect that had broken from Shi'ism in the mid-nineteenth century and had been hated and persecuted by the Shi'as ever since. There were then about three hundred thousand Baha'is in Iran, and they held many tenets that were anathema to the Shi'as: world peace, the unification of all peoples and religions, the equality of men and women and the value of science in a religious world. Under the Koran, heretics such as the Baha'is could be stoned to death if they refused to recant, and one of Khomeini's first acts was to outlaw the Baha'is, giving them the opportunity to rejoin the Shi'as or be punished. Most of the Baha'is refused, and the continuing acts of barbarity against them are an international scandal.

A gentle, erudite man much trusted by the Baha'is, Abdollah refused to leave the country when he still had the chance, even though his life was threatened.

Over dinner at his house I once said to him, "You know they hate you. Sooner or later they will come for you. Why don't you leave?"

He nodded sadly. "What will happen to the other Baha'is if I go? We can't arrange to get them all out of the country. I have to stay here to give them encouragement and support."

Khomeini made it illegal for Baha'is to hold meetings. One day, in the spring of 1980, Abdollah and eleven other leading Baha'is were holding a secret meeting when the Komiteh suddenly burst in and arrested them all. As weeks went by with no word of where they had been taken to, his wife held out hope for his safe return because there had been no official word of his execution. But months turned to years, and although she waited at home most days hoping that he would surprise her and just walk in the door, there was no trace of him or the others. International pressure has still not succeeded in discovering the fate of those Baha'is. Heartbroken, his wife eventually left Iran.

And so the revolution rolled on relentlessly. We were crazy, I suppose, but we still went to parties, wore bright lipstick, displayed our ankles and roared with an increasingly hollow laugh. I spent my time buying clothes, being manicured, preparing myself for another night of socializing with Hamid at the more risky gatherings. With alcohol banned and so many other pleasures denied, many of my friends took to smoking opium. In the Shah's days it had been the occasional drug of old-fashioned old men or the speedier jetsetters. Now no gathering was complete without a charcoal brazier and opium pipes. Although it was expensive and still illegal, opium was suddenly readily available on the black market. Under Khomeini, we had religion and opium.

Although I did not indulge in the pipe, some of my closest friends did, and one of our main sources of opium and other drugs was a *mullah* whom Hamid had befriended. It was an odd friendship. While most other *mullahs* were trying to become scowling copies of the ascetic Ayatollah and were proud of their robes and turbans, our *mullah* wanted to dress in Western clothes and often asked Hamid's advice on purchases. When he joined us for the weekend at the Caspian, as he liked to do, he would disappear for a few hours. He would return with cases of wine and liquor — and opium. I never knew how he obtained the contraband goods. He was so desperate to please, to fit into our crowd, and he ogled the women. Hamid once arranged for a very high-class call girl from Teheran to become the *mullah*'s companion. Months later he shocked us all by marrying her.

In the months after the revolution, Hamid and I became much closer, although he made it clear that he did not want to make any commitment. I was attracted by his recklessness, his love of partying. He could keep an entire roomful of people captivated by his humorous storytelling. He could drink prodigiously at night and wake up fresh, ready for more devilment the next morning. Women openly flirted with him, even when I was present. But the revolution began to close in on him as it did on the other young men in our crowd. Perhaps it was the young men who lost the most in the revolution. They had been raised to expect to inherit the wealth and position their fathers had secured for them, but now they were like disinherited sons sneaking into their own wine cellars to steal one last blissful sip before their houses were ransacked forever. By the time we had spent a year under the revolutionary government, most of my male friends had simply stopped going to work, either because the products of their factories were no longer needed in an economy brought to a dead stop, or because to show up for work had become too dangerous. Most of the older industrialists had left already, while it was still possible to get out legally, and had left their sons behind in the hopes that they would be able to salvage some holdings for the family. But the government was intent

on slowly taking over all the industries that had belonged to
the ruling elite. Any day, the Komiteh could arrive unexpec-
tedly and arrest the owner of the factory, business or retailing
company and cart him off to an uncertain fate.

Hamid was one of the many in danger. After the revolution
he had at first continued to go to his office in Saltanatabad at
odd hours, never giving his secretary or his second-in-
command any hint of his schedule, in an attempt to evade
spies among his workers. Both his parents had left Iran shortly
after Khomeini's return. Hamid had been out of the country
at the time, but had come back, hoping to hold together his
family's fortune.

His first task was to try to retain his parents' magnificent
mansion, which the long-time family servants—five of them
—were already beginning to treat as their own. Hamid preferred his own ultra-modern apartment in a landmark Teheran highrise, but he moved back into his parents' home just
to remind the servants that the family had not given up on
Iran altogether.

About nineteen months after the revolution, Hamid received his first unpleasant surprise from the regime. When
he went to the airport to fly to Paris where his parents were
then living, he was denied permission to leave, without explanation. In the chaos of the early days of the revolution, it
had been very easy to leave the country legally—or illegally,
if necessary. It was still possible to obtain visas for European
countries, Canada and the United States. If your name was
on the long list of people being sought by the Komiteh, you
could always resort to bribery. One very high-ranking *ayatollah*, nicknamed Mahmedringo because of his gunslinger
style, was known to be carrying on an active trade ushering
out of the country those wealthy enough to pay his fees, which
ranged up to hundreds of thousands of dollars for one family.
His technique was simple. We heard from friends of those he
had helped that he personally walked the wanted people right

past the Komiteh guards at the airport, who did not dare stop him because he was so high up in the new hierarchy. But on June 28, 1981, he was killed, along with seventy-one others, including the powerful revolutionary Ayatollah Mohammed Beheshti, in a bombing massacre at a political meeting.

Eventually, the Komiteh put out a public notice that they wanted Hamid for questioning and he did what so many others were forced to do. He went into hiding with friends and occasionally made quick raids on his apartment or house for clothes and supplies, while he decided whether to leave Iran for good in the only way now available to him — illegally, through Afghanistan or Turkey.

The revolution had another, I am certain, unintended effect. With so many families separated, with wives and children sent abroad while husbands stayed behind to take care of property, and with possible imprisonment or death hanging over us, marriages tended to suffer, and liaisons formed that might not have otherwise. Under different circumstances I would probably not have continued for as long as I did my off-and-on relationship with Hamid, which seemed for good times only and to have no serious intent.

During that first couple of years there were always a few women living with me and most had a boyfriend who came and went quite freely, glad to be able to relax in a household where the revolution seemed not to exist. One of the women, my cousin Chloe, took up with a separated man, a leading industrialist from a famous family, whose wife and two children were safely living in his European home. He was a frequent visitor because he had little to do with his time now that his entire family was under order to be arrested on sight. In pre-revolutionary days, we would never have dreamed of living such a hedonistic life; now we were pushing aside old rules of morality which said that a well-bred woman never, never took away someone else's husband.

In fact, in our small group, our attitudes to sex were considerably liberalized by the revolution. While the society at large was putting on veils and repressing any exhibition of love between a man and a woman, we were indulging our fantasies. There had been a time when, if a woman was known to have two lovers, I would not have deigned to talk to her. Now multiple affairs seemed quite normal to me. With Hamid, I became much more sexually active, truly enjoying our physical relationship. Friends used to joke that I used to choose cocktails by their colour, to match my outfit for the evening. Now I drank alcohol more freely and it helped to ease my sexual inhibitions.

In the spring of 1980, after a woman I knew claimed that Hamid had made a pass at her, I stopped seeing Hamid for about six months. During our estrangement, I met and became infatuated with one man and fell in love with another — and again, they were relationships that would never have flowered before the revolution turned our lives upside down.

I was at the one remaining restaurant of the Royal Club with Chloe and her boyfriend, Darvish, when a handsome construction owner, Fery, whom I had admired from afar came over to say hello to Darvish. We seemed to take to each other instantly, and that weekend all four of us went to spend a couple of nights at an Italian work camp north of Teheran in the Alborz, where an Italian-Iranian consortium was involved in a large building project. Darvish's and Fery's fathers were both partners in the consortium.

Fery was born of an Iranian father and a Swiss mother, and as a result he had a Swiss passport; I suppose that made him feel somewhat safer, because with that diplomatic passkey he would be able to get out of the country without problems. But his own father, a close friend of the previous regime, would not have survived a day under Khomeini — he was one of the very few people that the Shah took with him on his jet when he flew out of Teheran for the last time.

The family was a celebrated one, and I knew, as did everyone in our social circles, that Fery was engaged to a lovely Jewish girl, who had left the country soon after Khomeini's return, knowing of the Ayatollah's overt hatred of Jews and the likely persecution she would suffer. Even so, as I prepared for my weekend with Fery, I realized that I was not about to let that stop me from having so desirable a man. She was safely in the West. Who knew what would happen to us that day or the next?

That weekend was a reminder of happiness. Up at the camp, the Italian workers and their wives, isolated in their own temporary community and still untouched by the Komiteh, had created an island of sanity and fun. I suppose in the early days the Ayatollah still wanted some of the larger projects to go ahead, especially structures such as the dam, which would benefit the whole country. Perhaps for that reason, the contractors were permitted to continue their work and the Italians were left to follow their own customs.

We had dinner in a large, mess-type room decorated with bright tablecloths and fresh flowers picked on the mountains. Large barrels full of ice kept the beer cold, and wine flowed plentifully — in a country where the Komiteh had destroyed the $1.2 million wine cellar of the Intercontinental Hotel. A band put together by the Italians played raucously, and we danced with a joyousness I thought we had forgotten. Dinner consisted of fresh fish and game caught that day. That night Fery and I spent the night in a private lodge overlooking the lake. Everything seemed perfect.

But within a few weeks, the Komiteh put out an order for Fery's arrest.

"What will I do?" I moaned to the girlfriends who were living with me. "If he stays, I stand a pretty good chance of winning him. I know he loves me. But if he leaves now, his girlfriend is waiting for him on the other side. He'll be hers again. I may never see him again."

One girlfriend leaned over conspiratorially. "There is one thing you can do. You know perfectly well that if you call the Komiteh, even anonymously, and tell them the man they are looking for is about to leave on a certain flight, they'll stop him. Maybe they'll put him in prison for a few days. But they'll soon let him out again. And then, there he is, stuck in the country. What have you got to lose? If he stays, he'll fall more in love and he'll be yours."

I listened, both horrified and tempted. People were doing such things now—out of spite, to settle an old score, to hold on to a lover. It was just one little incident, but it was a devastating measure of how low we had fallen.

Fery finally left Iran, legally and with no obstructions at the airport, and when he called me a week later, I could already sense the reserve in his voice. Two years later he married his fiancée, and they now live in the United States.

Not long after Fery's departure I began a relationship which I would never — and could never — have contemplated before the revolution scrambled our lives and our morals. Chloe's boyfriend, Darvish, had a younger brother, Sufi, a Qajar prince, perhaps the best known and the wealthiest of their large clan. Their grandfather, once the rival of the Shah's father for control of the country, had had several wives and over twenty children who excelled in every area, from business to the arts. Sufi owned several manufacturing companies and extensive tracts of land. But apart from having been one of the most powerful men in the country, he was also a kind, literate man who became, and still is, one of my staunchest friends.

Sufi had been interested in me for months, but I never once thought of becoming involved with him—after all, he was a married man. His wife was living in their house in Switzerland and his two children were attending boarding schools in England and Switzerland. But with Fery gone and with our world becoming smaller and smaller, I became vulnerable to his seductive arts. One night, after a sumptuous dinner during which I laughed harder than I had in months, I fell into his determined embrace. It was the beginning of a passionate but troubling episode in my life, and it brought me face to face with the slow destruction of people such as Sufi under the new regime.

One night in September 1980, when I was just beginning to know Sufi, Chloe called me at home, terror evident in her strained voice.

"Stay at home, for God's sake," she commanded with little explanation. "I'm coming right over."

About fifteen minutes later she pulled up in a taxi and ran into the house, looking over her shoulder as if someone were chasing her.

At first she was so frightened and shaky that she was incoherent, but finally she blurted out, "The Komiteh came for Darvish. We were just sitting there in his house when one of his brothers called to tell him that the Komiteh were coming to arrest him. We didn't even have time to think. We just ran."

Several of the brothers had villas on a large compound in Shemiran, and Darvish's luck had been that the Komiteh had gone to the wrong brother's house. As they raced down the street in his car, Chloe and Darvish could see the Komiteh Range Rovers rounding the corner.

"He dropped me off. He didn't want me getting into trouble if he got caught. A single woman and a married man! He's gone to some friend's place. He wouldn't even tell me where. My God, Sousan, they're going to find us, I'm sure of it."

The following day, almost as if he were thumbing his nose at the authorities, Darvish joined Chloe and me for breakfast at my house, and later for lunch at the Royal Club. He was wise in a way: while the streets were dangerous for him, the old haunt of the rich was still a haven. No one there would spy on him or turn him in. I remember Chloe and him boasting that they had spent the morning making love — almost as if the danger was a turn-on for them.

Two weeks later the Komiteh put out a notice for his arrest and confiscated his construction business, with its millions in heavy machinery, and his mansion; several days later he escaped illegally through Turkey, Chloe and I being the only ones privy to his impending escape. Distraught at losing him, Chloe made the same trip shortly afterwards, and I lost one more friend.

By then all the women who had been living with me had left: they had escaped or married or returned to their families. Some time later, in order to feel safer in the house, I gave my basement apartment, free of charge, to the family of a long-time driver for the Seppehris, my Aunt Guity's family. Jalal Agha had been in the employ of the family for more than twenty years. I gave him, his wife Farah and two children full use of the basement. Occasionally, Farah would mind Farhad when I went out during the week, and he loved having two little friends near his own age in the house. What more trustworthy family could I have living with me?

But for the few months that I was alone in the house with my son, my privacy suited me well because of the clandestine relationship that I had embarked on with Sufi. Had my family and my more conservative friends known about that affair, I would have been ostracized, even though such liaisons were becoming commonplace. Every weekend, when Farhad went to his grandmother's, Sufi moved in quietly and we spent our days mostly indoors, away from prying eyes. At first I did not mind it. He helped by fixing gadgets that had broken down or sorting out my accounting files for household expenses. I cooked elaborate lunches and dinners and we played our favourite music as the fire blazed and we drank wines that we had bought on the black market. Farhad even came to know him as a family friend who occasionally dropped by during the week to take us hiking up in the Alborz.

Sometimes we drove into the mountains in search of out-of-the-way restaurants, where we would be unlikely to come across our friends and relatives.

But soon the Komiteh turned their attention to Sufi, and in the six months I knew him, I saw him go from a fun-loving, teasing charmer to a frightened and hunted man. In the beginning he was going into his office at irregular hours and still living sporadically in his mansion with its many servants. Then he started to move around with a couple of suitcases in tow, living with friends and relatives, always keeping just one step ahead of the Komiteh. Eventually, a friend of his took a great risk and rented an apartment for him in a middle-class suburb. He changed his Mercedes for a cheap Paycan, the working man's car, and took to wearing elaborate disguises because his face was as famous as his name. He grew a beard, and whenever he stepped out of the apartment, he wore a large scarf, a hat and clothes bought off the hanger instead of his tailored suits.

When I went to meet him during the week while Farhad was at school, I felt like a character out of a spy thriller. At his insistence I parked my car in a shopping mall not too far from where he lived, and he pulled up alongside me. After checking to see that no one was watching, I jumped in beside him and we sped off. He pleaded with me not to drive my Firebird, which was too noticeable, and to keep my long hair well covered. At his apartment building, he drove into the garage and we stealthily went up the back stairs.

For a man who had had every comfort, access to the best houses, even to the royal court, this life—the life of a common thief—was a nightmare. Slowly he became isolated from his friends and, because he feared that he might be found through wiretaps, he even stopped calling his family either inside or outside Iran. I was his only contact with the outside world.

But I began to resent a love that had to be kept hidden from everyone. And I had never been able fully to accept what I was doing—loving someone else's husband. Yet I suspected that his only reason for remaining in Iran — despite the growing threat to his life — was to be with me.

I said to him again and again, ''You have to go. I will never be able to forgive myself if anything happens to you. You will be on my conscience. Please go."

But still he stayed. One day the Komiteh, which had an order out for his arrest, announced that they would shoot to kill if he were spotted. Once again I begged him to escape, but it was only when I broke off my relationship with him that he finally made plans. What had started out as just another affair had become, for both of us, a wrenching emotional attachment. No other man had brought me alive sexually as he had. But with the realization that I loved him came the decision that I had to leave him. There was no future for us. He loved his wife, as he had always made clear to me, and I would never ask him to leave her. What was left for me? I broke from him and refused all his calls. I was cold and cruel to him, but I didn't know any other way of ending it. Shortly afterwards, he sent me word that he was escaping. The day I knew he was to leave Iran, I felt a vital part of me flowing away.

There were so many like Sufi, men finally chased out of Iran, even though no formal charges were brought against them. The Komiteh rarely spelled out why they wanted to interrogate someone. Charges were made regularly over the radio and printed in the state-controlled newspapers. They usually consisted of statements that the rich had profited unduly from their enterprises or had defrauded the state. I cannot testify as to whether such allegations were true. The powerful men who were my friends never discussed work with their women. I can only say that my family, my uncles and my husband operated their businesses according to the highest standards. As for the others I knew who were hunted, no proof of their alleged corruption was ever provided, although I am sure that there were many rich Iranians whose greed was a crime against the people.

What I do know is that for those of us still left in Iran, the circle of safety, the margin within which we could live unscathed, was becoming smaller and smaller.

Chapter Seven

Smugglers and
Other Useful Friends

No one thought of love anymore
No one thought of triumph anymore
No one
thought of anything anymore.

FORUGH FARROKHZAD

 On September 22, 1980, the skies were clear and the air was warm. It was a fine morning for a war. But no forecast could have prepared us for the long, bloody feud that even now causes my country to haemorrhage uncontrollably. When the phone rang at about 7:00 A.M., I expected nothing more than a friend calling about an invitation to lunch. Instead, it was the boyfriend of one of the women living with me at the time, and what he said stunned the household.

"The Iraqis have just bombed Teheran airport," he shouted excitedly. "Turn on your radio quick. The war has started."

The troubles with Iraq dated back to an historic disagreement over where the boundary should be drawn between the two countries near the Shatt al-Arab River; both countries claimed rights to the river. In 1975, the Shah and Iraq had signed the Algiers Pact, drawing the boundary down the middle of the river, with Iraq giving up its full claim in return for the Shah's promise to stop arming the secessionist Kurdish movement within that country. The Shah and Iraq's president, Saddam Hussein, had become so friendly that when the Shah had asked him to expel the troublesome Khomeini from the Iraqi holy city of Najef in the autumn of 1978, Hussein had complied quickly. With Khomeini in power, Hussein had much to worry about. The charismatic Ayatollah and his religious crusade posed a threat to his own rule. While Iraq's Soviet-backed, secular Ba'athist (Renaissance) government was led mostly by Sunni Moslems, more than half the Iraqi population was Shi'a. Already there were signs that the Shi'as would respond to a call from Khomeini to unite and spread the Islamic revival. But Hussein also saw an opportunity in a weakened Iran to regain some of the territories lost to the Shah, and in the process establish himself as the leading Arab ruler.

That morning, when the bombs fell for the first time, we knew that the war would be a tragedy for us all. Because Mehrabad Airport was about an hour's drive away and our house was soundproofed, we had not heard the booming impact of the explosions. But when we turned on the radio, we were given a vivid image of the spreading panic. The voice of the man on the radio was hysterical.

"Don't go out of your houses unless it's a real emergency. Stay indoors. The Iraqis may strike again at any time. The city is under siege. Tonight, do not drive or put on any lights in your houses. Keep tuned to the radio all day and we will tell you what to do. The Iraqis have bombed Iran!!"

If the voice on the radio was incredulous, so were we. Would Iraq really dare to attack the most highly armed country in the Middle East? Our fabled armed forces had 120,000 combat soldiers (down from 140,000 under the Shah), with another 400,000 reserves, 1,600 British and American battle tanks and 77 F-14 Grumman-Tomcat jet fighters. We had always said Iraq would never take the chance of facing our fighting power. But with Iran weakened by a year or more of political chaos, could Iraq win?

At that moment, with the radio shouting panicked instructions, I could think only of Farhad. He had gone to stay with a friend of mine who lived right across the city from me — a long and dangerous drive now that war had broken out. As the news worsened — the Iraqis struck nine other airports that day — I became more and more frightened that the bombing would cut me off from him. Even though the Komiteh had strictly forbidden wandering around in the city, I had to bring Farhad home. As I drove, I could see others rushing as purposefully as I was, getting ready for a long siege. In the distance, over the horizon, I could see a plume of smoke coming from the direction of the airport. When I had Farhad in my arms again, I cried to see how frightened he was.

"Are they going to kill us, Mummy?" he asked, his round face unusually pale.

For that week we hid in my house — Farhad and I, a couple of girlfriends and my father, who happened to be visiting Teheran at the time. Because we were fearful of sleeping alone in different bedrooms, we piled sleeping bags and blankets on the carpet in the fireplace room — called that because of the large, fieldstone fireplace that was always lit there in winter — and camped out. At first we dutifully kept all lights off, but later my father persuaded us to have a couple of candles and we spent our time listening to the radio and playing cards.

Every day brought terrible occurrences. The very next day the Iraqis set ablaze our oil refinery at Abadan, the largest refinery in the world. Iran retaliated by bombing Iraq's capital, Baghdad. The following day the enemy bombed the big oil terminal on Kharg Island. Soon, both countries cut off their oil exports, and in Iran it became illegal to sell gasoline and heating oil privately as the state moved in to control those suddenly even more precious commodities.

As the days passed, we began to move about more and the lights were switched back on in the city. Nonetheless, it was evident that the war, which threatened to become protracted, signalled a worsening of our lives. A curfew was imposed and strictly maintained, and we began to stay overnight with friends after dinner. In a country that had been the second-largest oil exporter in the world, we had to conserve all forms of energy; we got used to having only one light on in the house and to spacing out hot showers.

Food and fuel shortages became aggravated. For weeks at a time, staples disappeared from shelves and only the very rich could resort to the black market to buy them. Suddenly we would find that not a single store carried cooking oil and friends would tip each other off if they happened to find an out-of-the way shop with old stock. Or perhaps coffee, which had been plentiful the week before, would suddenly be scarce. We responded as most people would, by hoarding, only making the shortages worse. High-level business friends would use their muscle to get a case of dish-washing detergent or a brace of chickens. In order to get heating oil for the house, I would drive around Teheran trying to find a fuel truck that was on delivery, and then I would bribe the driver to divert his cargo to my address. Often the drivers were so unscrupulous that they watered down the oil and cheated us, even with the very high prices we were paying.

With the persistent bombing, Iran was not acquiring new housing, as Khomeini had promised, but actually losing it. And as the months went by, something far more irreplaceable was lost: a generation of young men. Khomeini has had no trouble recruiting ardent young men to die for his cause — which is to destroy Hussein and his government and install a fundamentalist Islamic regime in Iraq. But by the time I left Iran, two years after the war had started, there was already a growing realization by some groups that the price of Khomeini's *jihad*, or holy war, was too high.

Just after the war had started, Hamid came back into my life, as breezily and charmingly as he had left it six months before, and we went back to our casual dating. I missed Sufi, but I forced myself to date again because, whatever Hamid's drawbacks, he was eligible and we had a good time together. I could be seen in public with him and I could even eventually introduce him to the older members of my family. Only this time, even the light-hearted Hamid was different. He was more concerned about me and about what the regime might do to us.

Now he would say, "Sousan, you have to stop giving those parties. It's too dangerous. Too many people have an interest in getting you into trouble."

He refused to stay overnight at my house or even to visit me there for fear that the Komiteh would come unannounced and arrest us on the spot for having an illegal relationship. During the early weeks of the war, in order for us to spend more time together, Hamid invited Farhad, me and one of my girlfriends to go to live with a family who owned a large house not far from mine where he was staying. The man, who had been in the import-export business, had given up trying to run his company in the post-revolutionary chaos. He and his wife were only too glad to have company to pass the long days. We all had time on our hands and not much to do with it.

We lived with that family for two months, and during that time I probably did more for Hamid than for any other man in my life, including my lawful husband. So as not to give the servants in the house too much extra work, I washed all of his clothes by hand, cooked his meals and cleaned up after him. In all my life I had never washed my own clothes, let alone anyone else's, but somehow I felt it was my duty to serve him, and he simply accepted all my efforts as his due. After all, women had always taken care of him. And even if he had been poor, as an Iranian male he would have had every expectation of being properly served by a woman. Even in a post-revolutionary state, in the middle of a war, with all of us re-evaluating, under force, our social mores and habits, he could not bring himself to look at a woman as someone other than a person to have fun with or to take care of his needs.

Hamid also upheld the double standard of most Iranian men: he thought that he could flirt outrageously with women, but he became jealous and sullen if I even gave the appearance of enjoying another man's company.

Eventually, we became used to the idea that war was a permanent feature of the new Iran, and we adapted to the sirens that sent us scurrying for cover daily and to the jets streaking overhead on their way to a bombing run. Even the fear of being bombed while we slept became commonplace, though luckily for those living in Teheran, most of the damage was done to the oil fields and to the oil towns of Khorramshahr and Abadan.

Perhaps the one who suffered the most from the war was Farhad. Ever since the revolution, I had moved his bed into my room to give him a greater sense of security. He had been terrorized by the sound of sporadic gunfire during those first chaotic months. Then, with war and the night-time sirens, he started to have nightmares. Many nights he woke up screaming, "They're killing us, they're killing us." I kept him out of school for three months, and even after he went back, every time I heard a siren I ran from home to pick him up so that I would be near him should anything happen.

But two incidents sharpened my growing realization that we were in danger. About nine months after the revolution, there was a knock on the door and I opened it to find two Komiteh men standing there, their rifles by their sides. I kept outwardly calm as they asked me who lived in the house and who owned it. I told them that my husband had recently died and that I lived there alone with my child. After a few more innocuous questions, they went away, leaving me puzzled and unsettled. The mystery was solved a day later when one of the workmen from the gas company across the street from our house came over.

"I am so sorry about the Komiteh," he said apologetically. "A guy who works for us called them in. He kept complaining about this woman and her child living all alone in this big house. He said that Khomeini had promised everybody a house and that you didn't deserve to be living in such a big house all by yourself. The guy is a little funny. Anyway, the Komiteh came back and told him off for making them disturb you for no reason."

My husband had always been so thoughtful to the gas workers, personally bringing them treats from our kitchen whenever we had a party, and I continued the practice after his death. I was benefiting from the goodwill we had earned. Despite the anger of one individual, I knew I could trust the rest.

Later, however, a more disturbing incident made me realize that I was very visible to the Komiteh. One night, just as my dinner guests were about to sit down to their meal and everyone had a glass of alcohol in hand, my son came running in from the garden.

"Mummy, there are two army men coming in the gate," he yelled.

Within seconds my panicked guests were throwing their drinks down the kitchen sink. The men grabbed up the bottles of vodka, whisky and wine and in a frenzy emptied them into the toilet bowls and sinks of the various bathrooms. Several thousand dollars' worth of alcohol was destroyed in one minute or less. One woman fainted from fear and several others collapsed. All the time we scurried about in terror, the servants I had brought in for the night merely stared at us, a malicious amusement in their eyes. When the two men finally knocked on the front door (the gate they had entered by was a good distance from the house), they turned out to be policemen, not Komiteh. Under the new regime, policemen had been downgraded and their salaries cut and now about the only thing they were permitted to do was give out parking tickets. As a result, many of them had taken to supplementing their incomes by doing private security work or guarding people's cars.

"Good evening, madam," one of them said very politely. "We just wanted to tell you that one of the guests has left his car door unlocked."

Relieved, I went to tip him for the information, as he had hoped, and then he said more quietly, "You know, madam, the revolutionary committee has been keeping an eye on your house for some time. They're considering it for a possible headquarters."

After I had thanked him again and shut the door, I turned to find my white-faced guests still in a state of shock. No one could eat after that and the party was ruined, but, worse, the encounter graphically warned me that I would have to be more careful in future. My isolated little haven was no sanctuary after all. No doubt Hamid was wise to stay away from my house except in the middle of the day when there were other people around. I only wish that I had been as cautious as he.

By mid-1981 I knew that I would not be able to stay in Teheran much longer and I began to take the first steps to leave my much-loved country. My Aunt Guity had already left. Under a new law that was passed and then quickly revoked, parents with children under eighteen studying abroad could visit them—as long as father and mother went singly, leaving the mate behind as a kind of hostage. Guity's two daughters were studying in New York and she made it safely through the airport. My Uncle Ardeshir made his way out illegally through Turkey. Before leaving, they had sold their shares in *La Réserve* to Guity's side of the family, the powerful Seppehris who had good religious connections and were hoping to ride out the revolution.

La Réserve was no longer the restaurant they had proudly opened in 1975. At first, before alcohol was banned, the restaurant continued to do well, but the Komiteh showed up regularly to harass both patrons and staff for serving wine and spirits. Later, when alcohol was made illegal, clients were allowed to bring their own drink, and dark glasses were provided to disguise the liquids. A few months later, the Komiteh raided the restaurant without warning and destroyed many thousands of dollars' worth of frozen pork and seafood because they, too, were illegal in an Islamic state that applied the dietary laws of the Koran.

By the time I left Iran, no one went out to dinner in a restaurant anymore, partly because of the continual curfews, and partly because the Komiteh had a tendency to roam the streets at night looking for people to stop on any pretext. *La Réserve*, like most other restaurants, operated just for the lunchtime crowd. And my uncle and aunt—the only ones in the family who had supported the revolution — had left, disillusioned that the departure of the Shah had not brought the hoped-for enlightenment and improved quality of life for the poor.

With their departures, I started to pressure my son's guardians to let me send some of Farhad's capital abroad so that we would have financial support should we suddenly have to leave the country. At one point, after repeated meetings with my uncles, the guardians even agreed to allow me to sell the house. During the time that they had been resisting my pleas, the American dollar had risen sharply against the tuman and Farhad's money was worth less and less every day. My husband's remaining partner, Jamshid, agreed to send $70,000 to a Swiss account through the black market, but we never saw that money again. Jamshid told me later that, after I left the country, the Komiteh investigated Farhad's holdings, and in order not to reveal that money had been sent out of the country, he had been forced to replace the missing funds with his own.

Continually, we were victims of the manoeuvrings of Jamshid and the Aminis. Much of the money that my husband had left his son was used by his partner and his brother Ali to prop up the construction company, despite my entreaties not to put Farhad's only cash into such a risky venture. Construction companies were failing every day and even if they had been prospering, Farhad would not have benefited, because he did not own a single share in his father's old firm. The shares had all been given to the Aminis. Now they were using Farhad's money to save their own company and I could do nothing to stop it because my husband had not seen fit to give me, a woman and his wife, a single vote to help determine what happened to our son's fortune.

Jamshid and Ali even wanted me to sign a document listing the items in the house with the estimated value of each — three years after the law dictated that they, as the guardians, were to see that it was done. The list is made up so that if anything is removed, someone can be held liable — in particular the widow, who is usually allowed to live in her husband's house and use the furniture in it until she remarries, but is not allowed to sell a single item. Failure to make up the list is considered so serious that individuals who do not ensure that it is drawn up in time can lose their right of guardianship — and control of the money involved.

I could understand why the Aminis were frantic to have
me sign the list after so much time had gone by. They had
already stripped the house of some of its valuables and if I
signed a document now, not only would they meet their legal
obligation and keep hold of Farhad's fortune, but implicitly I
would be condoning their theft. Shortly after my husband
died, my Aunt Guity and I had actually seen Ali walk into my
living room, unplug all the stereo equipment and walk out
with it, without offering a word of explanation. I can only
conclude that he felt he had a right to it. My aunt and I said
nothing, too shocked to speak and unwilling to believe what
we were seeing. Later I saw the stereo installed in Ali's house,
but his wife insisted that he had just bought it.

Since Bijan's death, other valuables had disappeared: his
fine collection of gold, platinum and diamond-studded cigarette lighters, about six Nikon cameras with several thousand dollars' worth of lenses and a collection of jewelled cuff
links. The only ones who had had access to those valuables
apart from me were the Aminis.

My one defence against their possible charges that I had
somehow sold those valuables — and my only legal hold over
them — was not to sign that document, and I resisted their
considerable pressure to do so.

Because of their continual opposition to my desire to take
Farhad out of Iran, I set about finding my own way to smuggle money out. A friend, Anna, introduced me to her husband,
Paul, a diplomat with one of the Western embassies in Teheran. At first, he used his diplomatic status to take out jewellery
and furs for me. But eventually he introduced me to a professional smuggler, an Italian, who would be able to take carpets
out of the country and deliver them in Europe, where they
could be converted into cash.

One night, I invited Anna, Paul and the smuggler to dinner. I
wanted to judge the man for myself, in my own surroundings. No one in my family and not even Hamid wanted to

advise me as to whether I should try to smuggle carpets as a way of solving the financial problems that would await me, should I leave Iran. Under the Ayatollah, smuggling of any valuable — currency, jewellery, carpets or ancient coins — was punishable by death. We were even forbidden to have dealings with foreign banks, and external mail was routinely inspected to see if money was being shipped out. Those were laws aimed at the *taghouti*. I felt that if I could just talk to the man, I would have a good idea of whether I could trust him with my life.

An affable, kindly, older man, who liked pretty girls, the smuggler turned out to be someone that I immediately liked and trusted. He gave me his terms very frankly.

"I have a special storage place inside my trailer truck, and that's where I put the smuggled goods," he explained calmly. "It has never been discovered, even though I've made the trip from Teheran to Italy and back many times. Most of the time a little bribe gets me through the border without a check. It will cost you 750 Swiss francs per carpet."

When I explained to him that I wanted to get them to another Western European country, where my cousin Dara could pick them up, he whistled when he heard the name of the country.

"That's a bit more difficult. That border is the tightest one of all. We can do it, but it's risky. What we do is take the carpets up to the border area in a small van. Then, just before the border, we unload them and carry them across at a se-cluded spot. The driver takes the van through and picks us up on the other side. Your cousin will be telephoned and told a time and place for the drop-off. I should warn you that we might change the instructions at the last minute several times. We don't want an official welcoming party."

He laughed, relaxed and confident, as if smuggling were the most ordinary job in the world. And he proved true to his word.

As soon as I had found a good smuggling contact, I set about collecting the best carpets I could find. I plunged into a world that was totally foreign to me and yet one that was an integral part of Iran. The ancient art of carpet making had always been part of our history; carpets were one of the finest expressions of our artistry, one of the most visible signs of our love of colour and design. For the first time in my adult life, I donned a simple, flowered *chador* and took a taxi (so that my activities could not be traced through my car) to the bazaar. For six kilometres or so, narrow, winding streets covered with tin roofs were lined on either side with small shops. The bazaar occupied the heart of the city, and it was there that the more traditional Iranians did their shopping and their business.

The *bazaaris*, the merchants, had always played an important political and economic role in Iran. Behind the small, crowded shops, hidden behind the chaos of animals and people jostling for space, were some of the wealthiest homes in the country. Often from very religious families, the *bazaaris* still did a great deal of unofficial banking business for Iranians and many transactions were still made without documents — using only a man's word. The *chador* was essential not just to hide my identity, but also because the bazaar was a pocket of traditional Iran where the women appeared only when they were carefully covered up.

I spent days poking into the hundreds of carpet shops in the bazaar, hunting for the best deals and learning about the various types of Persian rugs. Those with hunting motifs came from Tabriz. The mosque dome was a favourite of carpets from Isfahan. Baluchistanis prized browns and dark blues, while Kashanis wove medallions on solid backgrounds. Some of the finest silk carpets came from Qom, while Isfahan had some of the best weavers. I had never shopped at the bazaar before, but now I was there almost every day, picking my way around the heavily laden donkeys and carts and learning to compete for attention with the shouting and gesticulating shoppers.

I sold everything I could get my hands on to acquire cash to buy the carpets. I sold my own wedding ring and my mother's for about $80,000, the furniture I had bought from the two panicked Americans, my clothes, my pots and pans — anything that I could rightly say was mine and not my husband's. I did not want to give the Aminis any excuse to attack me legally and take Farhad away.

Eventually, I smuggled out $400,000 worth of carpets, and Dara put them in storage and tried to sell them. My end of the smuggling was dangerous. For each shipment three men came to the house and, with quick professional moves, wrapped the carpets individually in plastic. Then they hustled them swiftly into a waiting Paycan. Rather than use a larger vehicle that might draw attention, they preferred to stuff every inch of the small working man's car. If they had been caught at any time while in my house or in transit in Teheran, they would have been jailed and I would have been executed.

In an effort to win some future considerations from my husband's partner Jamshid, who was looking for ways to get some of his valuables out of the country, I even told him about my smuggling contact and permitted him to bring his carpets to my house so that they could be shipped out with mine. I risked my life for him so that he could safely send out $2 million worth of carpets.

All the time that I was hunting for carpets to smuggle, I was also trying to sell my house. I realized the Aminis were giving me permission to sell only because they knew that they would have a much better chance of taking complete hold of Farhad's wealth if it was liquid. Trying to take away a house from a widow was a little too obvious, even in a society as anti-female as Iran's. But at the time, I put some effort into finding buyers and the experience gave me my only real glimpse of the new religious aristocracy of the country. When my husband was still alive, he had been offered about $7 million for the house and garden. Because of the revolution, the value had gone down, but we still requested $2 million for the house and a portion of the land attached to it. Dozens of people came to see the house, obviously prepared to spend the money if they liked it.

But they were not the rich of Iran that I had grown up with. Prospective buyers came in large family groups, the women shuffling in *chadors*, the children complaining loudly, the men dealing tersely with me. They were evidently newly rich: they gaped at the expensive furniture in the house and were amazed at our combined heating and air-conditioning system, which was relatively new to the country. I wondered how they had made their money so quickly and how they would fit into a place such as Shemiran. I knew too little about the regime to guess at the source of their income.

While I was still playing hostess to the newly powerful, Hamid was making plans to leave the country.

"Please, please leave. Don't stay because of me," I found myself saying to another man I cared for. "It's only a matter of time before they find you."

After months of living with friends and only occasionally going home to pick up clothes, Hamid had finally become the active target of the Komiteh. They had put out a warrant for his arrest. His company was in the hands of subordinates, and he no longer hoped to save his family's many properties. I remember with some pride how his attitude to me changed once I had made a success of my smuggling venture.

"You took a risk, all by yourself, and it worked," he said. His Sousan could think as well as wash his socks.

But even with that change, I was beginning to realize that I could no longer accept the subservience that so many Iranian men seemed to want from their women. Although my heart was still soft on Hamid, my head was telling me that he and I would not be able to survive together in the real world outside the revolution.

"God, how I will miss all this," he said one night. "Where else in the world will life be so sweet?" Where else, indeed?

Rich men in the West were not accorded the status of minor potentates as they were in Iran; wealth was more circumspect, and it did not buy you automatic respect.

We said our goodbyes sadly, and one snowy day in December 1981, he left Iran through the Turkish route, knowing he would most likely never see its deserts and mountains again. About ten days later he called from Istanbul to tell me he had made it safely.

"It was a tough journey," he said, but he gave no details, which was probably just as well — for then I might not have had the courage to follow in his footsteps just a few months later.

After Hamid left, I started to work almost exclusively on getting myself and Farhad safely out of the country. Discreetly, I let it be known to a few people that I was looking for various ways of sending money or valuables out of Iran. I still had quite a few personal possessions I could sell. One of my friends suggested that I meet a group of people who were also planning to escape and who were liquidating their assets and putting the money into old Persian stamps, which had the advantage of being light and easy to hide.

"It would be a lot easier than smuggling out carpets," she said, and I had to agree.

It was that initiative which first brought me into contact with the man who would become my second husband and who ultimately helped me escape. When I first met Kamal, he was sitting in a restaurant with a woman and another man, and I noted without interest his long, slim face and dark, dreamy eyes. I was intent on doing business, and those three strangers, whom my friend had come along to introduce to me, might just have the key I needed to escape. Hamid had been out of the country only three weeks and the last thing I wanted was an entanglement of the heart. But, as Kamal told me later, he fell for me instantly as I stood there earnestly looking at the group. While the others discussed the various advantages of smuggling out stamps and how to find the right contact to get out of the country, he kept his interest focussed on me.

At one point he suggested, "Look, if you're not ready to escape when we are, we'll delay our departure and wait for you." I could see that he meant it; even though he had known me for about an hour, he was already prepared to alter his life for me.

As planned, I took the group home with me so that we could continue our discussions and so that the second man, Kamal's cousin and an expert on antiquities, could evaluate a painting I had hanging on the second floor. During the hour or so that they were with me, Kamal repeatedly invited me to a gathering he was joining that night and refused to accept my refusals, unless my girlfriend and I promised to join him for lunch at his house.

The next day, we drove to Saltanatabad, one of my favourite suburbs, and found that Kamal lived in an exquisite airy white house with bay windows and french doors. The place was full of fine Italian and French antiques. His father, a construction man, and his mother had left the country, and Kamal had been left to protect the family holdings. Kamal himself had been a diplomat and had been working at the foreign office when the new minister had made it known that *taghouti* were not welcome. He had quit rather than be harassed out of his job. Since then he had been running his father's firm, while his father directed it from the safety of Paris.

Just four months before I met him, Kamal had been arrested in Shiraz, where he had gone to oversee a hospital-building project. His firm, like all the others, was heavily indebted to the banks and was not meeting its payments. It was also suffering from the government's refusal to pay for the project; officials said that the country could no longer afford the hospital, and that the company had probably overcharged the state.

After staying in prison for two months, Kamal was released by a local *ayatollah*, who gave him a letter exonerating him from charges of corruption and nonpayment. He carried that precious piece of paper with him always, because he never knew when he might be re-arrested on the same charges.

Despite my reluctance to become involved with him, Kamal used every means to attract me, including calling several times a day offering to help me with whatever problems I might have, dropping by unannounced with huge baskets of roses and continually inviting me out to parties. My friends all thought him a pleasant change from Hamid, who could never be counted on to show up when promised. After rebuffing Kamal repeatedly, I decided to invite him in for afternoon tea. He made full use of that opening and I ended up dating him.

"You know I am really ready to settle down, Sousan," he would say. "Marriage seems like a good idea to me." Later, he said, "You are the girl of my dreams."

How could he think of falling in love when our lives were shattered and we were about to turn our backs on our country forever? I had become so jaded with men and so confused about what I wanted from them that I merely laughed when he talked that way and said neither yes nor no to his many proposals of marriage. Perhaps it was cynical of me, but by then a man was merely someone to help me, protect me at a time that I was very vulnerable. I did not love Kamal, and I never told him that I did, but I did need him to help me escape.

By February 1982, I was certain that I would soon have to leave. Increasingly, my son was becoming a terrorized product of the crazy school system. He was learning little other than the Koran, and the teachers did not bother to hide their annoyance with him because he was a little rich kid. So many times he came home crying because he had been punished for talking out of turn, even though I knew that Farhad was a very obedient child. Because he had been mixed in with children from the poorer parts of the city, he picked up foul language. I sent him to school in old, patched clothing so that he would not stand out, but he was not spared the taunts of the other children.

At the same time, my house was becoming a target of surveillance, and the Aminis kept circling around me. They seemed to know a great deal about my whereabouts and occasionally my mother-in-law would make comments about my hectic social schedule. I had no idea how she could possibly know what I did with my days. But after my many run-ins with the Aminis, I concluded that they were looking for ways to get me into trouble so that they could prove that I was an unfit mother and take my son away from me by law.

Weeks before, I had decided to hold one last party, one last dangerous fling — only this time I would invite only women, and only women who wanted to laugh, not talk about the revolution or the horrible new Iran. I called together some friends and we made a list of dancers, musicians, singers and actresses who would welcome an afternoon of fearless entertainment. I set the day, and one February afternoon, about forty women showed up on my doorstep. For five hours we sang old Persian songs, danced traditional Persian dances, recited poetry: we laughed and we cried as we celebrated our love for our country and grieved over its plight.

One of the women was a well-known actress, who in the Shah's day had often recited on national television, in her famous sultry voice, the sensuous passages of many of our great writers. After losing her work, she had become a pariah under the Ayatollah and now she wept as, once again, her voice flowed mellifluously through the dark, emotional currents of our poetry.

She recited the verses of one of our modern, tragic poets, Forugh Farrokhzad, who in the 1960s had challenged the social and sexual taboos of Iran before dying in a freak car accident at the age of thirty-two.

From distances afar you came,
from lands of light and of perfume
setting me now in a ship
of ivory, of clouds, of crystal hewn
O take me, take me, heart-fondling hope,
to the city where verses and passions bloom.

I had bought quite a lot of alcohol on the black market for the day and by late afternoon we were all mildly drunk and hugely emotional. I suddenly regretted my decision to leave: nowhere else would I find such friendship.

That night I went to bed thinking, "Maybe I should stay. Maybe things will get better eventually. Why give all this up? My home, my family? Who knows what's on the outside and how we will survive?"

Chapter Eight

The Komiteh Pays a Visit

Would you that spangle of Existence spend
About THE SECRET — quick about it, Friend!
A Hair perhaps divides the False and True —
And upon what, prithee, may life depend?

OMAR KHAYYÁM

 When I woke up the following morning, having slept more soundly than I had in months, I did not want to stir from under my warm duvet. Outside, it was a cold and humid Thursday — February 18, 1982 — I have good cause to remember it. The new-found courage I had felt the night before was still with me. Overnight, I had decided to stay in Iran. The love and companionship of my friends had helped me overcome my fears. The regime was not going to chase me away. I was Iranian, proud of it, and rulers had come and gone. The *mullahs* would go, too — someday.

It was family card day. Various female members of the extended family were still getting together every two weeks for a day of gossip and low-stakes gambling. Today my Aunt Tootie was host and my cousin Fariba would be there along with a few other women — all of us family, well bred, still chic despite the times. I dressed carefully for the outside world — a combination of my old style and the new rules. No more short skirts. No more short-sleeved blouses. The radio and newspapers were still full of commands from Khomeini that women must be covered and the Komiteh regularly stopped cars to berate "improperly dressed" drivers and passengers. Along with my cousins and most of my friends, I had ignored the whole matter until a few months before when Fariba had come rushing into my house, white-faced.

"Sousan, have you seen what they are doing now?" she asked, waving a newspaper. "Some crazy men threw acid at the faces of two women just because they weren't wearing a *chador*. God, they are becoming worse than barbarians."

After that, we started dressing more carefully for the street and made certain not to forget our *hejabs*. But no *chador*. Never a *chador*, I swore, no matter what they did to me. That morning I put on a well-tailored, grey woollen suit with burgundy leather trim, high burgundy leather boots and a high-necked burgundy blouse with long sleeves that I had bought at one of the European import shops. Then, just before getting into my Firebird to make the ten-minute drive to my aunt's house on the Avenue Mirdamad, I put on a *hejab* that covered all of my blonde hair and most of my forehead.

That afternoon at my aunt's was uneventful, although I remember being more relaxed than I had been in months. According to the unwritten family code, we avoided any discussion of politics. We all left at about 6:00 P.M., just as it was beginning to get dark. We wanted to get home before the Komiteh started prowling around. I kissed everyone goodbye, covered my head and made the trip home with nothing more on my mind than plans for a long, hot bath, an early dinner with Farhad and a good night's sleep. Perhaps I would watch one of the five videos I had rented under the counter at my usual agency; maybe I would settle down to *Scruples* or *The Other Side of Midnight*.

I found Farhad playing with Jalal Agha, the driver, his wife and their two children in the basement. I thanked fortune once again for sending me such a nice family to live in the servants' quarters. I had only a couple of servants who came in for a few days a week now. It made me feel safer just knowing the driver's family was there in the house at night. Farhad came up and talked about the happenings at school that day while I started to get a light meal ready. Suddenly the telephone rang. It was Kamal.

"I am going to invite myself over for a visit tonight," he said jovially.

Kamal was becoming an overly aggressive suitor. The daily baskets of roses were lovely, the toys for Farhad even more thoughtful. But he was pushing too hard, too fast.

"Listen, Kamal, I am absolutely exhausted. How about tomorrow night?" I suggested.

"I'm going to be driving by your place anyway. I'm visiting a friend of mine who lives just a bit further on the hill there. I'll stay just a minute, I promise."

I was absolutely incapable of saying no, of being an ungracious hostess, especially to men. But I planned to make clear my displeasure by offering him only tea, not alcohol, and by keeping him sitting in the kitchen.

When I hung up, I berated myself. There I was saying yes to a man when I really wanted to say no. What was it about me that always felt the need to please? What was it about my culture that made it a sin to be ungracious to a guest? We are people to whom *taarof*, hospitality, is sacred. But it was more than that. I was beginning to realize slowly that I allowed men to rule my life. Hamid had been gone only two and a half months. When he escaped, I had sworn there would be no other men — not because I wanted to be true to him, but because I suddenly realized that I was fed up with men. How I had served that man for three years, right down to all those times I had washed his socks by hand — I, a woman who had never washed her own things. And now here was Kamal invading my life, while Hamid continued to call me from Europe. I had known Kamal barely a month. I agreed with all my friends that he was an improvement over Hamid, but he was taking it for granted that I would love him.

After I fed Farhad, I had no time for a bath, and I was still in my street clothes when Kamal arrived at about 8:00 P.M. When I saw him standing in the doorway, I was struck once again by how broodingly handsome he was. He had a mass of dark hair, but a very lean, pale face and soft, brown, intelligent eyes. Behind him I could see his silver Mercedes parked in the drive.

The sight of the car immediately angered me. He's done it again, I thought. Doesn't he realize the danger that he is putting me in? Every time he came, Kamal parked either in front of the house or in one of the alleyways where everyone could see him. During his last few months in Iran, Hamid had refused to visit my house when he was alone for fear of getting me into trouble. But, once again, I was too embarrassed to reprimand Kamal or ask him to take a taxi next time.

After joining me in the kitchen, Kamal started to tell me about his preparations for leaving Iran.

"I've pretty well decided to buy those old stamps. They're going to cost me about four and a half million tumans [about $700,000 U.S. then] but my cousin assures me that they're worth it. They'd better be. I'm selling my house to buy them."

"Whom are you buying them from? Who would be selling stuff that you can carry out of the country at a time like this?"

"Some old devout Moslem who has no plans to leave. I haven't even met the man yet. It's all being done through an agent."

We were still talking about his plans when there was a light knock at the front door. It was a gentle, almost imperceptible interruption. I sat up straight in my chair, my hands gripping the kitchen table. In those days, no one went to another person's house at that time of night without calling first.

"Kamal, I am not expecting anybody. Maybe you had better go. Take the door leading out into the garden. Down the hill, past the fruit grove, the wall is low. You can climb out."

"I am not going! And leave you here not knowing what's going to happen. If there's any trouble, I'd better be here."

It was chivalrous, but at that moment I would have preferred some common sense. Kamal knew it was illegal for us to be together alone. The three boys were in a ground-floor bedroom watching cartoon videos, and the driver and his wife were in the basement, but none of that would count under the new morality rules. Not even the bravest of us would go to restaurant with a man friend anymore. Didn't he read the newspapers? Women were being arrested for having lunch with unrelated male friends. But I had no time to argue.

Fortunately, I was still completely covered from head to toe in my carefully chosen outdoor clothes, and as I went to answer the door I put on a *hejab* that I always had handy in the main entrance hall. I was half expecting to see a contingent from the Komiteh, complete with curly beards, army fatigues and automatic rifles. Instead, there were two neatly dressed young men, with well-trimmed moustaches, and they carried nothing more dangerous than a packet of cigarettes. The older one, who must have been around thirty, was wearing a navy blue suit with a turtleneck. The younger one, in his early twenties, was in a brown suit and also wore a turtleneck. I was relieved for a moment. They could not be Komiteh.

The older one spoke first. "Salom. We want to speak to the people downstairs."

"Well, may I say who is asking for them?"

"Just say we are friends."

"May I say what it is about?"

"We just want to talk to them."

"Whom do you want to talk to exactly?"

"Just the people downstairs."

"How can you say you are friends if you don't even know their names?"

The younger one jumped in. "Just ask them to come upstairs."

Throughout the conversation they were very polite. I kept insisting on knowing what they wanted and they kept ignoring my questions. Finally the older one said, "Look, we've had a complaint about them. What kind of people are they?"

They still had not bothered to identify themselves. I thought quickly. If they were Komiteh, they might be concerned about whether the driver was a Communist or active in any political group.

"They're very good, honest people, very religious. They have never done anything suspicious," I insisted. But the men were adamant, and eventually I closed the front door, leaving them outside. All this time, Kamal had been standing in the hallway waiting to see what was going to happen. Before running to the door leading to the basement to call Jalal Agha, I said to Kamal, "You've got to go. I'm not sure they are Komiteh and they haven't asked for anything so far, but you'd better leave. I can't be found with you."

"Don't be silly, Sousan," he replied. "Nothing is going to happen. They have no right to bother you. Don't worry."

When I told Jalal Agha that he had some visitors, he was immediately nervous and suspicious. He went to open his own private doorway to the outside, which was near our door leading to the garage, and called the two men over to him.

I went to my own side door and went out to hear what they were saying. I felt a sudden chill that was not caused by the damp night air. I approached them confidently, as if I had nothing at all to hide.

The one in the blue suit turned and said to me, "We're going to search his house."

"What's the matter? Is there some kind of problem? What's going on here?" I tried to sound as impatient as possible, sure of my ground, even though my stomach suddenly felt queasy.

"We are from the Monkerat and we have a warrant to search his house," the younger man said. "And while we're here, we're going to search your house, too."

Before I could say a word, the younger one went downstairs with the driver and the older one just walked through my open doorway. With that began five hours of terror for me and my son.

I followed the stranger into my house, my mind racing ahead. The Monkerat was the notorious morality squad in charge of enforcing Islamic morals. I cursed myself for being lax. What would they find? How many of their laws had I broken? And then I gasped. I had completely forgotten about my Uncle Kurosh's letter. There it was sitting innocently on the console just to the right of the entrance, looking just like an ordinary letter waiting to be mailed. If nothing else, the contents of that letter would land me and my uncle in prison. I had spent months trying to get my uncle to trust my smuggling contact. The next day I was going to turn over the letter — addressed to my uncle's Swiss bank — to Paul, who was going to send it out of the country in a diplomatic pouch.

I stood at the open doorway, unable to move, but the visitor just walked past the console. His dark, unreadable eyes swept the hallway. Soon, the younger man came in, having already finished his search of the driver's basement apartment.

"Hassan," he called to the man in blue, "I've done." Then he switched from Persian to Turkish.

In Iran, Turks make up the largest of many ethnic groups within the country, and they tend to retain their language. Both sides of my family were of Turkish descent and I spoke the language fluently. I realized that I had to interrupt them quickly before I heard something I was not supposed to hear. Using my best imitation of the new revolutionary greetings, I said in Turkish, "Oh, brothers, so you are from the Turkish part of Iran, too. Then we have something in common."

They just looked at me very coldly, then turned to Kamal, who was standing by the kitchen.

"Who is this?" the man called Hassan asked. "What's his relationship with you?"

Kamal answered before I could, with the sort of contempt that only a well-bred *taghouti* can manage. "I am a friend."

I was furious. In front of two members of the Komiteh he was announcing with pride that he was my friend — a code word in Iran for lover or boyfriend.

"Well, actually, he is a family friend," I rushed in to explain, "and he has been helping me out with my late husband's financial affairs. I was so depressed by the confusion after my husband's death, and this gentleman is advising me."

The younger man looked at his watch. "At this hour of the night? At 9:30 at night? And you call yourself a good Turkish woman? Only sluts have men in their houses. Where is the party? Where are all the people?"

I was thrown off by the question. There were only Kamal, myself and the three children.

"We've had a report that there is a party going on here," he went on. "In fact, we hear there are parties all the time. Men come to meet women. Where are they hiding? Have they escaped already?"

What could he mean? Perhaps he had the wrong house. "There is nobody here except us. There is no party going on."

With childish whoops, my son and his friends came running out of the video room to see who our visitors were. Hassan glowered at them and then cocked his head as if to better make out something that he had heard. Emanating from the video room was that hated language — English. An English video! His eyes were suddenly eager. Now they had something! Both men ran in and found, still playing, a Sesame Street show that the children had been watching. They watched it for a while and then picked up the four videos sitting next to the television set and began to insert each one to see what the films were. Silently, they scrutinized disjointed segments of the films I had on hand: *Scruples*, *The Other Side of Midnight* and *Airport*. When they came to scenes of near-nudity, their faces hardened. I suddenly felt like covering my face. After they had finished, they turned on me, and the younger, more brutal one spat out,

"English, all English. And look at this filthy sex stuff. Aren't you ashamed to have this in your house?"

His hatred hit me like a blow. I could see myself in his eyes: a rich, spoiled woman, who could afford five foreign videos.

"Where did you rent this stuff?" Hassan asked. I gave him the name reluctantly — in any case it was written on the cassettes if he had bothered to look.

After watching the videos for about twenty minutes trying to detect more porn, in their terms at least, they brushed past me without a word and headed for the dining room. I was still worrying about the letter, sitting on the console for everyone to see, but they were more interested in finding a "party." In the dining room, they finally found something that confirmed their suspicions that my house was a pleasure palace: my large, round dining-room table that could seat twenty-four people.

"This is a gambling table," the short, young one said, hitting his hand on the dark rosewood. "This is where your guests play, isn't it?"

"It's just a dining-room table, that's all," I insisted. "Look how big it is. How could you possibly gamble at such a large table?"

But a quick search in the buffet revealed even more damning evidence. In one of the drawers they found all my illegal sets of cards and delicate handmade gambling jetons stacked in a beautiful lacquer case, now even more precious because such things were in short supply in revolutionary Iran.

"And so what are these?" he asked. "Food for your dining-room table? It looks as if this is a party house. We're going to collect plenty of evidence, I'm sure."

For the next four hours, they proceeded to search the house minutely. In every other respect they had seemed ignorant, inexperienced revolutionaries with a lot of indignation and bad manners. But now their professionalism became evident. They had obviously learned from an expert. They unscrewed the grates covering the air vents, checked through the flour and sugar in the kitchen, moved every photograph, every book, looked behind the stereo and cassette machines, looked through all my purses, fingered all my clothes. They unscrewed lamp bases, dug around inside the potted plants, squeezed cushions, checked under mattresses. Nothing hidden could have stayed that way for long. Hassan even found my most private letters tied up in an embroidered linen handkerchief in one of my bureau drawers. He remained impassive as he read the very first love letter that a man, really just a teenaged boy, had sent me when I was in the United States. Even my husband had never seen it. My face burned with anger and embarrassment, but I could say nothing.

Throughout the search, Kamal stood in the hall, watching silently. Farhad trailed me everywhere, asking me over and over again, "Who are these people, Mummy? What do they want?"

"It's nothing, baby, nothing. Soon they will go."

"But what do they want?"

The two men were in my favourite place in the house — the fireplace room. As they headed towards the bookshelves, I suddenly realized that they were about to find even more proof of my degenerate Western behaviour. My husband read a lot, and he had bought quite a few foreign magazines. Many of them were architectural magazines, but there were also one or two *Playboy*s. I had simply forgotten about them. The magazines were all neatly stacked up near the record player and tape recorder, in the high shelves on either side of the fireplace. The younger one pounced on them and started flipping through them. Every time he came across an advertisement depicting a woman with a short-sleeved dress or a man and a woman standing close together, he made clucking noises, his bushy eyebrows disapproving and his forehead frowning. As for the *Playboy*s, he took one look at the covers and tossed them on the ground as if he might be sullied merely by handling them.

"You know this is against the law?" he asked with condescension, as if I suffered from a streak of stupidity. "Don't touch a thing after we leave. Leave everything here. Tomorrow we will be back to pick up all this stuff. It's evidence against you."

I controlled an impulse to scream. Instead, I pleaded.

"Kind sir, please forgive me but I didn't even know they were here. Those magazines were my husband's. They haven't been opened since he died. I just never thought to throw them out, but, if you want me to, I'll throw them out tonight."

I was wringing my hands in supplication. I was still trying to placate them, be nicer to them than anyone had ever been, show them that I was really on their side, anything so that they would not take me to prison and separate me from my son.

The Komiteh man did not answer. Instead, the two men separated so that they could cover more of the house. Hassan grunted to me to lead the way upstairs, and the younger man stayed downstairs with Kamal. I realized that they did not ·

want to lose sight of either one of us, not even for a moment. As Hassan and I walked up the stairs, I was already scheming to find some way to make him like me. Of the two, he seemed the nicer type. He spoke a little less harshly. I thought if I could just befriend him, he might let me go without punishment. My head was filled with all the prison stories I had ever heard. As far as we were concerned, the Komiteh were just wild, violent and totally uneducated. I could see the contempt that they felt for me as they looked around the house, at its large, elegant rooms, its silk carpets and antiques. I could see them thinking, "Why does this bitch have all this when we have nothing?" They enjoyed degrading us. I remembered with a shudder the whip marks on my friends' backs out by the Caspian.

Most of all, I dreaded leaving Farhad, even for just a few days. Ever since his father died, he had clung to me even more desperately. Sometimes at night when I put him to bed he would say, "You won't leave me while I sleep, will you, Mama?" How could I have exposed a six-year-old boy to all this? A woman in my position in revolutionary Teheran was not supposed to have fun. I should have had no social life, and certainly no man.

Upstairs, Hassan went straight to my bedroom. He had just begun to search through my clothes closet when he pulled out a cigarette and started to fumble for a match. "I'll get you a match. I have some in the kitchen," I offered immediately. I was trying to make him like me and I still had in the back of my mind that letter sitting like a time bomb on the hallway console. I ran down before he could say no, went to the console, grabbed the letter, all the time terrified that the other, nasty one would see me, and ran into the small servant's bedroom next to the kitchen area. There I hid the letter between the blanket and the mattress.

I was halfway up the stairs again when I realized that the absence of the letter on the console might actually draw more attention to it than simply leaving it where it was. I ran down the stairs again—Kamal and the other Komiteh man were in the living room and could not see me — grabbed the letter again and put it back on the console. Then I hurried upstairs with the match I had fetched from the kitchen. My heart was pounding, I was panting and felt dizzy with fear. My future depended on my not making one wrong move.

When I got back to Hassan, he was in the projection room. He had one film unrolled and was examining it under a strong light. Without a nod, he took the match and kept frowning over the film. Photography and filmmaking had been my husband's hobby. He had spent a lot of time and money on it, and whenever we went to Europe he took hours of film on the beaches and at tourist spots. He had also taken film of all of us swimming and playing at the villa and in the outdoor swimming pool of the Teheran house. There was a four-hour video of our marriage ceremony; even the precious old film of my mother's wedding day that my Uncle Kurosh had shot was there, along with films of Farhad's baby years. A lifetime of memories were stacked up there, neatly labelled.

But I suddenly realized that in that room was even more evidence against me—evidence that I was not a good Moslem woman and that mine was not a good Moslem household. All those films of France, taken when topless bikinis were the rage, all those shots of me in a bikini! What would they say to that? There was even a porno film, *Emmanuelle*, that my husband had bought, still sitting on the shelves.

"Turn on the projector." It was a command.

"I am so sorry, sir, but I don't know how to do it and I think the light is broken." My voice had become smaller. I was about to vomit.

We both tried to fiddle with the machine, but we could not manage to turn it on. Instead, he started to unravel each film and looked at the frames under a strong light, searching for sinful scenes. For one hour, without making a single comment, he pawed through the films. Finally, he said, "What is all this filth? What kind of movies are these? Where did you find this garbage?"

"Sir, it is only family film, that is all."

"Don't you know what kind of trouble this stuff gets you in? These things are really bad." He shook his head. "If they see these films at the Komiteh, you'll have a lot of problems."

I must have turned pale because he seemed to take some pity on me. I ran to the bathroom. I vomited into the bowl. Then I wiped a cold cloth over my face and ran back to the projection room.

"Sir, what can I do? These were my husband's things, his hobby. Why should I be punished for that?"

Hassan seemed to relent for a moment. "All right. If you want to spare yourself, get some gasoline and we'll try to burn all this stuff."

Relief swept over me. Thank God, this man was kind. I had a second chance. "Of course, thank you, thank you, we'll do it right now. I'll get the gasoline right now."

I was scared that the other Komiteh man would come upstairs and change Hassan's mind. As quickly as I could, I ran downstairs to the garage where I kept the lighting fuel for the barbecue and ran back up.

"Where do you want to do it?" he asked.

"Right out on the balcony." We had a magnificent wide, tiled balcony on the second floor that linked several of the upstairs rooms, including our bedroom.

"All those films burning are going to make an awful mess of the tiles," Hassan said.

But by that point, I didn't care about the films, their personal or commercial value, and I couldn't have cared less about the balcony. I just wanted those men out of my house. I wanted to be left alone with my son. I didn't want a single man near me. I wanted to be through with all men for all time.

"Never mind the balcony. Let's just burn them," I said. I helped him clear the shelves and heap many of the films into

a big pile. I was too nervous, too shaky, to try to pick out and
save the family films, the film of my wedding, those of my
son growing, the films of my husband, my mother's wedding.
I have no idea how much of the family history ended up on
that pile. I was in a frenzy to burn them all. To cleanse the
house. I was almost gleeful in a crazy way when he doused
the films with gasoline. He lit the match and handed it to me.
For a moment, I stared transfixed at the tiny flame. Then I
tossed it on the pile. Immediately, huge flames lit up the balcony. Jalal Agha came up to observe. My son came, too, and
grabbed hold of my legs and watched silently. After a while
he said, "Mummy, are you going to burn the house, too?" I
cannot imagine what was running through his mind. Two
strange men had walked into his house, had made his mother
cower, and evidently they had the right to boss her around.

We all watched the films melt as they gave life to a strangely
coloured flame. As the fire leapt higher into the clear, cold
night, I felt that the core of my body was collapsing. I
crouched over Farhad and felt both our bodies tremble. It
seemed that we were all trapped in a strange quiet which no
one seemed able to escape: the Komiteh man standing there
looking at the pile, neither smiling nor gloating, almost businesslike; the driver who had come up to observe, his frowning
face glowing in the light; my son and I mesmerized. Finally,
the flames died out, leaving a gooey black blob of plastic.
I knew the residue had irretrievably damaged the honey-
coloured tiles of the balcony. But I was far from caring.

Hassan wasted no time on the memories that had just gone
up in smoke. He walked past me into the house and headed
for my bedroom. The younger man joined him there — I
suppose he was feeling safe about leaving Kamal alone downstairs — and the two continued their careful search. It was in
my bedroom, my refuge, my safe room where I curled up
and conducted my social life on my private telephone line
that they found the jackpot of guilt. Between the sheets and

the mattress of my bed they found an envelope containing my illegal gasoline coupons. That was where I always stored my coupons in case the house was broken into by a thief. Coupons were that valuable.

The Komiteh men could tell at a glance — I don't really know how, either through the serial numbers or the colour — that I had obtained the coupons illegally from a private taxi company.

The younger man turned to me. A fanatical glee distorted his face. "So, little lady. Where did you buy these? You know how illegal they are, don't you? Who sold them to you? Come, come, out with it. Who sold you these?"

He took the pile of coupons and pushed them into my face. I knew there was no point in lying. I was so scared that I could barely formulate the words. I gave them the name of the cab company that I always called. Later, when I had time to rethink the events of that night a hundred times over, I realized how much trouble that agency would be in. But there was nothing that I could do. Nothing in my life had prepared me for such an assault.

The two men went downstairs, taking the coupons with them. I trailed after them, Farhad holding on so tightly that I nearly tripped down the stairs. At the bottom of the stairs, Kamal stood watching us with unconcealed distaste on his face. The Komiteh men headed back into the living room — a room that they seemed to disapprove of intensely. They stood around frowning at all the stereo equipment, the tape recorder, the dozens of records and cassettes.

"What's all this music?" the perpetually angry young one asked me. "Why does anybody need so many cassettes? One or two would be fine. Why these hundreds?" He swept his arm over the shelves in a gesture of vast wastefulness. And then he said without irony, without a trace of levity, "You have too much music here. Music is against the law. Leave everything here. We will come back for them tomorrow and take them away with the magazines and the rest of the films upstairs."

It was then that they found the alcohol. My husband and I had always had an excellent cellar of wines and a very good collection of liquor in our house. Even after he died, there was a good deal left. Hamid had added to the supplies — even though after the revolution a single bottle of whisky cost almost 4,000 tumans on the black market (about $300 U.S. at the time). My cousin Kamron, a great connoisseur of wines, had also been very generous to me; he made regular trips to France to buy at wine auctions and had recently bought the wine collection of a wealthy Iranian who had just abandoned the country. Every now and then, he brought me French red wines that would have been rare even in Europe.

We knew the danger of having alcohol in the house, although, as with every other danger, we simply ignored it. But we did attempt to hide the bottles. The garden was full of little troughs and dips in the ground that were filled with the illicit stuff, then covered with leaves to act as a camouflage. There were little stashes of alcohol all over the grounds. Hossein, the old gardener who lived in a little house in the southeast corner of the garden, had helped me hide the bottles. In the house, I kept only a few bottles of wine and several half-empty bottles of hard liquor hidden behind some stereo equipment in a locked cabinet.

On one last sweep of the living room, Hassan noticed that they had not yet searched that one particular little cabinet.

"Open this," he directed me.

I cringed. "I have a box of keys in the kitchen but I don't know which one is the right key."

"Get them."

"Yes, sir." When I brought him the keys, he tried every single one patiently until he found the right one. After that, all he had to do was search behind the equipment to find the six bottles of hard liquor that I had there, along with a dozen or so precious wine bottles.

"All right, you can do one of two things with this stuff," Hassan said, pointing to the bottles of wine and alcohol and the pile of cards on the dining-room table. "You can take them out into the garden right now, with me watching, and break them and burn them. Or we will take them to the Komiteh in the morning."

As soon as he said that, I rushed into action. I could hardly believe my reprieve. With Jalal Agha's help, I carried the bottles outside through the door leading to the garage. Then we carried out the cards and all the jetons. Kamal just stood by watching, sneering at my frantic attempts, making no effort to help. I guess he still thought I had nothing to fear from those men. He appeared unconcerned.

Just as we were preparing a giant bonfire, Jalal Agha leaned closer to me and asked furtively, "Madam, these cards are so rare, so costly, would you mind if I took a pack?"

"Jalal Agha, go ahead and try," I whispered. "I'll try to distract them, but if you get caught, I won't be able to help you." Somehow he managed to sneak a pack away into his apartment while I made a great show of piling up the boxes of cards and the gaming rule books.

As we worked, the two Komiteh men went to the balcony off the bedrooms and watched us from there. I was left to destroy my own property, to be their instrument for hurting myself. I was almost violent in my actions. I smashed the bottles against the white stucco walls of my house. I threw every last card, every single delicately made mother-of-pearl jeton onto the fire. The wine splashed all over the side of the house leaving a deep red stain, like blood that had flowed freely. Even in my fear, even in my mad rush to burn the evidence against me, I shuddered at the sight and I was filled with hatred for my oppressors at the destruction of the beautiful jetons.

While everyone was still watching the fire burning, the two men called me to join them upstairs in my bedroom. I went up nervously, not knowing what to expect. Up to that point, they had said nothing about taking me to prison. They had said only that they would come back in the morning to confiscate my magazines, my tapes and the rest of my films. I kept praying that they would get out of my house so that I could shut the door and close myself in with my son. They had already violated our house. I thought that because they had let me destroy the alcohol, films and cards, perhaps they were showing some kindness. How wrong I was, how naïve. When I walked into the bedroom, I could tell immediately that what I thought had been mercy had been only a torturer's trick. They were angry and brutal. Hassan dropped the nice-guy act.

"Out with it, now. Who is this man and who is he to you?"

"I told you, a friend of the family, a business consultant."

"We know you sleep with this man. He is a lover, isn't he? Speak up! Where does your son sleep at night? You put him in the bedroom downstairs, don't you, just to get him out of the way? So that you can sleep with all your different lovers on that bed?"

He stabbed angrily at my neatly made bed. I looked blankly at its pale green silk covering, not seeing it as mine. My eyes strayed to the bamboo chairs, the glass coffee table with its bowl of multicoloured roses. Had I bought the roses that morning? Or the day before? Whose room was this anyway?

"Speak up."

"What lovers? Who? Where? What are you talking about? My son always sleeps in this room with me." I motioned to the little bed by the window where my son slept.

But the younger one insisted, "We want a list. A list of the people you sleep with. We want to know what people come here. Look," he said as he walked up and stood close to me, touching me with his breath, "we know you sleep with this man. We can have you sent to a doctor to check you out, to see if you have had sex within the last few hours."

I could feel myself about to vomit again, but I choked the feeling down. I was so alone in that room with those two men. I wanted to crouch in a corner. Hassan pulled out a list that he had written. There, in a scratchy script, were listed all my sins, all the illegal pleasures they had found in my house: the cards, the alcohol, the tapes and records, films and magazines.

"You are going to sign this."

"No!" I almost shouted it. If I signed that list, I knew it was my death. Those were major crimes in Iran. People had been killed for less if the newspapers were to be believed. Everything I knew about the regime so far had been from word of mouth, from newspapers. I had lived cocooned from the real effects. It was always someone else who had been arrested, someone else who had been forced to flee, somebody else's relatives who had never come back from prison. Now I stared at the reality of the Khomeini regime. I started to cry. I got down on my knees and begged them to let me go.

"I'll sign a paper that says I had the films, and the magazines and cassettes, too, but nothing else. You can't make me do that. You know what it means."

At that point, Farhad came in, and, seeing me kneeling on the floor, my face wet from tears, he, too, started to cry. "For Allah's sake, look at my son. You can't do this to him. Please, please, let me go." I cried and clutched Farhad but they only insisted that I sign the document.

"Sign this now," Hassan commanded.

I crawled towards him and I tried to kiss his hand. I thought that if I showed him my subjugation he would be moved in some way, have some pity or at least feel satisfied that he had put me through the shame. But when I went to touch him, he brusquely pushed me aside. "A Moslem woman does not touch a man."

I took another piece of paper and wrote my own list. I don't know how I managed to do it. My hands were shaking so badly that I could hardly make out what I had written. Then I signed it. "This is all that I am going to sign," I said, and I handed the paper to Hassan. He said nothing, but he took it and the two men headed downstairs.

Kamal was in the hallway, and they started to ask him one more time who he was. Throughout the ordeal, he had stood in the downstairs hallway, watching the search with evident contempt, saying little. He answered any question with an impatient scowl. And no matter what I said, he kept insisting he was a friend, saying it with pride, as if it were a safe thing to announce, as if we were in the Western world instead of in a country turned back in time.

This time, Kamal, to show them he was someone they could not trifle with, pulled out the letter given to him by the *ayatollah* from Shiraz, which essentially said that no one was to arrest him and cause him trouble. The letter made clear that Kamal was not just some rich young pup as the two men had thought, but a very rich man who was running one of the country's large construction firms.

Hassan took the letter, and a smile crept over his face. "Ah, the head of a big firm, I see. Interesting. And where is your father?"

"Out of the country."

"I see you have been in prison, a guest of the state. Why?"

"It's all in there," Kamal replied.

"Yes. So I see. Well, I think we will search the cars now."

The Komiteh was always very interested in cars—especially Mercedes-Benz and Range Rovers—and they confiscated them on the slightest pretext. The owners rarely got them back. We all went out into the garage. Luckily, my husband had sold both the Mercedes and the Range Rover just before he died, and my little Firebird was of no interest to them. But Kamal's was a fine silver Mercedes sports model. They searched the car thoroughly and found a fortune in coupons in the glove compartment.

"Look what we have here," said the younger man, holding them high in the air.

Kamal was furious. He had stood silently by, unable to help me, but now he could no longer control his anger. "They are perfectly legal. They were bought in a perfectly proper way. You have no right to touch them."

"Who are you to tell us what rights we have?" Hassan retorted. "You are coming with us and we're taking your car, too."

"You have no right to take my car or my coupons. Leave them where they are," Kamal insisted.

Kamal seemed to know no fear, but I was angry with him. They had been about to leave. They had said nothing about prison, and now, because of his blatant arrogance, they were mad. I had never dealt with the Komiteh before, but, from what everyone had told me, they loved the scene that I had just given them, with me crying and asking for forgiveness. It might have satisfied them — they might even have let me escape further punishment. Kamal's cool insistence on his rights hardened their attitudes. When he continued to protest the appropriation of his coupons, the two men arrested him on the spot.

I was standing beside Jalal Agha at the entrance to the garage when Hassan turned to me: "We are going to take this man in now. We are going to come back for you first thing tomorrow morning. Have everything ready."

Kamal would not give up. "What about my letter? You can't arrest me."

"We don't give a damn about your letter," Hassan said. And, sure enough, in Iran nobody and everybody was the law. If one *ayatollah* decided one thing, another just overruled him. Every section of the city, of the country, seemed to be run by little local chiefs. Kamal's *ayatollah* was going to be of no use to him here.

"I want to make a call," Kamal insisted.

"You will do nothing until we tell you to," the younger one said. "You are coming with us now."

Right at that moment, I have no idea why, the younger one went back into the hallway. Suddenly he noticed the letter to the Swiss bank sitting on the console. I almost stopped breathing. Everything they had found up to now was nothing compared to the dynamite in that letter. Next to former Savak members and the Shah's people, the regime hated most those rich Iranians who sent their money out of the country. Death was too good for such traitors as far as they were concerned. He picked up the letter and held it to the light, looking for money or what might be a cheque. Fortunately, most Komiteh members do not read Persian well, let alone English, because in bold black letters, in English, was written the Geneva address of the Union Bank of Switzerland. He fingered the letter with a look of distrust.

"What is this?"

"It's just a letter to a friend. I was going to mail it tomorrow."

He looked at it suspiciously for another moment and then, inexplicably, he put it back down again. I stood rooted to the spot for a moment and then slowly let out the breath I had been holding unconsciously in my tightened chest. I can only imagine that he set the letter down because he knew that all foreign letters were routinely opened. If there was anything worth catching, it would be caught. Internal mail was of no interest, and I suppose it had not crossed their minds that I would attempt to smuggle the letter out. My uncle, for a moment, had been spared and so had I. He stomped back outside to where Kamal was still arguing with Hassan. Again they told me to be ready first thing in the morning.

I don't know what possessed me, but I suddenly remembered that I had a doctor's appointment in the morning and said, "Could you come a little later in the morning, please? I have a doctor's appointment at ten."

"What time will you be home then?" Hassan asked.

"At eleven."

"All right. We'll send somebody at 11:30."

It seems odd now how, in the midst of such a frightening experience, that small, mundane domestic detail should stick out. How, after abusing me for so long, they would be considerate enough to let me go to my doctor's appointment.

As they were leading Kamal away, he turned to me and yelled, "Sousan, call my cousin at 64 . . ."

"Shut up. You call no one. You come with us."

". . . 3387. Call him. Tell him where I am. Remember 643387 . . ." and as they dragged him away, Kamal kept repeating the number. I kept saying it over and over in my mind. I was terrified I would forget it. I kept repeating it as I watched them pull away in their own Range Rover, and I kept repeating it as I turned and ran inside with my son and shut the door. I kept repeating it as I locked the door and held Farhad tightly. It was 1:35 A.M. The ordeal had lasted five hours and fifteen minutes.

Chapter Nine

Into the Darkness of a Khomeini Prison

Ah, voice of the prisoner,
will the plaint of your despair
never burrow a way to light
through any of this despised night?
Ah, voice of the prisoner
O, final voice of all . . .

FORUGH FARROKHZAD

I stood for a moment in the hallway, clutching Farhad fiercely, waiting for the flush of panic to subside. Farhad trembled and sobbed.

"What do those men want, Mummy? Are they coming back? Where are they going to take us?" He detached himself from me briefly and puffed up his chest in his best imitation of a strong man. "I wish I were Bruce Lee. I would destroy them. Chop, chop, you're dead. And they'd all fall down." His big, dark eyes were filled with tears and confusion. He had never seen me so upset before. He had never seen me on my knees begging for mercy.

"Don't worry, luvijun. Everything is all right. Mummy is all right. The men just had to look around the house. Maybe tomorrow I have to go to their place and answer some questions. But there is nothing to worry about."

I could not stop to comfort him for long. There was so much to do. The letter still stood on the console. I grabbed it and tore it to pieces. I had a crazy idea that I could chew the bits of paper and swallow them. It was Farhad who brought me back to my senses.

"Mummy, let's throw them in the toilet!"

We both ran to the ground-floor bathroom and watched the little bits of paper swirl out of sight. Then, before I forgot it, I quickly wrote down the number Kamal had given me. After dialling the number a few times and getting no response I started to call my relatives — in particular those who might help me — before I disappeared into one of Khomeini's prisons. Uncle Fayegh was first. Coming so late at night, my call scared him a little: only bad news comes in the small hours, it seems. He was immediately solicitous.

"My poor girl. Calm down a little. We have to think carefully about what must be done."

"What if I just leave early in the morning? What if I'm just not here when they come to arrest me?"

"And risk the chance that they will confiscate your house and everything in it? We don't really know what is going to happen. They may just ask you questions and let you go. If you leave now, you may never be able to live in your house again. If there is any way to get through this, better face it than live the rest of your life in Iran running from house to house."

I knew he was right. I had to be strong. But what if they really did take me away from Farhad? He would never understand why I was leaving him. He would never forgive me.

"You know I have no connections with this regime," my uncle said, "but I know some people who do. I'll do the best I can. I'll start making calls first thing in the morning."

I told him about Kamal's arrest. So far no one in the family had met him, except for my cousin Fariba. I felt foolish telling him that I had been caught with a man in my house late in the evening. But Uncle Fayegh was as tolerant as ever, and did not rebuke me.

"Take care of your little boy. Don't worry about Kamal," he said. "His family will get him out somehow. There is nothing any of us can do until the morning."

It was about 2:00 A.M. when I tried Kamal's cousin again, but there was still no answer. My Uncle Kurosh's wife answered my call right away. Horrified as she was at my news, she soon became practical.

"Now what can we do? Ah, I have it. I know a big importer. He has good connections in the bazaar and the bazaar is tight with the *mullahs*. I'll call him first thing in the morning."

Finally, I worked up the courage to call Kamal's sister. I had only met her once, in very formal circumstances, and I felt embarrassed and ashamed to be calling her in the middle of the night to tell her that her brother had been arrested in my house. What would she think of me? She would probably assume that I had lured him into visiting me. Fortunately, it was her husband who answered. He was remarkably sympathetic under the circumstances.

"Don't worry about Kamal," he said calmly. "We will take care of him."

My last call was to my cousin Fariba, and then all my bitterness towards Kamal came spilling out.

"Well, he finally got me in trouble. I told you he would."

"You can't blame him. I'm sure the poor man is mortified by all this."

"God, I hope so!"

All the while that I was making my calls, Jalal Agha and his wife, Farah, kept coming in and out of the room. Every now and then they would offer a word of support and tell me that things were not really so bad, but they seemed ill at ease about something. Farah kept shifting her eyes away from me and he kept pacing nervously.

With a shaking hand I started to list all the things that needed to be done before the Komiteh came back. Some of the alcohol that was hidden in troughs in the garden had to be gotten rid of and I asked Jalal Agha to dig the bottles out.

"It's dark out now," he said. "Wait until there's a little more light. Then we'll go out and see what can be done."

So instead, we spent about two hours going through all the magazines in both the photo library and the living room, ripping out any page that might prove offensive to the Komiteh. But even as I worked at the magazines, with Farhad curled up beside me, I could not stay sitting for long. I kept jumping up, remembering other possibly incriminating material in the house: a book that might be considered immoral, more gas coupons hidden in a drawer in the kitchen, even the remaining family photographs of us swimming at the Caspian. Months before I had cleared the house of photographs showing us with our powerful friends in the royal court, the army and business circles, but I checked once again, just to be certain. Eventually, we piled all the sheets torn from the magazines into the fireplace and lit a fire with them.

As I rushed around purifying the house, Farhad followed me everywhere, not wanting to be apart from me for even a moment. I wanted so much for him to go to sleep so that he could go to school in the morning. I was still imagining a normal existence, doing the usual things. And then I would be jolted. How can he go to school? Who will take him? As soon as his grandparents find out that I have been arrested— and they will find out soon because they always seem to know what goes on in my house — they will come and take him away. I shall have a battle trying to get him back from them. But Farhad was so scared that he could not sleep. Between making telephone calls, ripping up the magazines and re-membering all the things I had to do, the night passed.

At about 6:00 A.M. a cool dawn penetrated the sheer cur-tains, and I braced myself to face the day. My telephone started ringing as the news of my impending arrest spread and rela-tives and friends called to see what they could do, or to report on what they had already done.

Uncle Fayegh was the first.

"We've been making calls since first light. It appears the *mullahs* can definitely be paid off. Everybody says so. But you need to know someone that they trust. Otherwise they think you are a spy trying to catch them out doing some-thing wrong."

"How do we get the money together, uncle?"

"I'll worry about that. At this point we don't even know how much it would take to satisfy them — or even what they really have against you."

As soon as it was light, Jalal Agha went to rouse Hossein, the gardener. Together they checked out all the troughs where alcohol and wine had been buried under leaves. Where the hiding place looked a little too obvious, they removed the bottles, dug the hole a little deeper, then put the bottles back in and covered everything with soil. They spent over an hour working out in the cold morning air while I began to prepare myself for prison. Most of what I knew about prison had come from my Uncle Kurosh, but horror stories permeated our community. Those who had made it out described cold, dark rooms, little food and no communication with the outside world.

I got ready in the only way I knew how. First, I took a long, hot bath, washing my hair over and over again until it squeaked under my fingers. In prison I might not be able to

wash for a long time. Then I wiped the nail polish off my
nails and cut them back to the finger: in the new Iran, long
nails were seen as a sign of social decay. I removed the little
jewellery that I was wearing: my rings and the little gold chain
with the four one-carat diamonds that Bijan had given me
when we were first married. I tied my hair back in a bun and
scrutinized my face in the mirror to make sure there was no
trace of make-up left, no telltale signs of my corruption. The
face that looked back at me was pale, the eyes still swollen
from crying, the mouth tense. I was already a person that I
hardly recognized.

Then I dressed. First, I put on all my silk ski underwear,
followed by a pullover, a cardigan, a long woollen skirt and
another sweater on top of all that. I chose my oldest clothes,
the darkest colours in my wardrobe; I did not want any attention directed at me unnecessarily. Finally, I put on my warmest
boots. Because there was no telling when the Komiteh would
show up to arrest me, I was ready by about 8:00 A.M.

After asking the Komiteh to give me time to go to see my
doctor, I now found that I could not face up to doing it.
Besides, I wanted to spend what time I could with Farhad.
There were friends who wanted to come over and be with
me when the Komiteh arrived, but I would not let them. I
imagined the Komiteh were already watching the house. They
might not like it if I had too many people with me.

But I did call Seemin. Of all my friends and relatives she
lived nearest to me. We had remained good friends since
childhood, and I had often spent afternoons with her, gos-
siping happily. I needed her good sense, her calm support.
When I called, she did not hesitate for a moment to say that
she would come, even though she had a six-year-old son of
her own to worry about. Within minutes, they were at the
front door. I just hugged and hugged them both, unable to
let go. Even Farhad, happy to see a little friend, seemed to
cheer up.

Tucked under her arm, Seemin had what looked like an old rolled-up carton. But when she unfurled it with a conspiratorial flourish, I had to laugh. It was a poster of Khomeini at his fiercest.

"Here, put this up in the living room," she said. "It will make you look like a good Islamic revolutionary. They love this sort of thing."

At about 9:00 A.M. there was a knock at the door. I stopped in the act of helping Farhad tie up his shoelaces. Had they arrived already? And then I remembered. I rushed to open the door, and there stood Mansoureh, my masseuse.

"Mansoureh, I'd forgotten all about you coming."

"What has happened to you?" Her kind, old face was full of concern. "You look terrible. What have you been through? Has someone died in your family? Why are you dressed that way?"

I was determined to stay in control of myself.

"It is the Komiteh. They came last night. They're going to arrest me."

"Uh! They have nothing else to do, this government, than terrorize widows. Anyway, don't worry, they won't take you away."

"Mansoureh, you have to go. If they find you here I don't know what they will think of you. They think I'm some sort of prostitute. Anybody who comes in touch with me is going to be suspect."

"Me? Leave you? Ha! You think I am afraid of these people? I'm staying right here and I'm coming with you if they arrest you. Let's see if they can stop me. Now, first thing, you have to eat. You look as if you haven't eaten in days." Her spirit was so strong, so reassuring.

Indeed, I had spent much of the night in the bathroom with diarrhoea brought on by my nervousness. And my stomach would hold nothing down.

"I don't think I could manage it, really."

"A couple of nice scrambled eggs will do it. Light, nutritious. That will keep you going. They won't feed you anything decent in there, that's for sure."

Under her brisk command, I managed to eat the eggs and a little bit of bread, too. The three of us then spent some time carefully stacking up the requisitioned magazines and films by the door. At one point I noticed that I was still wearing my gold Rolex watch.

"I can't wear this in prison. It's too noticeable. But I want to know the time every second that I'm in there."

Mansoureh immediately took off her own battered watch and handed it to me.

"Here, take this. And don't worry about it if they steal it."

When everything was ready, we went to the kitchen to wait. I paced, babbled incoherently and wept. Calls were still coming in from relatives and friends. They all reassured me. If the Komiteh had been prepared to let me go to the doctor, maybe they would not come for me at all. Maybe their intention had been only to scare me. They had let me destroy the alcohol and cards, right? And they had confiscated the coupons, right? What else was there for them to do, friends asked. But somehow I knew they were wrong. I knew the Komiteh would come. And at 2:00 P.M. there was a knock at the front door.

The three of us got up to answer the door together, the children following at our heels. Once again, there were two strange men, but this time they were unmistakably Komiteh. Dressed in military fatigues and sporting dark, curly beards, the young men carried automatic rifles by their sides. I wondered what they must have thought when they saw us: three subdued women, their heads covered with scarves, and two little boys tugging at their legs. What could we possibly have done to merit arrest?

"Sousan Azadi."

"Yes."

"We have come to arrest you."

"Please come in."

They walked in and started to look around the house. They seemed surprised. Perhaps they were expecting something different. After stopping briefly in front of the poster of Khomeini, they walked around, looking about vaguely.

"Do you have anything illegal in the house?" one of them asked.

"No. Not at all."

"Your house was searched last night?"

"Yes."

"What did they find?"

"Oh, very little, very little. Just a few magazines, some films. I have them here." I pointed to the pile by the door. They seemed not to know what to do with me, so I offered them refreshments. I was determined to be civil. The *tagbouti* usually made the mistake of treating the Komiteh badly — and the Komiteh hated them for it. But I was surprised when they actually accepted some tea. The Komiteh, I had heard, rarely accepted food or drink when they were on assignment, fearing poisons from angry victims.

I felt strange acting the perfect hostess to two armed strangers. They took their tea standing, and then, without asking for permission, started to search the house. But it seemed they were doing so more out of curiosity than with any hopes of finding evidence. We watched in silence, not daring to say a word.

After about two hours they decided to call their headquarters and speak to the man who had searched the house the night before. He was at the Bon yad Monkerat. It was a huge, powerful Komiteh; other Komitehs were responsible for particular sections of the city, but this one covered the whole of Teheran, operating from a building downtown. Its job was to investigate prostitution, drugs, alcohol and gambling, and check out complaints about decadent partying.

Other Komitehs might concentrate on the political purity of
the nation, arresting suspected Communists and subversives:
this one was responsible for the morals of the revolution.
Who had spied on me? Who had complained to them? I could
only wonder.

"Hassan. Well, we're here. We don't see anything wrong.
Are we supposed to arrest the woman or what?"

Even standing a few feet away, I could hear Hassan's angry
voice.

"You idiot. What have you been doing all afternoon? Get
her here right away. We're waiting. Wait, put her on the phone,
now."

I recognized immediately the deep voice of the man who
had been somewhat kinder to me the night before. But now
he was furious. He accused me of trying to stall the two men
and warned me that if I did not go to the headquarters quickly,
worse things would happen. I had been hoping so much that
they would just leave; the Komiteh were chaotic and nothing they did made much sense. But now the two men became
very businesslike. They wanted me to get ready to leave.
Mansoureh came and put her arms around me.

"The little boy and I are going with her. I'm not letting her
go on her own."

"Nobody can go with her," the Komiteh man said. "Those
are the rules. She goes on her own."

Realizing that I was about to be taken away, Farhad started
to clutch my clothes fiercely, with all the strength his small
fists could muster. "I want to go too, Mummy. Me, too. Don't
leave me, please don't leave me."

His sobs must have had some effect on them because after
a while they relented.

"All right," said one. "They can come but only as far as the
entrance to the prison. No further."

Grateful to have at least this comfort, I hugged Seemin
goodbye and looked around the house one last time. I knew

that, even if I came back, my home would never again seem
like a refuge. As I walked out our front door to the Komiteh's
waiting car, Jalal Agha, his wife and children came out and
watched silently, without a wave of farewell, as we climbed
into the back seat of a light grey Paycan with large, white
letters spelling out KOMITEH and huge loudspeakers on its
roof.

Because the automatic rifles would not fit into the car, the
two men sat up front with their guns poking out of either
window. As soon as we started to pull out of the driveway,
they switched on the loudspeakers and the piercing drone
of a *mullah* filled the air for blocks around. Across the street
from our house the gas company workers came out to see
what was happening. I knew them very well; not long before I
had sent over a tray of food. They stared silently at us as we
passed, and my face burned with shame.

The car headed south, down the hills towards the city, but
we still did not know where we were being taken. Slowly,
leaving the quiet suburbs of Shemiran and Saltanatabad with
their large houses and rambling gardens, we descended into
the crowded chaos of the city. Along the way, people stopped
to stare into the car, and I could read the questions on their
faces, the distrust in their eyes. What had those two women
done? Prostitutes, probably. Or maybe Communists. Very
rarely did I see any sympathy or even a glimmer of anger at
the regime.

We had driven for half an hour, and it was already getting
dark when we arrived in front of an elegant mansion on
Takhtejamshid Avenue. I knew the large three-storey stucco
house with its swimming pool and large, walled garden. It
had belonged to a rich Iranian family but had been expro-
priated shortly after Khomeini took over. I had never known
the family personally, and now I envied them for having left
the country when it was still possible to do so safely. The
driver parked next to a side garden entrance. I could see into

the once-beautiful garden, now overgrown; the pool was empty and full of dead leaves. Still, it was a beautiful building with its large, leaded-glass, rounded windows, its intricate white-painted woodwork and its french doors leading onto the garden patio.

"It's time to go in," the driver said.

On hearing that, Farhad started to whimper. Mansoureh started to get ready.

"We're going in, too."

But this time it was obvious that the two men would not budge. I turned to her.

"It's cold out. Don't stand around here. Did you see that little grocery store across the street? Go in there and wait for me for about half an hour. If I am not out by then, take Farhad home. There is no telling what will happen when I get in there."

She was unflappable, even now.

"Don't worry about Farhad. I'll take care of him. And I'll get my son over to keep him company."

I gave Farhad one last hug, then the two men led me down a walk, across the garden and up the imposing steps of the mansion.

When we entered the Monkerat prison, I saw a long, wide hallway, crowded with gun-toting men and turbaned *mullahs* walking purposefully in and out of doorways to offices. But for the guns, the beards and fatigues, it could have been a scene in any office, the chaos inspired by too much paper-work. It was like any bureaucracy waiting for its tea-break. I was too scared to notice much, but I did become quickly aware that there were no women in sight. The two men led me to a small staircase on the right of the entrance. We climbed to the third floor and went down another long hallway. This time the men led me to a set of double doors. They knocked politely. This appeared to be the office of the head of the Komiteh.

Someone said, "Come in." My escort opened the door and I entered a spacious dining room, lined with large, gracious windows, that had been turned into an office. There were only two desks in the room; on the left a man worked quietly at a stack of files, and in the centre, sitting behind a simple wooden desk, was another man studying more files, while an older, more distinguished man bent over him solicitously explaining something or other. Here, then, was the leader of the Komiteh. As I approached, the seated man looked up. I was shocked. It was Hassan—the same man who had searched my house and had so skillfully alternated between comforting and punishing me. Part of me was relieved: he had been nice once before and maybe he could be again. But part of me wondered what I had done to deserve a personal visit by the head of the Komiteh. What kind of complaint merited his attention when he was in charge of the whole city?

"So you have finally arrived," Hassan said. "What took so long? Did they bring all the tapes and films?"

"Yes, I believe so," I said, and turned around to get agreement from my two escorts. I was still clinging to the hope that he would merely question me and then let me go.

"I destroyed everything you asked me to last night. Why am I here? I have done nothing wrong. My child is waiting outside. Please let me go."

I was determined to appeal to his pride and I became the frightened, humbled woman he wanted me to be. I promised him I would be a good Moslem woman. I promised I would not let any men into my house—not even my uncle, if he so ordered it. I promised my subjugation—anything to get out of there and not have to spend the night. I thought I was putting on an act, but I realized halfway through that I did not have to feign my fear, I was truly ready to do all those things. But after listening to me for a while, almost distractedly, he turned to one of the escorts and said,

"Take her down. Take her down." I felt the blood rushing to my face.

My two guardians led me out, down the two flights of stairs and into an office on the ground floor. The room was crowded, filled with rows of small desks, each with a man sitting behind it. The walls were covered with giant posters of Khomeini staring down stonily, unforgivingly. It was the interrogation room; I could make out the voices of questioners, sharp and angry, and of their victims, muted, in some cases terrified. I was brought to stand in front of one of the desks. In front of me sat a man who was in his fifties, corpulent and bearded. Even across the table I could smell his sweat. Without looking up he barked, "So who is this one?"

My escort told him who I was, but it was evident that he already knew. On top of a pile of files was one with my name on it, and he had clearly been informed about my transgressions. Once again he took me through the evidence discovered in my house. But after a few perfunctory remarks about the alcohol and cards, he turned his full attention to the subject I had least expected: the gasoline coupons.

"Have you finally decided to tell us the name of that driver you bought the coupons from? You'll have to tell us eventually, you know. You and your kind, thinking you can buy anything that other people can't afford. I want his name and the colour of the car he drove."

"I told the Komiteh already I don't know the name of the man. I don't remember the make of the car — I just remember it was red. That's all I know."

"Listen, you're going to stay in prison until you remember. Do you understand that?"

I started to beg him to let me go, but the words just dried up in my mouth. He signalled to someone behind me. "Take her away. Maybe she'll change her mind about talking."

An older woman dressed in a heavy, black *chador*, whose face was further obscured by a kerchief that covered most of her forehead and mouth, grabbed my arm and led me out of the room. I thought of Mansoureh and Farhad waiting for me in the small store across the street. I had been inside about forty-five minutes. Would they still be waiting for me there? I looked at the woman, trying to detect a hint of friendliness.

"My little boy. He's across the street. Please, I have to go and tell him what is happening. I have to let him know I'm all right."

"I can't do such a thing. Nobody calls nobody from here."

"Please, just let me go and tell him. I'll come right back. I'll pray for you and for your family. Please show some mercy for a young mother."

"What are you doing standing there?" the interrogator demanded when he saw us talking. "I said go, and you go."

His shout was directed at both of us. The woman quickly grabbed my arm and directed me towards the door. I started to shake and cry, begging her to get a message to my son. As she led me down a set of stairs into the basement, she whispered in my ear, "If I get caught I'll get into trouble. But I'll run over and tell them that you have to stay here. Don't say a word."

I started to thank her, but she shushed me violently.

Even before we got down to the bottom of the stairs I could smell human sweat on the damp, chill air. At the entrance to a long hallway stood several guards, young women who could not hide their brawniness even under their all-enveloping, thick *chadors*. After checking me out briefly with bored eyes, they turned away. Just one more woman entering the darkness and cold of the basement. On the right side of the hallway was a long, low table with a glass covering that was filled with the texts of Khomeini speeches and more of the ubiquitous portraits. In an alcove stood a bright red bed — a beautiful sight to me in the dark gloom of the basement — a clean plastic red bed. But then in horror I noticed the straps that dangled from the sides — straps for restraining flailing arms and legs. The whipping bed! I turned away from it. My guard led me down the hall. On either side was an entrance to a room, from which hung flowing cotton curtains. She turned into the first entrance on the left and parted the curtains. I recoiled. Looking desperately around me, I noticed a row of chairs along the hallway.

"Can't I stay out here on the chairs? I'm only going to be here a short time."

One of the younger guards down the hall looked up and shouted, "Get in there." Then she walked over and with one shove propelled me through the curtains. It took a moment for my eyes to adjust to the semi-darkness. Slowly I began to make out the outline of a large room — about fifty feet long and thirty feet wide — filled with women squatting on the floor. Dozens of pairs of eyes looked up at me briefly and then turned away. Many of the women were dressed in *chadors*, others in the traditional garb of the very poor — loose-fitting cotton trousers and small, flimsy, cotton tops. All wore at least a heavy headband to cover their heads and most of their faces. With their long, skinny arms and legs and their bulging stomachs, many of the women had the look of malnutrition that I had never seen except on television. Some were joking and laughing raucously, their mouths displaying the occasional glint of gold teeth.

Although there were several windows, they were so high up that the outside world was not visible to us. The floor was covered by a thin, grey carpet that squelched as I put my foot down on it. The odours of the day's lunch still hung in the air and mixed with the smell of women who had not washed for a long time. I shivered involuntarily — from the damp chill in the air and from the sight of so many women huddled together, their faces either blank or laughing carelessly, yet mirthlessly.

I spotted an empty corner of the room to the left of me and I made for it. Suddenly there was a loud howl from one of the women closest to me. She spoke Persian, but in a rough, crude accent I had not heard before.

"Take those dirty boots off. Who do you think you are walking with your shoes where people pray?"

As I looked behind me to where she pointed, I noticed a pile of sandals and shoes at the entrance to the room. I quickly took off my boots and felt the dampness of the carpet through my thick stockings. Hoping that no one would see me, I hugged my boots under one arm and headed for the far corner of the room. There I found a little spot of cement that the carpet did not cover where I put my boots down. Imitating the women around me, I curled up on the floor.

From my little recess, I surveyed the room slowly, not wanting to catch the eye of any of the women. The last thing I wanted was attention, someone who would ask me who I was and what I was doing there. It was quite likely that my fellow prisoners hated the *taghouti* as much as Khomeini did. Each woman seemed to possess one blanket, using it as a mat to make a bed, as a badly needed blanket or as a pillow. Only one blanket each, and, by the look of them, they were filthy, smelly ones. No matter how cold I was, I had no intention of ever using one. I removed my coat and used it as a covering, then cautiously put on my boots as well.

But the blankets were precious to the other prisoners. A fight erupted almost immediately between two women over the ownership of a blanket. Standing facing each other in the middle of the room, the two hurled insults and then started to shove each other, to kick and pinch. The commotion brought in a guard, who quelled the two with one threat: quiet or else.

As the room settled down again, I noticed that everyone seemed to be talking at the same time. It was as if each woman were telling the story of her troubles. Some were joking, as if they were used to their prison. Others were crying terribly. Just to the left of me was a woman crouching under her *chador*. Although no one seemed to be paying much attention to her, she kept telling and retelling her troubles, rocking herself back and forth like an abandoned child.

"Why did they bring me here?" she asked. "Why was I arrested? Why?"

To my right, a very young girl—maybe fourteen or fifteen—who was in the last stages of pregnancy, was crying quietly to herself. She was wearing a light-cotton dress, and every now and then she clutched at her swollen stomach, as a pain—perhaps a contraction — seized her. With her wispy, light brown hair and large, hazel eyes, she looked even more vulnerable. She, too, was moaning softly: "What have I done wrong? Where is my husband? Why am I here?"

She spoke in Turkish, the only language she knew, it turned out, and she was evidently from a village, not from Teheran itself.

The rest of the prisoners ignored the two crying women. We three were the latest additions — somehow we had all sought refuge in the same corner. I could hear some of the women telling stories in the centre of the room. They were not addressing anyone in particular. They just sat on their haunches, looked up at the ceiling and talked and talked, like old-time storytellers, who pay no attention to the audience, only to the story that has to be told.

A toothless, middle-aged woman started.

"They killed that short, dark woman just a little while ago. They called her outside, to the garden. Then they killed her. Shot her, yes, and we all heard the shot."

Another woman in flowing cotton trousers joined in.

"They killed a woman. She was maybe three, four months pregnant. They were supposed to wait until the baby was born. But they didn't want to wait. They took her to the bottom of the empty swimming pool. They shot her there."

Another woman pointed to a young girl who was sitting very close to me. With her short hair, unusual for a Iranian woman, the girl had a very mannish look, and she, too, wore the flowered trousers of the poorer women of the city. "Do you know what her penalty is?" the woman asked. "Death.

She is married, and they caught her with another man."
The victim herself seemed unconcerned. She joked with
the women closest to her. Perhaps she enjoyed her brief
notoriety.

The stories went on and on. About whippings, disappearances, the cruelty of the young women guards. After a while
I began to suspect that the women were getting a terrible
pleasure from telling the newcomers about the victims of that
prison. And I began to think that if I got away with merely a
whipping, I would be lucky.

All around the walls of the room giant posters made certain
that we could not escape Khomeini. Also taped up on the
walls were sheets with quotations from his speeches in large
print and drawings depicting the various positions to be taken
during prayer. I remembered my Uncle Kurosh telling me that
in prison, inmates were often asked to pray in order to prove
that they were true Moslems. I had never learned how to pray
the Namoz. In between the moans of my desolate neighbours,
and after taking furtive glances around to make sure that no
one was watching, I began to memorize the prayer and the
various stances. Who knew what spies were in prison with
us? And who knew when I might be asked to perform? Because I was scared and still shaky, I found I could scarcely
concentrate, but the effort at least helped me to focus on something concrete, not just on my fears.

Soon I had my first run-in with the guards. My body was
still unsettled and I desperately needed to go to the bathroom.
I tiptoed out to the hallway and peered out, looking for a
guard.

"Hey, you," one guard yelled. "Where do you think you're
going?"

I tried to look at her face. She could not have been much
more than eighteen.

"Sister, I have to go to the bathroom. Could you please
show me where it is?"

"Don't 'sister' me," she said, and then, turning to the other guards, she laughed. "We've got a well-mannered one here, girls. It's on your left down the hall. But be quick about it or I'll come in and pull you out."

Where had they found such women? Barely older than schoolgirls and already so mean. I found the bathroom and was very nearly sick again from the stink and filth. There was one small sink that was plugged up and filled with dirty water from a leaking tap. A dribble of water was falling to the floor, which was wet and slimy. There was one cubicle with an Iranian-style squat toilet that was smeared with human faeces. If the other room down the hallway had as many women in it as ours did, that one toilet probably had to serve about 130 women. I got out quickly.

After a while — it was around 7:30 P.M. — the guards brought in supper. They distributed small, plastic bowls filled with a strange-smelling soup and spoons that had not been washed from the previous meal. Even before I was handed mine, I knew I would not be able to eat the meal. I looked at the plate and tried to decipher what the soup was made of. It became obvious that it was a combination of two standard meals, *obgousht* made with meat, potatoes and chickpeas, and *osh*, made with little meatballs and greens. Everyone else had eaten upstairs and the prisoners were now being given what was left over — all mixed together.

The other prisoners were not so finicky. They eyed the food hungrily. Some of them carefully unfolded dirty little plastic tablecloths, which they spread out neatly on the floor. Others unravelled little bits of cloth that hid precious hunks of old, mouldy bread. They ate with gusto and satisfaction. I turned away not to see and not to be seen.

But the young Turkish-speaking girl, even though her own misery was so great, noticed that I was not eating.

"Sister," she said, "why are you not eating? You must eat to keep strong."

"Don't worry about me, really. I am just full. I ate just before coming here."

"If you don't eat, I don't think I'll be able to take a bite. Please eat."

"No, really. I just can't."

Then, shyly, she said, "Well, if you are absolutely certain that you won't eat it, could I have it?"

"Of course, take it. Please, I would be so glad."

She moved closer and sat beside me. Over the humble meal she told me her story.

"I come from Azerbaijan. From Ushchi. I have been married just ten months. My baby is due now. Two days ago my husband's brother offered me a drive to the countryside. I was so tempted. I leave the village only every year or so, and I just wanted to see something different. I suppose I shouldn't have gone. He brought a friend along. But when they got me away from the village, they raped me."

Her voice still held a little of the surprise she must have felt to be betrayed by a relative by marriage.

"I just wanted to drive into the hills. They left me there. I walked back — maybe it was ten miles. I told my husband. It never crossed my mind to say nothing. He was angry. He shouted at me. He threatened murder to everyone. He brought me all the way to Teheran, to this place, to make a complaint. The Komiteh went and arrested my brother-in-law and his friend. This morning they whipped them eighty times and then they let them go. Then they put me here. I don't know what they are going to do to me."

She started to cry again. I tried to comfort her, but there was so little I could say in the face of so much injustice. My own problems seemed so small by comparison.

Moved by the story of the young girl from Azerbaijan, the woman in the *chador* who had been arrested that afternoon started to tell us her troubles.

"What was I doing wrong, I ask you? I was just riding in a taxi. I was going home from the market. I was in the front seat. A man got in beside me. It was tight in the front and he put his arm over the back of the seat, like this." She showed how the stranger's arm had been placed on her shoulder, on the seat. "Then the Komiteh stopped the car. No special reason. They just wanted to check up on everybody. Well, they asked me, 'Are you related to this man?' I said, 'No, he's just somebody who got into the taxi.' And they said, 'He can't be. Look at the way he's sitting. He must be your lover.' And so they arrest me then and there. And they arrest the man and they insist that we are lovers. What can my husband be thinking? I've got five children at home. One is just three months old. She needs my milk. My breasts are heavy and spilling milk. They won't let me call home. How will they know where to find me? They'll be checking all the hospitals, wondering if I've been in an accident. How will they guess that I am in prison?"

She, too, started to cry and beat her chest. I muttered some inadequate words of consolation and then fell silent.

At around 9:30 P.M., one of the women guards came into the room and called my name.

"Sousan Azadi. You are wanted."

I jumped up quickly. Finally, my uncles had managed to find a way to get me out. I would not have to spend the night with this wretchedness. I still did not know if Farhad had received my message. I would rush home and comfort him.

Just as I was about to set off, the woman in the black *chador* said to me: "You can't go without a *chador*. They won't interview you unless you wear this."

She kindly removed her own and held it out to me. As I gingerly took the robe, I realized that I was about to wear a *chador* against my will for the first time in my life. The revolution had finally forced me to wear its uniform.

As I pulled the *chador* over me, I felt a heaviness descending over me. I was hidden and in hiding. There was nothing visible left of Sousan Azadi. My long, blonde hair, which I loved letting blow in the wind when I drove out to the Caspian. My

husband used to take hold of my face gently and then run his
fingers through my hair right down to the ends. My full lips
which I always kept tinted a deep rose. My slender limbs. I
had always dressed carefully to stress my wrists and ankles
and my small waist. Even my eyes, the only part of me still
visible, were no longer mine. They were puffy from crying,
the skin ringing them a bruised blue from lack of sleep. I felt
like an animal of the light suddenly trapped in a cave. I was
just another faceless Moslem woman carrying a whole inner
world hidden inside the *chador*.

As soon as I got to the entrance, I put on my boots, which I
had concealed under the *chador*. The guard led me up to the
ground floor and into the interrogation room. There were
fewer people about now, and neither of the two men who
interviewed me was the one I had spoken to earlier in the
day. The upstairs room was so warm after the chill of the
basement. It had a little gas burner. I was grateful for the few
moments of heat.

I expected more surliness and insults from my interrogators.
This time, though, they were almost kind in their questioning.
Once again they led me through the reasons for my arrest,
the origins of the coupons and my relationship with Kamal.
Once again I explained to them that he was just a business
friend who had come to offer me advice.

One of the Komiteh, who seemed to know a great deal
about my case, was puzzled at that reply.

"But we have talked to the gentleman in question and he
assures us that he has every intention of marrying you, that
he has been courting you and that he came that night to
propose marriage to you. In fact, he is suggesting that we get
the *mullah* to marry you right here in prison."

I was shocked. What was Kamal trying to do? What was he
telling those men about me? I had no intention of marrying
him. Was he trying to bully me? I was scared at the thought
of being forced into a marriage right there in prison. The

Komiteh could, if it suited them, make a marriage a condition of my release.

"No, no," I hastened to assure them, "there has been no discussion of marriage, and I certainly have no desire to marry. My husband died only three years ago and I do not know the gentleman well enough."

"We'll have to clear all this stuff up, but I don't see any reason for detaining you any longer. In the morning you will probably be released."

I was so relieved that I almost jumped up to shake his hand, but then I remembered how insulted Hassan had been.

"May I go now? My little boy is waiting for me. He must be wondering what is happening to me."

"Now? At this hour? A good Moslem woman going out at this hour? Nonsense. How would you get home?"

"By taxi."

"By taxi? A woman? Absolutely not. You will wait until the morning."

Even though I tried to change their minds, the two would not budge. Then they asked me one last question. "What does your father do?"

"He lives in Azerbaijan. He is a landowner."

What a stupid mistake! Their attitude, which had been comparatively friendly, suddenly turned nasty. The interrogator put his hands on his hips and sneered, "Oh, so you are the daughter of a filthy, oppressive landowner, one of the leeches on the country, are you? Get the hell downstairs. You'll go when we tell you."

When I got back downstairs the guards were beginning to distribute blankets to the new prisoners. This time I did not shun them. Even with my coat over me and my boots on, I felt the cold deep in my bones, so that I ached no matter how I sat. Once again a squabble broke out. That was how I noticed that on the other side of the room several women had children with them. One woman had what appeared to be a ten-month-old child, and she had somehow managed to get an extra blanket for her. Another prisoner was accusing her of stealing her blanket, and a fight broke out. The guard soon silenced them. Then I saw another woman with a three-year-old child lying beside her and a tiny baby in her arms.

I was so shocked to find that children were living in such cold conditions that I said out loud to no one in particular, "My God, there are children in this place. How can they do such a thing?"

I had an image of Farhad in that dark, cold room and I was angry. I was so lucky that there had been someone around to take care of him, unlike those unfortunate mothers.

I took my blanket as it was handed to me, trying to touch as little of it as possible, and I used it as a mat to put some insulation between me and the cold floor. With my boots safely back on, I was trying to find warmth under my coat. Not far from me, lying unnoticed was an unexpected gift — an extra blanket. I looked around carefully to make sure it did not belong to anyone, then I reached for it secretively, and hid it under my coat. After making a pillow out of it, I tried to settle down as comfortably as possible.

But there was little rest or peace to be had. The young Turkish-speaking woman had been struggling all night to control her pains, but there was nothing to stop the labour. In a desperate attempt to stifle her groans she bit her lips, bit her hands, held both hands over her mouth, but her pain found voice despite her. Every time a moan escaped her, the prisoners sat up and yelled.

"Shut up. Who wants to hear you? If you can't shut up, go out into the hall."

"That's right, get out, get out, we have our own worries. We don't want to hear yours."

She lumbered to her feet with great difficulty and waddled outside to the hallway. I turned and asked the woman who had lent me the *chador*: "Who are these women? How can they be so mean? Imagine having a baby in this hell. She needs sympathy, not curses."

The woman looked at me quizzically. "Don't you know what these women are? They're prostitutes, drug addicts. The Komiteh rounded them up right after the revolution. Those who haven't been here for the last two years have been in and out. They don't have much sympathy to spare."

From out in the hall we could hear the pregnant girl let out a cry. I went out to have a fast look at her. She was walking up and down the hall, every now and then bending over, holding on to the walls to steady herself so that she would not fall. Her face was tight with pain. Whenever the contractions were severe, she let out a yell. What would the *mullahs* do to both those two children—the one giving birth and the one being born? Soon the prison guards started to curse her as well.

"If you're going to make that kind of noise, get back inside the room," said one of them. "We sure don't want to listen to you all night."

The girl came back in, carefully sidestepping the bodies of the women who were now lying down, getting ready for sleep. At a quarter to midnight a guard came in and told us that lights would be out in fifteen minutes and if anyone wanted to go to the bathroom, now was the time. After that the doors usually kept open at the curtained entrance to our room would be locked until 6:00 A.M. I ran up to the guard, a young woman with pimply skin and bad teeth. How could I stay locked up for hours when I had been running to the bathroom all night long?

"That's not my problem," she said. "You can ask to go out once, but that's it. And I don't want to hear any more complaining."

At midnight sharp the lights went out. I could hear the rustle of bodies turning over, trying to find a spot of comfort that was not to be found. The pregnant woman lay down beside me, and I could feel the warmth of her young body, like that of a gentle animal. She would surely have a child within twenty-four hours, one way or another. My thoughts went to Farhad. Had the old prison guard gone to tell him that I was all right? That I was staying for the night? I had asked the guards repeatedly, but they said they didn't know and they quickly got tired of my asking them. I hugged myself in the little corner of the room, tucked my old coat under my chin. My mind was filled with terrible images of what the Komiteh would do to me. My fate was in the hands of men who hated women. There was no such thing as justice here, just the arbitrary rule of the guards. As I berated myself once again for having taken such chances under the Khomeini regime, I started to cry quietly. With the sounds of bodies shifting, the pregnant woman moaning low next to me, I felt myself slipping away from reality. I had been without sleep for twenty-four hours. I had eaten and drunk almost nothing all day. I had voided any food still in my system long ago. Depleted, exhausted, frightened, filled with terrors imagined and real, I could barely remember the previous day when life had seemed so promising. From the darkness of the room I faded into the darkness of sleep.

Chapter Ten

Freedom—at a Price

The wheel of fortune's sphere is a marvellous thing:
What next proud head to the lowly dust will it bring?

HÀFIZ

 Allah-u Akbar, Allah-u Akbar. La illah illa Allah . . . God is most Great, God is most Great. I testify there is no other God but God and Mohammed is His Prophet. . . .

The voice of the *muezzin* calling us to prayer from loud-speakers attached to the walls of the room jolted me awake at 6:00 A.M. For a second I was confused and stunned by the loud, penetrating wail. But memories of the previous day quickly flooded back to me. I sat up and looked around. The other women prisoners were beginning to stir. A pale morning light filtered through the high, grimy windows. I heard the guards unlock the door to our room, and one of them, the young woman with the pimpled face, came in and yelled that breakfast was coming and we should get moving. Just as she was turning to leave, she looked down at the ground by the doorway and started to screech loudly enough to compete with the *muezzin*.

"Which pig did this filthy thing?" she asked, pointing to the floor. "Who did it? If I don't find out, you will all be punished. Three more days will be added to your time here. So speak up."

A loud murmur went up in the room and word came back to us in the corner that someone had urinated by the doorway. Some poor woman had obviously been unable to wait until the doors were unlocked. It could just as easily have been me. Now there would be trouble.

The prisoners all looked at each other, and for a while nothing happened. I was too far away to see what occurred next, but in a few minutes a guard was leading away one of the poorest-looking creatures in the place. I do not know if someone had reported her or if she had just confessed to spare the others the punishment. She was a tall, skinny woman of about thirty, obviously malnourished, with a protruding abdomen and bones that seemed about to break through her skin. She was almost toothless and hairless and she was dressed in long, baggy trousers and tunic.

She had been brought in just the night before, a few hours after me, along with another woman. The prisoners quickly learned that they were prostitutes who had been caught right in the act with a couple of men and had also been in possession of heroin. They had breezed into our room without evident concern, having, according to the prisoners' gossip, already been inside a number of times before.

The younger of the two was led off without any protest. Soon she became the first prisoner of the morning to lie on the soft, shiny, new whipping bed.

We were silent and watchful as she followed the guard out. It had grown so still that we could hear the slap-slap of the leather straps as they belted her onto the bed. Then came the horrible sound of the lash cutting through the air. The woman screamed. Another lash, the sound of flesh ripping. Another scream. On and on it went. Eighty times. The guards took turns, each giving ten lashes. When their whipping arms tired, they passed their weapon on so that the victim would feel the full force of the punishment. We could make out the differences in each guard's style. One was swift and reckless, another more precise. One seemed to linger over each stroke. I was crouching on the floor. I cringed with each whip stroke, as if the lash were landing on my own back. After a while I just could not bear to listen, so I put my hands over my ears.

They whipped her eighty times, the standard punishment, and then, because she could not stand up, they lifted her off the couch and threw her into the room, where she lay in a bleeding lump. The prisoners quickly surrounded her to have a look. I could only stand to have one glance, but it was enough. Her back was covered in welts. In some places, the skin had been torn off completely. I knew from the experience of Reza and his friend at the Caspian that the welts would probably become infected and her back would become dreadfully swollen. She would have the marks for more than a year, even after they had finally healed—if they healed. That prostitute would likely have little money to buy the antibiotics needed to keep her back from becoming infected.

One of the prisoners offered to put cream on the woman's back. But no matter how gently she applied it, the woman screamed with pain, unable to withstand even the slightest touch. After a while she must have fainted because I heard no more. And by then more dreadful sounds were coming from the whipping bed.

It appeared that the bed served the entire prison. Upstairs, guards began to bring down some of the male prisoners who were housed in the upper floors. Their yells pierced our part of the prison. All morning there was a steady stream of victims, with just a few minutes' break between each beating. All the while, the *muezzin*'s voice continued to pray on the loudspeakers. In all that chaos, our guards brought us breakfast: a weak tea, a mouldy piece of bread and a small piece of cheese. I was so hungry and thirsty that this time I gulped down my food.

Towards the end of the morning, the guards brought another woman to be whipped. She came from the other large room in the basement and we never found out what she had done to merit the punishment. But we heard her screams and pleadings even before she made it to the bed.

"You can't whip me. I'm sick," she yelled. "You'll kill me. You can't do this."

She screamed those words over and over again as the guards hustled her and strapped her down on the bed. I clenched my fists to my chest waiting for the horror to begin again. But after her violent screams with the first few lashes, there was one long wail and then silence. The whip flew, landing with that terrible tearing sound, but there was no animal reply. In a way, that silence was worse. Terrorized, we waited. The whip kept landing, and still the woman said nothing. Had she fainted away or died? The guards did not stop to find out. The full eighty strokes were given. Then the guards started to unstrap the inert body. But the woman's anger must have been great because all of a sudden we heard her yell and curse her tormentors as she struggled violently with them. Somehow or other she threw something on the glass table which held Khomeini's speeches and we could hear the sound of glass shattering. Several other guards came running down the hall to reinforce the two who had done the whipping, and soon the woman's screams of anger were drowned out by the sound of fists and feet pounding her body. The prisoners were crowding around the doorway to get a glimpse of the fight but it did not take long for the guards to overwhelm the woman. They soon dragged her off and threw her back into her room.

"Did you see her?" asked one woman who came back to my corner after watching the fight. "She was covered in blood from head to toe. It must have taken some guts to fight those bitches."

So many times that morning I had wanted to curse and strike those guards as that woman had done—but I knew I would not have the courage. And I knew that the same thing would happen to me if I tried. No other prisoner would lift a finger to help me — just as we had sat there petrified while that prisoner was being beaten up.

Eventually, the guards brought lunch, some weak soup and rice leftovers from other meals, but once again I could not touch it. It was about 2:00 P.M. when the pimply, brutish guard called out my name and led me to the first floor to be interviewed again. My interrogator was the same paunchy man with the perpetual sneer on his face who had first interviewed me. Once again, he wanted to know about the gas coupons and which driver had sold them to me. I repeated that I did not know the name of the driver and that I had already given him a description of the car and the man.

He leaned over towards me so that I could smell his sweat and said, "You will not leave this place until we find that man."

Then he turned to a guard and motioned to him to bring forward three men who had been standing nearby. I looked at them closely for the first time and recognized three drivers of the private cab company I had used regularly. It is odd what a person can feel in such frightening circumstances, but when I saw those three men, drivers who had taken an elegant Sousan to parties and to afternoons at the Royal Club, all I felt was embarrassment. There I was, hidden under layers of the *chador*, my eyes so swollen from crying that I could barely open them. Even my face felt bloated from crying.

"I did not buy the coupons from any of these men," I told the interrogator. Then I turned to the men and apologized for having caused them to be brought to prison.

Just as the drivers were being led away, Kamal walked into the interrogation room accompanied by another man. As soon as he saw me — and I have no idea how he recognized me in that *chador* — he smiled, waved and made as if to come in my direction. But the man he was with pulled him away and led him out of the room. My embarrassment at being seen reduced to a featureless blob grew, but the interrogator was shouting at me again to tell him who had sold me the coupons. Again I told him I did not know the name — and I had long ago given them the colour of the car. The company must have whisked the driver away — and for that I was grateful.

"You will stay here until you recover your memory," the interrogator finally spat out. "Go back downstairs and stay there."

As the day passed, it became evident that no one was going to rush in to save me. Where was my family? Where were my aunts' and uncles' many contacts? Would they really let me stay there one more night? In the basement, the pregnant woman continued to cry out in pain and the lady whose *chador* I kept borrowing for my interviews cried quietly. I cried, too, off and on. And all the time the whipping bed was kept busy and the screams of men and women filled the basement.

At about four in the afternoon, a guard came in looking for me. She told me that Mansoureh, the kind masseuse who had accompanied me the previous day, was upstairs in the waiting room. When the guards told her that she could not talk to me, she had asked if she could leave me toothpaste, towels and soap. But there seemed little point in having soap and a towel when the only sink in that filthy bathroom was plugged up and full of dirty water.

"No. Tell her to take the things away again and please thank her."

Then the guard gave me dreadful news.

"The woman asked me to tell you that your son is with his grandmother."

Such an innocent-sounding message, yet I knew how serious it was. The Aminis had Farhad. They would use every available means to keep me from getting him back — including arguing in court that I was not a capable mother because I had been thrown into prison. Taking my son away would merely be the first step in taking everything else as well: my use of the house, my monthly allowance from the estate, the car — everything that had been left to me.

I blessed Mansoureh for her visit and for the warning, but once again I wondered where my family was. If someone who was not even a relative would take the chance of coming to the prison, what had happened to my closest family? Were they just frightened? Had Khomeini made us so afraid that we would not even help each other?

As the day faded imperceptibly into the gloom of evening, I again refused the gruel that we were served, and this time even the pregnant girl was too overcome with abdominal pain to eat it. After the lights were turned off at midnight and the door to our room was locked, her wails grew as her pains intensified, and she cringed beside me. I felt so badly for her, but there was nothing anyone could do. Her cries kept us all awake until finally, at around 3:00 A.M., one of the guards came to find out what was happening. After glowering at the cause of the commotion, she went to call a doctor who lived on the prison compound and, in a short while, two guards led the pregnant woman away to see him.

Looking no less frightened, the Turkish-speaking girl was back within a quarter of an hour. One of the guards reported to us that she was in labour but the doctor had estimated she would not actually have the baby for another day or two. She would have to remain in prison until she was ready to deliver.

The girl seemed to have hardly any sense of what was going on, focussed as she was on the unstoppable labour pains. As the lights went off again, she crouched on the floor and began her rhythmic wails.

My second morning in prison began much as the first: with prayers and the curses of people being whipped. During the night I had sworn to myself that I would get out that day — no matter what it took. At about 9:00 A.M., after once again accepting the tea and cheese that was my only nourishment in prison, I heard the telephone ring in the hall.

The room hushed. The telephone could bring release—or dreadful punishment. We could hear clearly what the guard was saying.

"So you are going to send over a couple of people to take her to hospital?" the guard asked. "Finally we will be rid of all that noise. . . . And then, after she gives birth? . . . Oh, she's to be brought back here and shot. Fine. All right. We'll be expecting you."

We looked at each other wordlessly. Most of us had understood. But the young girl spoke only Turkish and she did not realize what her fate was to be. As we watched and said nothing, the prison guard came in and told the girl in Turkish that she was to be taken to a hospital.

"Oh, thank Allah," she said in her innocent way, a smile on her face for the first time in many hours. "Now I can have the baby and everything will be fine."

She gathered up her few belongings like an excited child setting off to get a treat. So many times I started to tell her what we had overheard, but I looked around at the other prisoners, many of whom, no doubt, were spies. Would they report me? The guards did not tell her about her impending execution. Should I? The more experienced prisoners said nothing, I noticed. Perhaps they knew what would happen to anyone who warned her. And yet the guard had spoken loudly enough for anyone to hear. She could not possibly care who knew.

Then I thought, what if I do tell her? All through her labour she will think of the child she will be permitted to see for only an instant and ponder her own death. Would it be right to give her that extra burden? The guards came and led her away and I said nothing. Was I right? Was I wrong? I still don't know. Her only mistake had been to accept a ride with her brother-in-law, and the state blamed her for the rape she had been subjected to. I never knew what happened to her. She was like hundreds of prisoners in Khomeini's prisons, faceless lost creatures who faded quickly because there was no one to look after them or to weep at their disappearance.

Sometime around 1:00 P.M. I was called once again for an interview, but this time I harboured a desperation I had never known before. I would be a victim, the same as the pregnant girl, unless I could get out soon. The interrogator put me through the same routine, and again I had nothing new to tell him. Partway through the interview, he was called out of the room. As soon as he had turned his back, I ran up to another interrogator, one who seemed to have a kind face.

"Please, please, tell me where I might find Hassan. I have to talk to him," I pleaded and reached out to touch his hand in supplication. But as my hand brushed his, he drew it away as if scorched. I had forgotten, once again, that a Moslem woman does not touch a man — ever.

"You are filthy, filthy, filthy," he spat out.

I could feel my anger rising. I, filthy? When those murderers were killing young mothers for no reason? I felt like slapping him across the face, but I needed that self-righteous man at that moment. Instead, I begged him again to tell me where Hassan was.

"I can't take you."

"I am only begging you to tell me where he is. I will go on
my own."

Finally, grudgingly: "He's in his office, it's on the third floor.
But I'm not taking you there. If you make it, fine. If not . . .
take your own risks."

There were risks, indeed. Up and down the halls, in the
interview rooms, there were almost no women, and the men
were armed with rifles or handguns. A figure in a *chador* running upstairs would surely arouse suspicion — she might even
be mistaken for a man who was trying to hide something
under those voluminous robes. But I took little time to make
up my mind. Both my interrogator and my regular guard were
momentarily occupied elsewhere. It was my only chance.

I ran out of the interrogation room and made for the stairs.
I took them two at a time, breathing hard as I neared the top
of the third landing. But suddenly from below, a voice bel-
lowed harshly and the sound seemed to bounce off the walls
in a spiral all the way up to the ceiling.

"Stop. You. Where do you think you're going?"

For one mad moment I thought that I would ignore the
order and keep on running. I had only three more steps to
go. But I realized it would have been certain death. I looked
back down the stairs and saw my interrogator, a rifle drawn.

"I have to talk to Hassan. I just want to go to the third floor,
that's all."

"You're going nowhere but the prison. Now get moving."

Again I started to beg and plead, offering to pray to Allah
for his family if he would just let me go to Hassan. I talked
and talked, not letting him get a word in, and slowly I slipped
up one more stair, then another, then another, and when he
said nothing, I just thanked him and sprinted into the hallway
of the third floor.

The large doors leading to Hassan's room were just in front
of the stairwell as I emerged, still breathless and shaking from
my escape. I was dismayed to see a long line of people, all

men, waiting patiently to see Hassan, as if they had been there a long time. A three-hour wait would probably not have gained me access to the prison leader. I did not have even five minutes of freedom upstairs, let alone three hours. Once again, I braced myself, walked boldly up to the entrance, which was guarded by two Komiteh men and, without giving them a chance to react, pushed the door open and walked in.

Hassan was sitting behind his massive desk, which was piled high with files. The room was full of activity, but I ignored the others and, relieved to finally get a chance to put my case before him, I launched into my plea.

"Hassan Agha, I have learned my lesson," I began, addressing him formally. "I've suffered enough. My poor child doesn't even know what is happening to me. I must go home. I promise you that I will never do anything against the law again. I won't even have my father or brother in my house, if that's the law. Just let me go home, please."

Just then, my interrogator walked in behind me, probably to make certain that I did not say anything against him. No doubt, should Hassan be furious with me, the interrogator would be quick to blame me. But when he heard Hassan say, in Turkish, "All right. Be quiet for now. I'm busy on a file," and motion me to a chair on the side of the room, he, too, sat down without saying a word and watched the proceedings with a careful eye.

While I waited for Hassan to finish his consultation with an older man, I had my first opportunity to look around the room. I was sitting close to one of the large windows that looked out onto the street. For the first time in almost two days I could see something other than the walled garden of the prison. There was life out there — traffic making its way noisily up and down the street, pedestrians walking past unhurriedly. The noises of the city rose up to us. I wanted so badly to be out there walking on the street or speeding past in a car, not even noticing the mansion that had become a place to hide people away and destroy them. I thought, my God, how wonderful it is just to be able to do simple things like walk down a street freely and without fear. It was probably the first time in my life that I realized the meaning of freedom. And I realized how fragile a gift it was because, as I looked at Hassan, I knew there was still a good chance that I might not enjoy my liberty for some time.

I was immersed in the life down below in the street when I realized that everyone in the room was rising respectfully. I looked up and saw a *mullah* entering the room. He was a giant, good-looking man with dark skin, a beard and a white turban on his head. Even Hassan stood up and bowed reverentially to the newcomer. I did not know how to behave in front of a *mullah*. Did a woman stand as the men did? Should I say a greeting or was that out of place for a woman? My mother-in-law had once told me that according to Moslem law, a woman's voice should not be heard by a man because he would find it sexually exciting. I did not want this evidently powerful leader to think that I was snubbing him. I stood up — but only halfway and only briefly, and I muttered something under my breath, a greeting that he may or may not have heard. Then I sat back down and hid under my *chador* with my eyes gazing on to the ground.

Hassan started to bring the *mullah* up to date on the details of certain prisoners and held up several files for him to peruse. But the *mullah* kept glancing in my direction and I could hear him asking about my file. Hassan continued to talk to him about other prisoners but the *mullah* returned to my case. Who was I? Why was I in prison? Finally he requested my file and then, turning to me, asked me to follow him.

Just when I thought I might be safe in Hassan's office, a powerful *mullah* was leading me off. I disliked *mullahs*. I knew nothing about them, nor did I care to be in their presence, but this *mullah* had the power of life or death over me. He could decide whether I was to be merely whipped or put to death.

He led me to another office just two doors down from Hassan's and, as we walked down the hall, everyone stopped what they were doing and bowed. I heard someone calling him Hojat Al Islam Tabatabai, giving him the respectful title that placed him just below *ayatollah*, the highest religious rank. I was in the hands of the religious head of Teheran's morality squad, a *mullah* from a powerful Iranian family.

We entered another elegant drawing room that had been converted into an office, and he motioned me to sit on a wooden chair by one of the two desks in the room. I was so frightened that I started to shake violently with an unnatural coldness in my limbs. My mouth was dry, and I found that I could neither swallow nor open my mouth easily. He must have seen the bad state I was in because he offered me tea. I was so shocked that I immediately said no. Thirsty and hungry as I was, I could not think of drinking when so much hung on saying and doing the appropriate thing. Tabatabai asked one of the men standing in the room to go for tea anyway.

As the *mullah* sat behind his desk, I noticed that it was littered with dozens of files—all of them containing stories such as mine, no doubt, all of them seemingly untended. The room was spartan, with just the two plain wooden desks and several wooden chairs. Whatever paintings, rugs and furniture had been here when the house was confiscated had long before been sent to the central auction warehouse set up by the Komiteh to sell off the "contributions" of the wealthy to the new regime.

Tabatabai seemed concerned about my state.

"What's wrong?" he asked me, more politely than anyone had spoken to me in ages, it seemed. "Why are you so worried? We'll take care of everything. Leave things to me."

His voice was warm, rich and reassuring, but still I could not speak. When the tea was brought, I took a few sips to wet my tongue and throat and loosen my jaw. He started to ask me questions. When had I come to the prison? Who had brought me there? What had I been charged with? Those were all matters explained in the file, I was sure, but he did not seem to be bothering with the papers in front of him. When he heard that I had been in prison for two nights, he was incensed.

"That's what happens when I go away for a few days. You should never have been brought in here. These people are so disorganized. I don't dare go away for too long."

As he talked, I became bolder and stole quick glances at him. He was, without doubt, a finely featured man. He had delicate, well-manicured hands and youthful brown eyes.

"Now, tell me what is worrying you," he said after I had drunk some more tea.

I told him about my fears of losing my son. "Even if I get out of prison, I now have to face my husband's family. As soon as they heard that I was in prison, they came and took Farhad away. And now I am going to have to hire a lawyer and fight to get him back. They have been trying to take him from me ever since my husband died."

He wanted all the details of my husband's death, how well off he had left me, who my in-laws were. I told him the suspicion that had grown in me while I was in prison that it had been my in-laws who called in the complaint against me that had brought the Komiteh to my door. What I could not understand was who had told them that Kamal was with me. In my mind, there was no question that the Komiteh's visit had been timed to his visit, when I would be compromised by his presence in my house.

Then he asked me why I had alcohol and cards in my house. I could tell from his questions that he had known all about me, even before finding me in Hassan's office. And he knew all the details of the search, although Hassan had promised me that some of the findings would be left out. But he did not behave with me as the others had. His questions revealed curiosity rather than condemnation.

I answered in the same relaxed way. I stressed my complete

ignorance of the things that my husband had left behind, that I had never thought to get rid of the alcohol, that I was blameless. How much he believed, I don't know. He nodded as if everything I was saying was just fine. I did not stop to consider what his behaviour might mean. I was just relieved not to have another man berating and threatening me.

Then he changed tack. "Tell me about this man Kamal who says that he wants to marry you."

Again I was on guard. "He is nothing to me. He is just a friend who came to help me sort out my husband's affairs. I am not at all interested in getting married to him or anyone else."

"But he has told us that he went to your house to propose to you and that he wants to marry you very much."

For a moment I thought that the *mullah* was considering forcing me to marry Kamal, in prison. I hardly knew Kamal, and in that moment I realized my heart was not yet finished with Hamid.

"I am a widow," I replied as firmly as I could, "and my main concern is for my son, to educate him and raise him properly. I don't want to get married."

The *mullah* seemed very understanding. "Well, in fact, in your situation, I wouldn't advise you to get married again. As a widow, you can live in your husband's house and you get a monthly support payment. You would lose all that if you married. Now, if you were to make a pleasure marriage with someone," he continued, "you could keep your house and car, and you could still have . . . sex."

The word, coming from a *mullah* and spoken within the walls of that prison for the enforcement of morals, flushed me with alarm.

He went on. "You are young. You must have your sexual life. If a young woman does not have her sexual life, her prostate would be damaged. So the best way is to have a *siqeh*, a pleasure marriage, with someone. The *siqeh* is a great aspect of the Moslem faith. You know, you should read some books on the Moslem faith. You would find them very interesting.''

I began to realize slowly where this strange *mullah*—who had power and influence and came from a wealthy family but who still did not know that women did not have prostate glands—was leading. He could not be contemplating having me killed because he seemed so interested in my well-being. But he was also making an unmistakable suggestion. Was the price of my freedom to be in a *siqeh* arrangement with him? Did he want me as his concubine? Although a concubine has no rights to property, her children have inheritance rights equal to those of the children born to the man's wife. The *siqeh* was once a popular method for a man to get around the Koran's ban on adultery. Usually a man would make a pleasure marriage with a servant in his household or a woman of the lower class. He would rarely do so with a woman of his own class that he might otherwise marry properly. In recent decades the *siqeh*, approved in the Koran, had grown out of favour and it was actually illegal under the Shah. But Khomeini had reinstated it—another setback for women under his rule.

While the *mullah* subtly made his proposition, all I could think of was to get out somehow and retrieve my son. Sex, which seemed uppermost in the *mullah*'s mind, was far from mine. But I was not about to tell him that. First I had to get out.

"You know, under this regime," he said, rolling his eyes up in exasperation, "you can't have a boyfriend or girlfriend. So it's better just to *siqeh* someone. This regime . . . you know, sometimes I wonder about the things they do." And he tittered as if we were both on the same side.

Just then, two guards came in, bringing with them a middle-aged man who looked around the room in a perplexed manner.

One of the guards spoke up. "This man has come to pick up his wife."

"Well, then, give her to him," the *mullah* said impatiently.

The guards looked at each other and then the same one said, "But, sir, she is no longer here."

"Why not?"

"Well, she was executed ten days ago," he said, hesitating, then added, "by mistake."

The *mullah* turned to me. "There, you see. I go away for a few days and everything falls apart." Facing the guard again, he asked, "So what happened?"

Speaking for the first time, the aggrieved husband said that he and his wife had argued ferociously a couple of weeks before. Angry at her for talking back to him, he had complained to the Komiteh, who immediately arrested her and put her in prison. "But now I want her back. I have four children. The youngest is just three months old. I need a wife."

The man did not seem unduly concerned that his wife had been killed. He was more concerned that he had been left with no one to care for his children.

The *mullah* smiled expansively, and then, with a glance at me, made a generous suggestion.

"Well, the solution is simple," he said to the guards. "Take this man downstairs to the women's prison and let him choose whatever woman he wants to replace his wife."

I became rigid. Even now I wonder whether, if I had been downstairs at the time, I, too, would have been lined up for selection by that paunchy, stubble-bearded man.

The guard pointed out that the man was also due to get eighty lashes for having abused his wife during their fight. But the *mullah* was positively magnanimous now. "I will forget about the whippings. Just let him take his new wife home." The man went off, happily enough, to make his choice. I never found out what happened. "You see," said the *mullah*, "you can't leave your work for one moment."

I hastened to flatter him. "You are such a kind and generous man. God bless you."

But there were still a couple of men in the room, and I suppose that I had gone too far because he suddenly turned on me.

"You, be quiet," he said.

As soon as the men left the room, he again became friendly.

"You can go back downstairs now. I will send your release papers down right away and you can leave prison."

At first, I did not believe him. Was he really going to let me go? Even if he let me go, they would surely whip me first. But I was too scared to ask if I was to escape being a victim of the bright red bed: I might just remind him to order up a whipping.

As he wrote the letter of release, he added, "As soon as you get downstairs, this letter will be brought down and they will let you go." I did not trust the prison's efficiency. The day before, a young woman had been told that her papers would be coming down soon, but at 4:00 P.M. sharp, everything shut down in the prison and no more work was done. The woman was forced to spend another night in the prison. But when I asked the *mullah* if I could take the letter down myself, he was adamant: by law, the guard had to take the letter downstairs to my keepers in the basement.

"If I had been here, none of this would have happened to you. I will give you my telephone number so that if you need anything at all — especially if you need help in dealing with your husband's family — you can call me."

I had visions of having made an important contact in the new regime. Perhaps if my uncles got into trouble now, I would have a powerful connection to invoke. And if my in-laws tried to hold on to Farhad, they might regret it. Perhaps it was best that I had met this *mullah*. After all, how much longer could any of us survive in the new Iran without such contacts?

I was even emboldened to ask who had turned me in to the Komiteh.

"Well, if you stay around a few more hours, I could find out and you could also have back all your films and photos," he offered.

But nothing could be worth several more hours in that place, during which the rules might suddenly change, or another *mullah* might come along to replace this one. Not wanting to take any chances, I thanked him and told him I wanted to leave right away.

As the guards escorted me back downstairs, I made plans for my release. I could not let the women guards downstairs know that I was about to leave. The other prisoners had told me that they often contrived complaints against women about to be freed, just to keep them there for two or three more days. I prepared a sad face. When the women guards and a few other prisoners asked me how my interrogation had gone— I had been upstairs for so long — I said that nothing much had happened. I found my spot in the corner again near the woman who had been arrested in the taxi. I handed her back her *chador* and thanked her again for the loan. After what seemed hours, but was in reality just fifteen minutes, a guard called out my name.

"Sousan Azadi. You're to be released."

As I scrambled to pick up my belongings, the woman next to me immediately started to cry.

"What will I do now?" she wailed. "Please, you must call my husband. Please. Let him know where I am. He will never believe that I am innocent. What will he do to me when I get out?"

The woman was both frightened of staying there and of being released to the mercy of her husband.

"Shush. Not so loud. You know it's not allowed to take out telephone numbers. But tell me what it is. I'll write it down on this piece of paper." I whispered for fear of being caught. The guards reminded us from time to time that we were not to take numbers to make calls for prisoners and we were not to buy things for those left behind. But I could not say no — even if it meant more risks.

Confused by her overwhelming fear, the woman kept trying one number after another, but she could not quite remember her home number. Finally she remembered the number of a friend, and I wrote that down and stuffed it inside my panty-hose to keep it safe. A couple of other women asked for yoghurt and cookies. Then I wrapped myself in my coat and left, without escort and without so much as a backward glance.

I ran up the stairs and out the side door I had entered two days before. I took a deep breath of the cool winter air and flew down the stairs and out of the garden door. I went straight to the grocery store across the street, the one Mansoureh and Farhad had visited the night that I was brought in, and bought ten yoghurt containers, cookies and juice with money that I had stashed in my pantyhose before leaving home. I went back to the side door of the prison and left the groceries with a guard, saying they were from the families of the prisoners (relatives, but not former inmates, were permitted to drop off food). I stayed to make sure that he called downstairs and had the women guards inform the prisoners.

After returning to the street, I flagged down a passing public taxi. I climbed in beside a male passenger in the back seat and could hardly stop myself from bouncing with excitement. Finally the driver looked around and said, "You seem to be very happy about something, don't you?"

I looked out the window at the bright sunshine, a clear Teheran winter day, and the world had never seemed more beautiful and fresh to me.

"You will never believe where I have been," I said to the driver. "I'm so happy because I have just come out of prison. Can you believe that? And do you know why I was in prison? Because I had too much music in my house. Imagine that. Too much music in my house. I had too many cassettes and too many illegal coupons. And for that I was in prison for three days. That's the kind of regime this is. I'm just glad that I made it out alive.''

The passenger and the taxi driver just looked at each other but did not say a word. I realized that although I had stepped out of prison, I had not really stepped into freedom. Those two men in the taxi were locked up, too. As long as I stayed in Iran, I would never be free.

Chapter Eleven

The Revolution Closes In

When a moth threw itself into a fire
  it was consumed.
The moth dying said, "I am fire,"
  but the words were from the tongue of the flame.

JONEYD

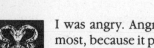 I was angry. Angry at the regime, first and foremost, because it punished a woman for entertaining a male friend in her home. Angry at myself for having been so stupid as to take that sort of chance. Angry because I had once again let a pushy man cause me trouble. And I was furious at my family. Where had they been when I had sat crying for three days in prison? Why had they not managed to buy my way out?

When I arrived at my Aunt Tootie's place, I poured out all my anger on her before she could explain.

"Where were you all?" I shouted. "Why didn't you help me?"

Much as she tried to calm me down, I refused to listen. "We did what we thought was best," she persisted. "They didn't know that you were part of a powerful family. If we had put pressure on the Komiteh, it could have backfired. They might have held onto you longer and demanded a lot of money to let you go. As it was, you were just another woman who got herself into trouble."

Still fuming, I rushed to my son's school in the hope of intercepting him before the Aminis could pick him up and take him home. But when I arrived, I could see no sign of Farhad. When I asked the principal where he was, he spat out, "Your son hasn't been to school in three days. Are you so disorganized that you can't even get your son to school?"

The Aminis became the focus of my growing rage. They were the ones who had always made a big scene if Farhad missed his classes because of skiing or other activities. Now, just because the school was far from their house, they had not even bothered to drive him there.

As soon as I arrived home, I called their number. Farhad answered and when he heard my voice he started to cry. "Mummy, when are you coming to get me? Why do I have to stay here? I didn't know where you were. Come soon, please."

I did not dare promise him I would come to pick him up because I knew that there would be trouble with the Aminis. Instead, I asked him to put his grandmother on the line.

Mrs. Amini was very cool.

"I'm coming for Farhad," I said boldly.

"No, you are not," she answered with equal force. "You must be very tired after being in prison. You take care of yourself and we will take care of Farhad. The way you live is no life for a little boy. He's going to stay here and that's the way it's going to be." Then she hung up.

It was evident that my in laws were finally going to make an attempt to get custody of Farhad and, with Khomeini in power, I had few defences. By going to prison, I had just handed the Aminis the perfect proof against me. Without thinking about it for even one second, I picked up the telephone and called the private number that Tabatabai had given me. I left a message with a male secretary and expected to wait for a day or more for him to call me back, but within minutes he was on the phone, smoothly promising that I would soon have my son.

About fifteen minutes later, Farhad called me and Mrs. Amini came to the telephone. She told me curtly that I was to come and pick him up, but gave me no explanation for her sudden change of mind. I rushed over, my only desire to get Farhad in my arms and never let him go again. He was waiting outside the Aminis' front door, a tiny, forlorn boy, holding his tote bag and looking in every direction until a big smile broke out at the sight of the car. Hovering in the background was his grandmother, but she disappeared as soon as I got out of the car and caught Farhad up in a huge embrace. Never, ever again was I going to jeopardize being with my son, I swore.

While I had been in prison, both Hamid and Sufi had called from Europe looking for me, and Kamal had been over the night before to pick up his Mercedes. Now, as I arrived home with Farhad, Farah came out of the basement apartment, wringing her hands nervously.

"Madam," the woman said fearfully, "Mr. Kamal has called again. He has this idea that somehow we are responsible for your troubles. He threatened us. He said that if he ever found out who spied on you and called the Komiteh, he would kill him. But, I swear, madam, we had no part in all this."

I was so angry with Kamal at that point that I had very little sympathy for his wounded pride. I reassured the woman. But I had barely settled Farhad back into his home when Kamal called again.

"I would never have left that prison if I thought you were still in it," he said hotly. "They promised me that you had already been released."

Kamal had been kept overnight in a room similar to mine, but he had been released shortly after I had seen him in the interrogation room, thanks to the intervention of his cousin, a highly ranked *mullah*. He admitted that he had told the Komiteh that he had plans to marry me. After being admonished not to visit an unmarried woman, the Komiteh let him go. His only punishment was the loss of his coupons, which the Komiteh refused to return to him. I was too annoyed with him to give him much comfort and I got off the phone quickly only to have it ring again. This time it was the *mullah*.

"Well, I sorted things out for you. I called your in-laws and you should have no problems bringing your son home," he said, rather pleased with himself. Then he added in a reverential tone, "I had no idea that the Aminis were such a good family. Mrs. Amini is the daughter of a famous *mullah*."

I said nothing about his notion of a good family. But he was right — they belonged to his order, not mine.

"Now, I have to see you," he went on. "You need instruction in the Koran and in Moslem ways."

After I agreed, we discussed various places where we might meet. He ruled out his place, which was in a poorer area of the city and "not the sort of place a woman like you should visit." My house had already caused enough problems.

He finally hit upon an idea: "I have some friends who live in your area. I'll arrange with them to meet you there."

It seems mad now that I was so naïve, but I truly believed that I could turn him into a friend, an important contact who would benefit not only me but also the entire family. I would be so proud if I turned out to be the only family member who could aquire an important ally in the new regime as insurance against times of trouble. Even though I knew he would try to make me his concubine, I was actually looking forward to seeing him and felt sure I could talk him into being a business contact. But when Kamal called again soon afterwards and I told him about my planned encounter, he was adamantly opposed to it.

"Don't for one second consider meeting that filthy man," he commanded. "All he wants to do is get his hands on you."

I dismissed Kamal's outburst as jealousy, but when I called my Uncle Fayegh and told him, too, he was even more agitated.

"You have no idea how much trouble you might be getting yourself into," he said. "That man has plans for you, of that I'm sure."

"But couldn't I turn him into a friend, an important contact for the whole family?"

"It's nice of you to think of the family, Sousan, but a man in his position does not get interested in helping you unless he wants something from you. He wants to make you his concubine and, when he asks you, you will not be able to say no, because he has the power to destroy your life. Not only will you get yourself into trouble, but probably the rest of us as well, if you say no. The man is quite capable of making love to you right then and there, and there is nothing we would be able to do for you."

"I'm sure I can talk some sense into him and make him a business proposition," I insisted. "He could be a conduit for bribes if we need help sometime."

"Sousan, you still don't know about Iranian ways," my uncle replied with a deep sigh. "There is only one reason that a *mullah* becomes interested in a woman — and that is for sex. A *mullah* doesn't sit down and talk business with a woman."

After counselling me never to take a call from Tabatabai again and to avoid all contact with him, he broke the bad news that the Aminis had demanded a meeting with us for 4:00 P.M. that day.

At the meeting, held at the Aminis' house, were two of the guardians — Jamshid and Ali — and the psychologist, Parviz, who seemed to be sitting in for Mr. Taslimi, whose fate was still unknown. They carefully avoided looking at me, as if I were too insignificant, or perhaps too vile, to contemplate. Instead they spoke to my uncle.

"Sousan can do what she wants with her life," Ali began, "but Farhad is another matter. He was traumatized by the arrest and we are not going to let that happen again. We want him to move in with his grandmother where he will be better cared for."

When I protested vigorously, they gave me two options: to move into the basement apartment in the Amini house or to a modest apartment in a middle-class section of town not far from them. My house had become too eye-catching, they said, and there was no reason for me to continue living in such a large place all by myself. I did not dare remind them that it was my husband's house, which he had passed on to his son, and that under Moslem law my right to live there was guaranteed. The trouble was that they were Farhad's guardians and they controlled the money we needed to keep the house operating. In the end, I agreed to move out of the house and keep Farhad with me. It would only be temporary, I decided inwardly. Soon I would find a way to leave Iran.

At the insistence of my family, who feared Tabatabai, I essentially moved out of my home that very day after packing a suitcase for me and Farhad. We began to live as many other Iranians did — on the run, staying overnight with different friends and relatives and returning home by day after checking with Jalal Agha or his wife to make sure that there was no emissary from Tabatabai waiting for me. Every day, Jalal Agha reported that Tabatabai had called repeatedly. After a week had gone by, the *mullah* started to send the Komiteh to see why I was not returning his calls. Eventually he put out an order for my arrest, even though I had been fully discharged at the prison and had no outstanding charges against me. A simple task, such as taking Farhad to school, became dangerous because my movements could be too easily traced that way. Friends had to take turns ferrying him back and forth.

Kamal was equally insistent. Everyday he would berate Jalal Agha and then do his best to track me down. When he finally found me and heard that Tabatabai was pursuing me, he exploded and decided to take matters into his own hands. Despite the danger that it posed to him, he went directly to the prison and asked to see the *mullah*. He was accompanied by the *mullah* who was also his cousin. When he confronted my pursuer, he made it very clear that he was marrying me and that he wanted Tabatabai to leave me alone.

"I have nothing to talk to you about," Tabatabai replied. "It is Sousan Azadi I have business with. There is no point in your coming here."

Kamal was so insistent that I marry him that I considered becoming his legal concubine just to deter the *mullah*. I had no intention of truly formalizing the relationship or of becoming emotionally involved, but my family disapproved of my suggestion. To be a concubine, even in the disjointed world we were living in, was not proper, they said. I would be better off getting a quick marriage and an even quicker divorce.

I felt a deep visceral revulsion at the notion of marriage — to anyone. But I had few options. It would take weeks to arrange an illegal escape through Turkey. In that time, Tabatabai would have plenty of occasions to track me down. Marriage to Kamal might be the only way to evade him.

But there was one other option, and I decided to make one last attempt before giving in to Kamal. According to a Khomeini law, an Iranian woman married to a foreigner was free to leave the country with her husband. If I could just find a dependable person with a foreign passport who would consent to a marriage of convenience, I would be able to get Farhad and myself out of the country safely and legally, without resorting to the expensive and dangerous route through Turkey.

Through my cousin Dara in Switzerland, I obtained the name of an Iranian man, married to a Swiss woman, who now had a Swiss passport and was temporarily in Iran. Dara called the man's wife in Switzerland and detailed the strange request before asking her permission to approach her husband. Sympathetic to the problems of Iranians caught in Khomeini's theocracy, the woman readily agreed to allow her husband to take a second wife. It was perfectly legal in the new Iran, where men could once again marry four wives, as outlined in the Koran.

"But I can't get through to the man in Iran," Dara said. "I'm afraid you will have to call him and put the case to him yourself."

Somehow I managed to overcome my embarrassment and called the man at his brother's house, where he was staying. In very vague terms, I suggested that he come to visit me at the house.

"Please drive only a modest car and don't park anywhere near the house," I told the man, who must have been baffled by my sudden interest in him and my odd instructions.

The day he was to come, I asked a girlfriend to be in the house with me just in case the Komiteh made another surprise visit and found me with another man. By now I thought the Komiteh knew of my every move. They had become my recurring nightmare: I spotted them everywhere I went and half expected them to walk in on me no matter where I was staying.

It was early in the afternoon. The visitor had been with me for only fifteen minutes — and I was still working up the courage to put my strange proposal to him. I was pouring tea in the living room, when my gardener suddenly burst in on us, white-faced and breathless.

"The Komiteh!" he panted. "I've barricaded the gate near my house to keep them out. For God's sake, run."

I grabbed the hapless visitor by the arm, pushed him out the door and pointed him in the direction of the gate on the far side of the house, at the opposite end of the garden from where the Komiteh were now banging to get in. There was no time to explain what he was running from — only that he must get away as quickly as possible.

My girlfriend and I ran up to the balcony to see if we could spot the Komiteh at the gate. They were not in our view, but we could see my visitor's orange Paycan car standing on the road to the west of the house, with its doors wide open. Several revolutionary guards were walking around, inspecting it.

"He must have got away," she said, scanning the garden. "Let's make a run for it. My car is right out front. I'll go out first, start the motor, and then you just jump in."

"But what about Farhad?" I suddenly remembered in a panic. "His school bus should be dropping him off any minute."

"We'll intercept it," she said without a moment's hesitation. We had all become used to the unusual, to escaping from our own houses in the middle of the day.

We did as she suggested and, luckily, just as I was about to get into her car, I saw Farhad's bus pull into view. I grabbed him as he descended the steps and shoved him into the back seat of the car. We sped off, looking back for miles afterwards to make sure that we were not being followed. We carefully avoided the road where the Komiteh were still swarming over the Paycan.

What had happened to the man who might have been my next husband? As soon as we reached my friend's house, I started to call the man's family home to see if he was safe. But his brother knew nothing. Half an hour elapsed before I was able to find out what had befallen my visitor. He had walked right into the arms of the Komiteh at the gate to my house. It was merely bad luck that had caused him to be arrested, it turned out. Apparently, he had not been taken in because the Komiteh were looking for me. That morning, an important *mullah* had been assassinated by a couple of men who drove off in an orange Paycan. In the course of their investigation, the Komiteh had routinely checked the man's car and merely wanted to ask the owner some questions. He was arrested when it became apparent that he was driving around without ownership papers. The car belonged to his brother's firm and the papers were locked up for the night at the company offices. It was late at night before they released the frightened man, but not before they forced him to sign a document in which he promised to return to the jail if he was summoned.

I spoke to him that night and what he told me frightened me even more.

"They kept asking me about you," he said, still shaken. "About whether you ran a whorehouse. They asked me how much I paid you. I told them that I hardly knew you, that I was just a friend of your father's and had looked you up hoping to see him. What's going on? No, better still, don't tell me."

There was no question of telling him what my plan had been. He left Iran a few days later, well ahead of his planned departure and with his business left undone.

By now I could trust no one. Who had called the Komiteh? Why were they there within minutes of my visitor's arrival? That night I moved in with a close girlfriend whom even my family did not know. I told no one where I was staying so that no friend or relative would be in a position of betraying me under force. As a precaution, another friend took Farhad. It seemed that almost everyone was protecting a friend or relative, providing a hiding place for someone on the run, despite all the dangers. Some of my girlfriends took risks on my behalf that I know their husbands resented — and yet they did it willingly and I was never turned away.

That night I spent many hours dreading the sudden appearance of the Komitch. I was certain they would take me back to prison and I would be at the mercy of the *mullah*. How I hated all men just then and the society those men had created, where women were safe only if they were protected by men and where their main function was to provide sex in return. I did not want another man to come anywhere near me. Pacing back and forth in the room my friend had given me for the night, I became hysterical with fear. I was shaking as if suffering from a deep and permanent cold; my teeth chattered and, as much as I tried, I could not stop myself from crying.

When she saw me so distraught, my friend grabbed me by the shoulders and shook me. "You have to stop this, Sousan," she shouted. "You can't do this to yourself. You have to calm down."

She cried with me but nothing could take away my fears.

"They're going to get me," I chanted. "It doesn't matter what I do or where I go. They're after me and they're going to get me."

With the help of tranquillizers I eventually fell asleep. When I called Farah the next day, she told me that the Komiteh had once again come with a warrant for my arrest. I realized then that I could not go back to my house under any circumstances. When I called and told Kamal about the latest threat, he decided to confront Tabatabai again.

"Don't go," I begged him. "They'll probably arrest you on the spot." When he insisted, I made him promise that he would go only if he had his *mullah* relative with him. "I've already made trouble for enough people."

He promised — but then with typical stubbornness went off to Takhtejamshid Avenue by himself — just a couple of weeks after we had been released from prison. Later he told me about the encounter.

"The man was unbelievable. Here I'd come to tell him that I wanted to marry you, and by all rights he should have been pleased. After all, according to the Koran, the fact that I want to marry you is supposed to clear you of all past sins! Even if a man marries a prostitute she becomes clean, or so they say, because she gives up her old profession. And instead he tells me, 'You shouldn't marry that woman. You have no idea what she is like. She has all sorts of parties. I'm sure she runs a whorehouse.' So here is a religious man who should be praying for your salvation and instead he wants to damn you. But I know why. That man can't get you out of his mind—I could see it. He's determined to make you his concubine. But not while I'm around."

With the continued pressure from Tabatabai, the fear that the Aminis might at any time make a grab for Farhad and my difficulties in finding a smuggler to get us out of the country, I found that I was being thrust into Kamal's arms — for protection at the very least — even though I felt only repugnance for men.

"Look, why don't we just get married?" he said. "I can't stand not seeing you every day. I need you. I love you. And that way a lot of your problems will be solved. The Aminis would leave you alone. The *mullah* would back off. Then we'll escape together—I promise you. The revolution seems to be throwing us together. Maybe it's for the best. Maybe it was meant to be."

After worrying about it for days, I finally agreed. I would marry him—but with some important conditions. I was not at all sure I wanted to continue to have a sexual relationship with him. And I fully intended to leave Iran with Farhad.

"As soon as I find someone to take me out, I'm going, whether you are ready or not," I told him. "I want you to understand that."

He agreed to everything happily. This man I hardly knew, whom I had met only two months before, wanted me no matter what, it seemed. I didn't know what his hobbies were or what food he preferred. Our discussions had mostly been about how to find a smuggling contact to escape. He was quiet, almost morose, although when he was around me he cheered up noticeably, his friends said. He was punctilious and well-mannered and quite the opposite of the witty, devilish Hamid.

Two weeks later we were married at my Aunt Tootie's house in a small, subdued ceremony attended only by a few close family members and friends. I was still trying to keep the news of the marriage from the Aminis because I wanted some time to organize plans to leave.

On the morning of my wedding, I cried. How different from my fairytale marriage to Bijan when I had awakened excited, on the threshold of my adult life! I had been massaged, coiffed, made up, outfitted, cosseted — prepared to be the wife of a man I hardly knew but who fitted every girl's dream. But this morning I could barely apply my make-up for tears, and my eyes remained puffy all day. I dressed in a simple ivory silk dress and saw to the details of the wedding myself. I was marrying a man that I did not love. But I knew it was the only way for me to survive in Iran.

Just a few weeks before, I had gone to see a lawyer to ask him to fight for the limited rights that I had as a widow and a mother. Early on in my conflicts with the Aminis, I had wanted to go to a lawyer, but my uncles and aunts counselled against it, saying that a long and difficult fight with my in-laws would be a public display that was foreign to our family. But now I had little left to lose.

I told the lawyer — a long-established, respected professional — that I would do anything to hold onto my son. He amazed me with the kinds of suggestions he made.

"I have contacts with certain authorities," he said casually. "People whom we can bribe to go and beat up Dr. Ali and threaten him if he continues to bother you."

"Much as I hate those people," I replied, "I couldn't do that to anyone."

"Well, then, we can bribe a *mullah* that I know who will put the Komiteh onto the Aminis and harass them, maybe even throw them into prison for a few days — just to give them a taste of what they have done to you." But again I could not order such a punishment.

The one step to which I agreed was to start a court action charging the guardians with improper conduct in regard to my son's finances—both their failure to have the list of household contents written up and the misuse of his money by the construction company.

Two weeks after my marriage, after I had slowly and discreetly moved into Kamal's house, we called a meeting with the Aminis and told them of our marriage. They did not have to feign their joy, although they were also shocked that such a respectable man would consider me worthy of marriage. Now I was no longer eligible to get an allowance from Bijan's estate, I could no longer live in the house or have claim to it, and Farhad's wealth would be entirely in their hands to use at their discretion until he turned eighteen.

Furthermore, because I had never claimed my *mehrieh*, my dowry from Bijan, they would not have to pay it now that I was remarried. Whatever small share of my husband's land was mine by law I lost in the same way. They had been slow in selling the land and distributing the money, and now they had no obligation to give me any proceeds of the sale.

"Now we will take Farhad," said Ali.

"No, you will not," I replied. "I got married so that I could hold onto Farhad. Try proving that I am a bad mother now that I am so respectably remarried."

The Aminis said nothing, but I should not have underestimated them.

A short time later I provided them with the perfect weapon against me in their fight for control of Farhad.

Ever since the revolution, I had been storing in my house various valuable items for friends and relatives who had been forced to leave the country, as well as the rattan furniture I had bought from the two American men. I was slowly selling off some of the pieces both for my friends who needed the money abroad and for myself. Anna, the wife of my embassy friend, Paul, decided to buy some of the furniture, which was now quite valuable because foreign-made items were almost impossible to buy. One day I made arrangements with Jalal Agha for her to pick up what she wanted at 4:00 P.M.

At about the time she should have been there, I called the house. Farah answered. She sounded very odd, and was guarded in what she said, as if someone were overhearing her conversation. She said that Anna had already left. After five minutes, I called again, worried that something might be wrong. This time she told me that Anna had still been there when I had called the first time but that now she was truly gone. She hung up before I could ask any questions.

"Kamal," I said, "something odd is going on."

"You'd better call again," he suggested, "and if things look bad, I'll go up and see what I can do."

As soon as she answered, it was clear that Farah was very distressed. "I'm sorry, I just couldn't talk to you," she said. "The Aminis were all here and they had your friend arrested for theft. The police even searched your room."

When I heard that, I knew we were facing the most serious trouble yet. In a drawer by my bedside was a booklet that contained all the dates and figures, written in code, of my shipments of carpets out of the country. In my haste to leave the house, I had stupidly left it behind and had not been able to go back to retrieve it. Had they found it? Did they already know about Paul? Was that why they had called the police to arrest poor Anna? What did they know?

Kamal grabbed me by the hand and together we rushed out of the house, unaware that I was still dressed in an old jogging suit that I only wore indoors. We drove madly from house to house, visiting friends of Kamal's whom I was meeting for the first time. Without waiting for introductions, he blurted out that I was his wife and was going to be accused of smuggling and that we needed help. It was a mark of how dislocated our society was that no one so much as blinked at the news: they immediately sat down to talk about what could be done. The people we visited that afternoon all had good connections in the police department. It was apparently this arm of the state, and not the Komiteh, that had arrested Anna. They all promised to call their friends to find out what was going on and where Anna was being held.

All that afternoon, as we rushed from house to house, I kept dialling Paul's number, hoping to hear that Anna was fine, but there was never any answer. Then I remembered one other person who might be in danger should Anna talk: Jamshid, my husband's partner, who had smuggled carpets with me. We went to his house.

"You have to escape from Iran tonight," he shouted, scared and not thinking very clearly. "I'll come with you. My wife will have to get out later."

"Wait a minute," Kamal said. "This is my wife you happen to be talking about. We just got married. I don't want her to go so suddenly. Use your power with the Aminis to make them back off. You have a lot to lose, too, don't forget."

"There is only one way to make them stop," he said, turning to me. "Give them your son. That's what they really want. Until you give him up, they will keep your friend in jail, I promise you."

Kamal seemed to think that was a reasonable suggestion. "Why don't you just give him to them for a few days to get Anna out? He'll just start to cry and make a big fuss, and they'll be only too glad to get rid of him."

Jamshid was so reassuring: "Dr. Ali is planning to send Farhad to school in Switzerland. Once he is there, it will be so much easier for you to get custody. You can do anything you want once he is out of the country."

With both of them looking at me as if I held the key to end all our troubles, I told them that I would consider the idea — but that I wanted time. It would take much more than one pressured moment to decide to let the Aminis have Farhad—even for a few days.

When we called at about 10:30 P.M., we finally found Paul and Anna at home. I had known Anna for years and she had often attended my parties. Even in good times, she was a skittish woman, a skinny, child-like wraith, although she was in her mid-thirties. Between sobbing and hysterical screaming Anna managed to tell us what had happened. When she arrived at my house, Jalal Agha and Farah had started to help her load up the furniture in a van she had brought. But within minutes, Dr. Ali, my mother-in-law and Bijan's two older sisters showed up and accused her of being a thief. They immediately called the police.

"I told them, 'You know me. I'm Sousan's friend. I'm not a thief.' And the mother said, 'She's not a worthy friend to have. She's a bitch. All she did was give parties in the house that my son sweated his life out in the desert to build. What gives her the right to take pleasure in what he died to earn?'

"I begged and begged them on my knees not to call the police, but they did and the police took me to the station. I was so afraid to tell them that I was married to a foreigner, in case that caused us even more trouble. So I told them I wasn't married at all. I didn't know Paul had come to bail me out. He'd told them I was his wife. My God, I thought I would never get out of there. And, Sousan, they have a little book of yours. I'm sure that woman Farah pointed it out to them. Then I heard the police and your in-laws talking about smuggling. That family hates you, Sousan. They're not going to let me go."

Farah. Jalal Agha. Finally, so much that had been inexplicable made sense: why the Aminis seemed to know so much about me; why the Komiteh always arrived when I could be caught in a compromising situation with a man; why the driver and his wife had seemed so nervous the night the house was searched. Did they fear they would finally be exposed? The spies, probably paid by the Aminis, were right in my own home. Had I waited at the prison and obtained my file, I would have seen their names listed as the ones who had lodged the complaint against me.

The police had released Anna, but only on condition that she report back to them first thing in the morning. She was to continue to report back and be interrogated until either I showed up at the station to claim the property as mine and answer questions about my carpet-smuggling activities or the Aminis dropped their charges. For me to go to the police was tantamount to turning myself in to the Komiteh. The death penalty awaited me if the Aminis succeeded in proving that I had smuggled out carpets — and with the little book of accounts I had so carefully kept, it would not be difficult. If I gave them my son for a few days, they might leave Anna and me alone.

"I can't go back," Anna was screaming. I felt my heart being squeezed. It was my son or my friend. I had to sacrifice one of them for my liberty.

For days I walked around the house unaware that I was talking to myself out loud.

Once Farhad heard me on the telephone discussing my terrible choice with Uncle Fayegh, and he came to me afterwards, his eyes filled with tears.

"Mummy, is Aunt Anna more important to you than I am? Do you love Aunt Anna more than me?"

"No, my little darling," I replied, heartbroken. "Whatever gave you that idea? It's just that maybe you might have to go and visit your grandmother for a little while so that Aunt Anna doesn't go to jail."

He pulled away from me. "You must love her more or else you wouldn't be sending me away."

How could I explain to a six-year-old that our lives were just not normal anymore? How could I tell him that I had been doing everything possible to hold on to him, but that I might lose the fight?

Everyone in my family advised me to turn Farhad over.

"Give him up for a little while," said Uncle Kurosh. "The Aminis will take good care of him. They'll send him to the best school."

"Yes," added a friend. "You are so young. You have a fine, new husband. You can have another family, and soon you may even be glad that Farhad is taken care of here."

I almost jumped up and hit them. Didn't they understand? This was my only child, my baby, they were talking about. I would sooner die than leave him behind. If I gave him up, it would only be for a short time, until I could arrange our escape.

Eight days after Anna was arrested, I made my decision. I turned Farhad over to the Aminis and they agreed to drop the charges against Anna. I still had to make a formal visit to the police station to deny charges of smuggling and I faced the death penalty if they did not accept my denials. I had read many accounts of the executions of smugglers caught near the Turkish border. But a relative by marriage, who happened to know the police chief, smoothed the way by assuring him that I was an honest woman from a good family. When I arrived at the headquarters, I looked around nervously, half-expecting the Komiteh to pop up and re-arrest me. They still had a warrant out for my arrest and I wondered if the police, which acted independently of them, had informed them of my whereabouts. I was shown into the police chief's office. For three hours he berated me for attempting to sell property belonging to my husband and grilled me on my little book. I used all my skills to persuade him that I had meant no harm, that the furniture I had intended to sell was mine and that I had never contemplated smuggling. He sat stonily through it all, giving me no hint of what his ultimate decision would be. Finally, just when I thought I would be put behind bars, he got up and dismissed me abruptly.

Saying goodbye to Farhad was the worst part. He held onto me until the last possible moment and cried pitifully.

"Now, remember what I said," I reminded him. "Start complaining, all the time. Wet your bed at night. Demand that you be sent home. Make life miserable for them. And memorize our telephone number. But don't tell them where we live or what the number is."

After marrying, Kamal and I had taken the precaution of not revealing our whereabouts to the Aminis in case they came up with some flimsy reason to send the Komiteh after us. Later, Farhad told me that he carefully memorized the number I had written on a little piece of paper and hidden in his pocket. For days he had been unable to destroy the paper because his aunt or grandmother had always been with him. But one morning, when the schoolbus came to pick him up and take him to his new school — one closer to his grandmother's house — he had ripped the paper into tiny pieces, and when his aunt wasn't looking, dropped them into the gutter. "The water took the pieces away really fast and she didn't see a thing."

I hated myself for putting such a heavy burden of secrecy on him.

At first, the Aminis were so happy to have Farhad that they promised I could visit him anytime I wanted and have him on weekends and public holidays. I could telephone him anytime at all, they said. But it soon became apparent what their real intentions were. They restricted my visits with Farhad to Fridays from 10:00 A.M. to 4:00 P.M. and my calls to one a day. If we missed each other on the phone because I was out or he was busy, the Aminis would not permit us to call again that day. Often on weekends they made excuses not to let me see him at all — he had a cold, or was too tired, or they wanted to take him to the country.

During the first couple of weeks, Farhad cried on the phone that he wanted to come home, holding onto the line until his grandmother pried him away. But slowly he became more and more guarded with me, as if he were afraid. He would mumble one-word answers to my questions. His voice became flat, almost depressed-sounding. His characteristic boyish cheerfulness disappeared. Even on the few occasions when I managed to tear him from the Aminis, he seemed introspective and unwilling to talk about his life with them.

Finally, one day I asked him, "Luvijun, is there something you are afraid of? What's the matter?"

In a torrent of tears it came out that the Aminis had terrified him into not talking when he was away from them.

"I'm afraid to tell you. They have cameras everywhere and they can see everything I do. They can hear what I'm telling you and now when I go back they're going to be mad at me. They're going to know."

My child was so sure the Aminis could spy on him that it took me several hours to calm him down and make him believe that nobody could keep that kind of watch over him. As he became more assured, he told me between teary hiccoughs that he had to spend an hour a day with his Uncle Parviz, the psychologist. The Aminis were making a serious attempt to turn my son against me.

"They told me you're a bad mother because you don't feed me and don't help me with my homework," he said.

The Aminis were not the only ones pressuring him to be secretive. I had instructed Farhad not to reveal any details of my life with Kamal.

That afternoon, when Farhad left, I cried for hours and I told Kamal, "My poor baby. He's being torn to pieces. I'm losing more of him every day. I have to leave Iran. Get ready, because I'll go with or without you."

So many of us were abandoning Iran. Various statistics are used by observers to give a sense of the vastness of the changes that occurred in just a few years. One figure commonly cited is that over a million Iranians from the middle and upper classes have become emigrés. More than ten thousand were executed under the revolutionary banner. The war with Iraq has killed upwards of 100,000 people, while the refugees it has created are numbered in the millions.

The Iran I wanted to leave was in chaos at every level. Khomeini and his *mullahs* had succeeded in obliterating any threat to their rule — from the moderate middle class, the Communists, businessmen and even the more level-headed religious leaders. The purges of the armed forces and the civil service had been massive and bloody. Khomeini had turned Iran into an Islamic republic, with revolutionary Islamic bodies operating side by side with the remnants of the old order. A well-equipped Revolutionary Guard fought alongside the regular army at the front; the Komiteh had usurped much of the role of the police force; revolutionary tribunals and Islamic judges were imposing Islamic law on the judiciary. Anybody who resisted, anybody who attempted to oppose was bludgeoned into silence by thugs directed by the only sanctioned party, the Islamic Republic Party.

Even old Khomeini supporters such as former President Abol-Hassan Bani-Sadr quietly left. He sneaked out after he was impeached in Parliament for being unfaithful to the revolution. One of his mistakes had been to want to restore some civil liberties. In July 1981, Bani-Sadr set up a government-in-exile in Paris, fuming that the revolution he had helped to launch had gone astray. Khomeini's former foreign minister, Sadeq Qotbzadeh, was less fortunate. In April 1982, as I was making plans to escape, he was arrested and accused of plotting to overthrow the regime — a charge that he only partly refuted — and was shot.

The universities had been closed down for two years while educators struggled with Khomeini's command that they Islamize the curriculum. Indeed, the state was struggling to make all aspects of society conform with Islamic beliefs. The penal code was about to be revamped to apply the Islamic *hadd* punishments: in the case of theft, hands were to be cut

off, and adultery merited stoning. But on many issues it was
not clear what the proper line should be. In banking, the long-
awaited Islamization created turmoil as people waited to see
if interest — forbidden in the Koran — would be eliminated.
By the time I left, nothing had been done, and even now the
issue of interest on loans has not been tackled. Right through
the society, attempts were made to check out the Islamic
credentials of workers. Students were not permitted into
higher education if they were left-leaning or suspect Moslems.
Prospective teachers had to pledge to follow the Imam's line,
while civil servants were interrogated on their beliefs and
living habits. A whole new elite had risen from the slums,
through the revolutionary bodies, and was making its way
into government, while the nation's top leaders were over-
whelmingly religiously educated: Khomeini's handpicked
mullahs.

That spring of 1982, the government also launched a new
offensive against the Kurds in the northeastern part of the
country. This group had taken the opportunity, while the
central government was in confusion, to press their long-
standing desire for an autonomous state.

State violence continued unabated. It wasn't until after I
left that some attempt was made to put a curb on summary
arrests and executions, illegal searches of homes and con-
fiscation of property. It was not that the regime relented. It
was only that it made its repression more orderly.

My first attempt at finding a contact to smuggle us out of
the country ended in disaster. I met a man at a party who had
been involved in Hamid's escape. A political firebrand who
was implacably opposed to Khomeini, he ran a ring which
smuggled out political activists like himself who were being
sought by the Komiteh. He had crossed illegally to Turkey
and back a number of times and was only too glad to help
out a friend of Hamid's. Any time I needed to escape, he said,
he would arrange it. But about three months after I met him,
not long after my second marriage, I read in the paper that he

had been caught by the Komiteh while hiding out in the city. A neighbour had tipped off the authorities, and although he had made a valiant dash when he saw them coming, he was wounded and captured. After being tortured and refusing to the end to recant in public, he was shot.

In May 1982 I turned to my father for help. If we were to escape through Turkey, we would have to pass through the daunting, snow-capped Zagros Mountains along the border, where the rebellious Kurds held control of the passes and of hundreds of small villages scattered amongst the high hills. The rolling plains of Azerbaijan, the region where my father's family had been so influential, rise into that mountainous border region. Surely, my father would know someone with connections to the Kurds in the mountains.

Talking about such matters on the telephone was dangerous. When I called my father in Sabbalon, I spoke in code.

"It's time you visited your daughter to talk about family matters," I told him. He promised to be in town the following week.

Understanding well from previous conversations what I needed, he arrived with the name of a good contact: a former senator in the Shah's government who, like my father, had been a major landowner and was now having to find other ways of making money. He had hit on the perfect business— the smuggling of human cargo — and was now getting even richer, thanks to his old contacts with the Kurds who once farmed for him. He charged high fees merely for an introduction to the Kurds who were prepared to lead the way safely through the dangerous mountain route into Turkey.

The Kurds did not want the money for luxuries: they lived a simple life raising goats and making yoghurt and cheese. But they needed to finance their long, and so far fruitless, struggle for autonomy.

With my father at my side, I visited the landowner, Marjani, at his opulent apartment in Teheran. We sat in a waiting room while he finished with a group of people who were without doubt on the same quest. The smuggling business had become as regimented as a dentist's practice. When he finally received us, Marjani turned out to be a gregarious man—bald, rotund and cheerful — with a fine taste in clothing.

"Get you out of Iran?" he boomed happily, obviously unconcerned about untrustworthy ears as an ancient servant came in with tea. "No trouble at all. I will arrange everything with a Kurd I know and you'll get VIP treatment all the way. You'll be in Turkey within the day and in Istanbul the following morning. You can even go straight on to Paris that same day. Nothing to stop you."

He made it all sound so easy—at a cost of $6,000 per adult and $3,000 for Farhad ("We normally charge full fare, but as a favour to your father . . ."). Kamal gladly paid. I had almost no cash left, and now that I had remarried, no property left to sell. I certainly could not hope to liquidate any properties belonging to Farhad. We would have to make do with what I had already managed to smuggle out.

"There is one problem," I said, breaking into his confident recital of our escape. "I can't go by the smugglers' schedule. I know they always call at the last minute and expect you to be ready to go, but I have to wait for a weekend when I can have my son with me. I'm having trouble getting him at all, even for visits, so first I have to find some way to take him away from my in-laws. I'm not going without him."

"That's fine," he said expansively. "For you, we'll make an exception. Let us know when you're ready to go and we'll do it that day. We'll be on standby, and if you have to cancel the plans, we'll just wait for another weekend. I'll make the exception for your father's sake."

We set the date tentatively for two weeks thence, and Kamal and I began the mad scramble to be ready in time. We were to be joined on our trip by an old friend of my family, Shery. Some time before, she had told me that should I make a dash for Turkey, she wanted to accompany me. Shery's sin, according to the new rulers, was that her schools for the disabled had been a favourite charity of the Shah's wife, the Shahbanou Farah Diba. Once Khomeini took over, the state had disbanded Shery's schools, claiming that she must have been corrupt to have received money from the Pahlavi Foundation, a fund set up by the Shah for charitable works, which his critics said was used to enrich the Shah, his family and friends. Ever since, Shery had been living in hiding with her sister in Teheran, while the Komiteh periodically inquired about her at her old home.

Both Kamal and Shery had to sell their houses in that two-week period and convert their funds into transportable assets — in Kamal's case, some old stamps his cousin was arranging to buy. I collected what remained of my valuables. On one of my early trips back to my house when I first went on the run, I had been smart enough to take with me a pouch containing all the jewellery I had not already sold or sent out with Paul in his diplomatic pouch. The Italian smuggler who had taken my carpets had also carried out three fur coats and other clothing. Thanks to Dara, whatever valuables I had managed to send out to the free world were sitting safely in a safety deposit box in Western Europe.

The two weeks sped past. Dozens of newly rich Iranians came to inspect Kamal's house. The rest of the time was spent making arrangements to buy foreign currency on the black market (we finally decided to let Marjani buy whatever currency he could for us), saying goodbye quietly to relatives who were not to know that it was the last farewell — and trying desperately to get a visa to any country willing to take us in temporarily after Turkey.

Getting a visa was almost impossible in the new Iran. By now, most foreign countries, with the exception of Turkey and Spain, demanded that Iranians produce a visa for entry. But the state had ruled that unless an Iranian had proper exit papers, provided by the Komiteh, embassies were not to grant them visas. That meant that anyone in trouble with the state had little chance of getting a visa. Because of that, there were already thousands of Iranians languishing in Turkey while they waited for another country to permit them to settle down permanently. We had decided that it would be best to live in Paris: Farhad had an apartment there and Kamal's parents lived there. And now, somehow, we had to get a visa before we, too, became stranded in Turkey.

I was the major hitch. Even though the police had let me go and the *mullah* had stopped trying to find me, the Komiteh still had a warrant out for my arrest, and on the night she was arrested, Anna had heard that a photo of Farhad and me was on display in a Komiteh headquarters. The incredible chaos of the Iranian justice system had allowed me to slip away from one arm while another was still trying to grasp hold of me. But for me to go and simply request a legal exit document was far too risky.

It so happened that a French businessman, a friend of Kamal's parents, was coming through Teheran, bringing new instructions from them about how Kamal was to conduct the construction company. When we met him, I prodded Kamal to ask him if he could help us get a visa. The only way would be for a connection within a Western European embassy to slip me one without asking questions about my exit documents.

"It's odd you should ask me," he said. "I sat next to an ambassador on the plane coming in, and he said he was only too glad to help Iranians wanting to get out. I'm sure he would give you a visa. I became rather friendly with him. I'll call him and ask him to see you."

While we were waiting to hear back, I was frantically trying to fit the last — and most crucial — piece into place. Before I could escape, I had to arrange to have Farhad for the weekend. Not only did I have to succeed in getting him for the usual six hours on a Friday that the Aminis permitted, I had to make them agree to give him to me the previous Thursday night, as well. The smugglers would come to pick us up at 6:00 A.M. on Friday. I tried asking the Aminis to allow him to attend a special friend's birthday party on Thursday night, but my mother-in-law said, "He's not going to have his routine disturbed just because you want to take him to a party."

In desperation I turned to my lawyer, who was one of the few aware of my escape plans. He came up with the solution.

"We are going to serve them with notice that we are going to take legal action against them as guardians of his money and property. That should shake them up a little. We'll see if we can pry your son out of them that way."

He was right. As soon as the papers were served, three days before we were to leave, I received a call from Jamshid. The Aminis were worried. Up until now I had not fought them in any way. I had been the perfect Persian woman and had let them walk all over me.

"Sousan, what is this silly thing you are doing?" he said. "Surely we can work things out without going to court and spending a lot of money on lawyers? We don't want the Komiteh to notice us too much, do we? Look, you say you want to take him to his friend's birthday party. I'm sure I can talk them into giving him to you for the weekend if you'd just sign a document saying that you withdraw the charges against the guardians."

"Fine, I'll do that on Saturday. But first I want my son."

By Saturday, God willing, I would be gone. Now that I had them on the run, there was no way I was going to stop the action — even if I was out of the country.

"You'll have your son. I'll call you," he said. I began my wait.

By now it was Wednesday, two days before we were to leave. I still did not have Farhad, Kamal and Shery had not sold their houses and we did not yet have visas. The strain was showing. I couldn't sleep or eat. In ten days, I lost ten pounds. It seemed as if we would never meet the deadline. Quietly I made up my mind that if the Aminis loosened their grip on Farhad for the weekend I would leave even if we did not have visas, even if Kamal and Shery had not succeeded in selling their houses. If I got Farhad this time, there would not be another chance.

That morning we heard from the Frenchman that everything was set up. We were simply to go to the embassy — and he named the nationality of the helpful embassy — and pick up our visas. When I went there, I saw the long line-up of people that was typical now outside all the foreign embassies. If I waited in line, I might not make it into the embassy before the noon-hour closing time. Taking courage, I walked up to the guard at the entrance and explained that I was there to see the ambassador. I was motioned inside to a reception area, where another line-up had formed.

Once again I asked a secretary if I could see the ambassador, and she asked me to join the end of the queue. After I had waited half an hour, a woman called my name. I cringed at the sound of it and felt very exposed. What if a Khomeini spy were in the waiting room? Spies were said to be posted at all embassies to check on who was trying to leave the country.

I rushed up to the woman who stood behind a protected counter. She demanded loudly, "May I have your documents, please."

I was stunned. The embassy was supposed to know that I did not have any documents. I made a show of looking for them in my purse. "I have them here somewhere, I am sure," I said for the benefit of anyone who might be listening.

The woman, a greying, middle-aged Iranian, became impatient. "Well, do you have them? I can't issue you a visa without them."

"I must have forgotten them at home," I said lamely.

"You'll have to come back, then. Next."

I stood absolutely still for a moment: I had just lost our last opportunity to get a visa before leaving the country. The embassy would be open for only a couple of hours the next day, Thursday, and on Friday we were to go. I had to either get the visas now or face a months-long wait in Turkey for some country to be kind enough to grant us entry. I spotted another secretary walking through the reception area towards the door leading to the guarded section of the offices. Aware of the risk I was taking, I stopped her and in hushed tones explained why I had come.

After telling me to wait, she disappeared behind the door. Again I waited, another twenty minutes, all the while expecting the Komiteh to appear, until another secretary came and demanded to know my circumstances all over again. Every time I repeated my request — visas without documentation for three people — I felt more and more exposed in that crowded waiting room. I began to suspect that the Frenchman had never spoken to the ambassador — or else why would the papers not be ready?

As the closing hour approached, I again walked up to the security door and knocked. The same lady who had originally sent me away peered out at me, cautious, even scared when she recognized me.

"Who are you? What are you still doing here? I sent you away."

I rushed to calm her down. I knew what she must be thinking—that I was a terrorist or one of Khomeini's people come to make trouble.

"I don't mean any harm," I said in a whisper. "I've come because the ambassador has promised to give me a visa and I am escaping from Iran Friday morning with my small son. Help me, I beg you."

In an instant, the frightened, angry expression on her face changed to one of sympathy. She opened the door farther and grabbed hold of my arms: "My dear woman, come in here and sit down. We'll take care of everything."

Immediately she produced papers for me to sign, then

instructed me to return the following morning when the visas would be ready.

That night my father arrived from Azerbaijan to say a final goodbye. I had called him a few days before and passed on a coded message.

"Your daughter is ill."

"Is it critical? I was planning to visit next month."

"I think she will need an operation this weekend."

"I'll be right down, then."

We all met in Kamal's house that night — my father, Kamal and my cousin Fariba. Everyone thought I had taken too many risks at the embassy.

"It could just be a trap," said Kamal. "You might find the Komiteh waiting for you tomorrow morning. Don't go."

But I had to. I did not want to live with Farhad for months in Turkey wondering which country we would be able to call home. On Thursday morning, the day before our departure, I still had no word on whether I would have Farhad that afternoon. Kamal and Shery had not sold their houses, although some buyers had expressed interest. When I walked up to the embassy, I fully expected men in army fatigues, carrying automatic rifles, to jump out and arrest me.

But when the same embassy woman saw me she hurriedly took me into the office area and handed over the three precious visas. She hugged me again: "God bless you. Have a safe journey to the other side."

I left quickly, not looking back, but I shall always remember the bravery of that woman in trusting me. Such trust in a country when you could hardly be sure of anyone — not servants, children, relatives or friends — was rare and courageous.

It was noon when I arrived at Kamal's house. He was excited and nervous. He had found a buyer for his house but they were bickering over the price. He would not know until later in the day if the sale was going to proceed. We had already sold all the expensive antiques in the house, and his cousin was on standby with a collection of old Persian stamps to make a swap quickly once the money for the house came through. When Shery called shortly afterwards, she was in a similar situation — an interested buyer but nothing absolutely certain.

After packing the rest of our belongings into the two small bags that Farhad, Kamal and I were permitted to take on the journey, I checked once again that I had hidden well my remaining jewellery. I had carefully sewn my gold necklaces, bracelets and earrings, my diamond pendants and earrings, my strands of pearls into every item of clothing that I was taking with me: my belt, the collar of my shirt, the hem of a skirt, the shoulder pads of my light jacket. I searched out, especially, the turquoise ring that my grandmother Roghieh had handed down to me. I prayed to her to give me luck.

All afternoon there was no word from Jamshid. Perhaps, after all, I would not be leaving. Then, at about 4:00 P.M., the phone rang. It was Jamshid, sounding pleased with himself.

"The Aminis have agreed. You can pick Farhad up at 5:00 P.M. You see, they are capable of being reasonable," he purred.

It was hard not to cheer out loud. I thanked him politely and hung up.

We had arranged to spend our last night in Teheran in my cousin Fariba's house because with any luck Kamal's house would be sold by then. Now I took a moment to have one last, lingering look at the house that had been my home for only a few weeks, a beautiful jewel of a mansion, white and delicate with its mouldings and patios. I knew that no matter what happened, I would not return, nor would I ever lead again the life of beauty and ease that I had led there. At 4:45 P.M., I went out to the street and hailed a public taxi—I avoided taking a private taxi because I didn't want my movements to be traced later when many would be searching for me. When I arrived at the Aminis', Farhad was waiting outside the front door. His aunt stood beside him. I said goodbye to her and then just scooped him up, put him in the cab and drove off. I did not look back.

I kissed Farhad over and over again.

Puzzled, he asked, "Is there anything wrong, Mummy?"

Until we were safely away, I did not dare tell him of my escape plan in case the Aminis found us and forced him to give us away. The taxi dropped us off several blocks away from Fariba's house — so that we would not put her in jeopardy — and we walked the rest of the way there, our arms swinging with happiness.

Apart from my father, Fariba and her husband, no one knew where we were that night. It was too dangerous for my uncles and aunts to visit us, and we said our goodbyes on the phone, careful not to talk too explicitly. Eventually, Kamal called with wonderful news: he had sold his house. Just fifteen minutes later, Shery called and said, "The patient has been cured." She, too, had sold her house. Later they told me that they had accepted much less than the asking price, just to be rid of their properties. But at least the last obstacles were gone.

Chapter Twelve

Escape on Horseback

O Traveler, strike and fold the tents of dawn:
Already from this caravanserai the scout moves on.

MANŪCHERĪ

 Our last night in Teheran was one of long and sad goodbyes. When we woke early the following morning, we made haste in hushed voices. Marjani and the Kurd arrived on schedule, announcing themselves with a light tap at the front door. They made an odd pair: the short, stocky former politician wearing a casual, pearl-grey suit, and the Kurd, tall, gaunt, his skin burnished from a life spent on horseback in the northern mountains, where he was a chieftain. We were never told the Kurd's name, and he said little all the time we were with him. By six o'clock

on that July 4 morning, we had already left Fariba's house —
after she had checked to make certain that there was no one
around to mark our departure. Marjani, at the wheel of his
Range Rover, guided us through the almost-deserted sidestreets of the city. It was a tense quiet, not the early morning
peace we had once known. In the distance we saw the occasional prowling Komiteh car. The few pedestrians we encountered looked up in fear and then looked quickly away
when we passed. But before leaving the city, we had to make
a lengthy and dangerous detour to Marjani's home to pick up
the German marks he had absent-mindedly left behind. As
we wove through the backroads of the city, I worried that
our escape would be aborted before we ever made it to the
highway.

But no one took an interest in our early morning movements, and we arrived at Shery's place safely. By 7:00 A.M.
we were on our way out of the city, on the highway leading
northwest, towards Azerbaijan. We knew almost nothing of
the escape plan. Our lives were in the hands of two men we
barely knew.

The seven-hundred-kilometre drive to Tabriz, the old capital
of the Mongolian and Qajar empires, was uneventful. We
passed a few checkpoints, but our story that we were going
to visit relatives in the country was plausible enough. Because
the highway served a number of large communities and was
well travelled, the guards at the checkpoints gave the car only a
cursory search and waved us on our way. Beyond Tabriz we
expected the situation to be tenser. Everyone, including the
Komiteh, knew that the favourite escape route was through
Azerbaijan, over the rugged four-hundred-kilometre-wide
Zagros range. There was only one road out of Tabriz in the
general direction of the border. Tabriz was a highly religious
centre, where the streets were full of women bobbing under
flowing *chadors*, and about an hour from the city Shery put
her *chador* back on and I pulled out one I had packed for a
moment such as this.

Our first indication that the trip would not be as easy as Marjani had promised came when we arrived at the outskirts of the city.

"This is where we leave you and you change cars," Marjani announced. "It's too dangerous for us to proceed beyond this point." Then, reaching down into the car, he pulled out a big box. "Here are your passports and your foreign currency."

"What do you mean?" Kamal demanded. "Those are supposed to be waiting for us on the other side of the Turkish border. You yourself said we should not be found travelling with this stuff."

But we had no time to argue. With a great deal of jostling, Marjani attempted to push us into a waiting Paycan. As he did so, the box fell open and all the money fluttered about.

"This is dangerous," he yelled. "Pick up the money quick and get moving."

We rushed to gather up the bills—about $13,000 in Turkish lire and German marks. Then, still objecting, we piled into the car and our new driver sped off, giving us no time to understand what was happening. The city was a minefield. Checkpoints seemed to jump up at every turn. Fortunately the driver was a local who knew his way around them.

"We can't go on like this," Kamal kept arguing. "We have to go back. They were supposed to take us all the way to the border and now suddenly, they change cars and hand us our passports."

The driver was equally nervous. "I've told these people I won't work for them anymore if they continue to do this. I'm risking my life having these passports and money. I've got a wife and a small child."

For about twenty minutes, weaving through sidestreets of the dusty, crowded city, we deliberated.

The driver kept yelling, "Stuff the money in your clothes. They won't see it under the *chador*."

Frantically we tried, but the money was so bulky that I could not zip up my trousers and we gave up on the idea. Luckily, we made it safely out of the city, but we were only slightly relieved because we knew we still had to decide what to do. For me to go back now meant losing Farhad forever. And yet I could not insist that the others risk their lives on my behalf. I said little and prayed they would choose to continue.

On the highway leading out of the city, the driver suddenly noticed a Mercedes approaching from behind at a fast pace, guns protruding from the windows on either side.

"My God, they've followed us," he said, almost fainting at the wheel. He slowed down sharply.

"Don't slow down. They'll notice us more if you do," I yelled, but there was no way to make him speed up. He pulled over to the side, panting as if out of breath. The Mercedes, the latest model, sailed past. A couple of bearded men, obviously Komiteh, glanced back at us with little interest.

After the danger had passed, our driver pulled over onto a small sideroad leading to the entrance of an orchard and there we sat, discussing our future. At first, Kamal was all for going back. The ride through the city had shaken him and he was becoming increasingly irritated that Marjani had not delivered what he had promised. Still only newly married to him, I was beginning to notice how extreme was the punctiliousness he must have acquired as a civil servant. He did not like deviations from set plans. Shery was calmer, advising caution, but was prepared to take some risks and make adjustments if necessary. I thanked God for her reassuring presence.

Where could we safely store the money and passports? After checking the muffler and every part of the engine for space, Kamal hit on the idea of pulling apart the back seat and stuffing the money, now stashed in a burlap bag we had brought with us, between the springs. The bills safely hidden, we put the seat cover back on. It seemed the perfect place for our damning evidence should we be stopped at the checkpoints. To my great relief, the group decided to go on. The Aminis were expecting Farhad back that afternoon, and it was now already about 2:00 P.M. The border was still four hours away.

Marjani had told us that we would be driven to a point very close to the border; then we would have a three-hour horse ride over the mountains and across the border. On the other side, a car would be waiting to take us to Istanbul. It had sounded so easy. But I was beginning to sense that Marjani had not been completely truthful. No wonder he was — and, to my knowledge, still is — such a successful smuggler. He made sure that all the risks were taken by his clients. What other surprises would be in store for us?

Still scared about being caught with us in his car, the driver told us that we would meet the next contact just outside of Shahpur, a small town about fifty kilometres northwest of Rezayeh and the last major habitation before the border. If we had been leaving legally, he would then have driven us another eighteen kilometres from Shahpur and we would have been at the border crossing. But we were to turn off the highway onto a smaller road that was heavily patrolled by the Komiteh. We were to be at that junction at exactly 7:00 P.M. We made such good time on the highway that we had to stop at a café for tea just to slow down our pace. Due to the driver's skill, we were questioned only once. He contrived to reach the checkpoints when the guards were facing the Holy City of Mecca, a thousand miles away in Saudi Arabia, for one of the day's five prayer sessions, or when a long line of cars forced them to wave us on. Once he hid behind a large transport truck. At the last minute, while the guards were busy with the truck, he whisked past, waving to the guards as if he had been cleared.

At the café, while we were gratefully drinking our tea, a policeman pulled up and joined us at our outdoor table. We could barely be civil, but our driver spoke to him amicably, and the policeman smiled and nodded at us from time to time. I hid deeper and deeper in my *chador*, afraid that he might recognize me from posters. But the policeman left without incident. When we went to pay our bills, we found that he had paid for our tea.

Safely back in the car, we asked the driver who the man was.

"He's a friend of mine," he laughed. "He knows I'm smuggling you out. He just wanted to wish you luck." Such gestures are what I prefer to remember of my last hours in Iran.

Throughout the day, Farhad had not asked us a single question. He must have realized that we were not really going to his grandfather's village for a picnic, but something about our furtiveness must have told him it was better not to ask. It was typical of him that in times of stress, he became quiet and introverted, accepting everything that happened without comment. For hours, he stared wordlessly out the window, watching the orchards, fields of wheat and red, mud-brick villages flying past.

At the fork just beyond Shahpur, a man was to be standing if it was risky to proceed. As we approached we strained to make out the figure of a man standing in the shadow of a clump of trees. But there was no one. We turned onto the sideroad and finally came to a stop next to a walled orchard. Straight ahead of us was a shallow but fast-flowing river. It was a dead end.

"We're here," the driver said.

But where was our contact? I had expected to see five tall, heavily armed Kurds, and their horses, ready to carry us across the border. The driver seemed nervous, and we began to suspect a trap. What better place than at a dead end? After a few minutes we noticed that a couple of men were working at a nearby *qanat* — probably changing the direction of the water to irrigate the fields. Were they Komiteh in disguise? Or were they robbers?

"All of you start moving towards the river," Kamal suggested. "Take the suitcases. I'll get the money out." If it came to it, we would have to make a run for it across the water.

Shery and I took off our *chadors* — they would only en-
cumber us now. Impatient with the wait, the driver went off
in search of the Kurds, and in a while we saw him approaching with two men. We picked up our bags, tensed and ready
to run. The workers at the *qanat* looked up in our direction.
But the newcomers turned out to be our contacts. The contingent of Kurds that was to take us to safety consisted of
two young boys — teenagers by the looks of them — dressed
in dark trousers and sweaters. Despite their youth, they quickly took charge of us and led us to the river's edge. They took
turns carrying us across the water so that we would not get
wet. When we got to the other side, one of the Kurds said,
"You won't be able to carry your bags and your purses, so
give them to me." And without another word, he grabbed
hold of them and ran off into a nearby field of wheat.

"I have everything in that purse. Be careful," I yelled at
him as he ran off. I was full of misgivings. Kamal had not yet
crossed the river. Shery, Farhad and I were alone on the edge
of the river. I was so relieved when I finally saw Kamal being
ferried across. We all held hands, met up with the first fellow
and started running across the huge field of wheat. Although
it was already past 8:00 P.M., there was still plenty of summer
light and the field was surrounded on three sides by higher
ground, from which we were easily visible. Our guides kept
cautioning us to bend down so that our heads would not be
above the wheat stalks. We had dressed in city shoes under
instruction from Marjani, who had said that walking boots or
shoes would be suspicious if we were stopped. As a result,
we were not prepared for a fast run through a field rutted
with animal holes and full of prickly thistles. We tripped and
fell repeatedly, but the two men refused to stop.

"How far is it?" I kept asking.

"Just a few more minutes to the horses, just a few more
steps," they answered. Throughout our entire trip Shery and I
had to do most of the talking because our only common
language with the Kurds was Turkish, and Kamal and Farhad

did not speak it. Those few minutes stretched into almost three hours of running in a bent position, all the time wondering if we would be shot at from behind. At one point, when I was close to Kamal, I whispered to him about the strange behaviour of the Kurd who had run off with my purse. "As soon as we stop, I'm going to check my purse to make sure nothing is missing."

It was dark when we reached the edge of the field where the ground began to rise up towards the mountains.

"We're here," one of the guides said. Again, there was no one in sight. We felt terribly vulnerable sitting on the ground under a stout chestnut tree in the middle of nowhere with night approaching. The two Kurds asked us if we had anything to eat and, as reluctant as I was to share the little food we had left, I had no choice but to offer them some of our precious sandwiches.

After about half an hour, we heard the rustling, clumping sound of horses approaching and, in the gloom, we could make out three men on horseback. Dressed in traditional Kurdish clothes — large, blousy shirts, baggy trousers and waistbands, with large, colourful jackets worn on top—they better suited my image of the men who would be strong enough to lead us to freedom. Without so much as a greeting, one of them hauled me and Farhad onto his horse; the second took Shery, while the third helped Kamal up. Still without a word, we rode off at a gallop while the two younger Kurds ran alongside. They took a route parallel to the western edge of the town of Shahpur, which twinkled down below, but after a while the Kurds yelled something at each other in their own language and switched direction, sharply speeding up as if running away from some danger.

"What's going on? What's happening?" I asked vainly, speaking into my rider's back.

I looked around and could see no sign of Kamal. He and his rider had disappeared into the night. "Where is my husband? Stop until he catches up."

"Don't worry, he'll catch up," my rider said tersely, but I had little cause to trust him. Were they trying to separate the three of us from the only man in the group before robbing us? After about half an hour, Kamal and his rider came up behind us, and I was momentarily relieved. But I kept pestering them to tell us where the car was. My rider said, "Soon, soon. Just a little further." We rode at a fast pace for four and a half hours, without saddle, on a track we could barely make out in the starlight, climbing higher and higher. I could already feel my bones and muscles aching terribly.

"We have to be out of Iran by tonight," I insisted. "We can't stay here even one more night."

But they said nothing until we approached a Kurdish village high in the mountains and they told us to dismount.

"We can't take the horses any closer," one of the Kurds said. "We don't want the villagers to hear us."

Again they took our hands and ran with us through darkened fields and into narrow alleyways in the village until we came to the low entrance of a small, mud hut. They knocked lightly and then, without a word, pushed us inside. It took a few moments for our eyes to adjust to the smoky gloom. In a large room which was both a kitchen and a bedroom I saw six men sitting smoking cigarettes. A woman who was boiling water for tea over a small fire looked up and smiled. They made a place for us to sit down and asked us to join them for a hot drink. As my eyes began to pick out the subtleties of greys and shadows in the room, I noticed that there were more like fifteen people, all warming themselves in that crowded hut.

I began to take stock of our situation. The Kurds are a handsome people — generally tall, slim, with high cheekbones and thick hair. The greenness of their eyes adds to their startling beauty. The women are festooned with all the gold the family owns — in fact, jewellery is usually the only thing of value the family owns apart from its animals. Kurds prefer portable assets. The women wear several dresses, one on top of the other, and hitch up their flowered skirts into a tight band on their waists, accentuating their slimness and litheness. The group seemed friendly enough and much more relaxed than we were. We gladly accepted the tea and began to chat with them.

An older Kurdish man explained the situation to us. "You have to spend the rest of the night in the village, but you can only sleep here for a couple of hours. Then we will have to move you to just outside the village. We can't trust anyone now. Khomeini has set up a special armed group that patrols this area. They come to the village and actually pay Kurds to spy on each other."

The news of a move terrified me. I knew the Azerbaijan hills and the many poisonous snakes that lived there.

"You can't just leave us out in the open like that," I protested. "It's so cold this high up and we'll be in danger all the time from the snakes."

The men seemed to consider the problem for a while and then after consultation another of them said, "I am ashamed to tell you the only thing we have is our stable. You would be safe in there."

I gratefully accepted the offer. After we turned down their invitation to eat with them, the Kurdish woman put out a small blanket for us to sleep on the we settled down. I checked my purse and most of the Turkish lire were missing. When I told Kamal, he wanted to get up and confront the young Kurd who had probably stolen the money, but I begged, "Don't do such a foolish thing. It's just money. We'll be lucky to get out of this alive."

We were so tired that soon Kamal, Shery and Farhad were sleeping soundly, but I kept a wary eye on the rest of the Kurds who were also settling down to sleep. Fatigue proved to be an even stronger master than fear, however, because eventually, I, too, slipped into an uneasy sleep.

Just two hours later they woke the four of us and led us out into a moonless night. Dizzy with exhaustion, we made our way to the stable, a couple of miles outside the village. Morning was just tinging the horizon with light when we got there and we could see how elementary our temporary lodging would be. The stable consisted of one room packed full of dried dung patties with just a hole in the ground for a toilet. Another very small clearing with a rough, dirty blanket made a bed for us all. We slept until 8:00 A.M., while two Kurds kept watch over us, and we were awakened by the Kurdish woman of the previous night and two younger girls, evidently her daughters. They smiled and nodded, unable to speak to us in our language, and offered us hot tea, yoghurt, cheese and bread, all freshly made, and the flask of water that I had requested. But we were all dismayed to hear that we would have to spend the entire day in the stable.

"You will not be able to leave even once, not even to poke your head out," one of the men said. "You must keep talk to a minimum and whisper. Don't let the child make any noise. The villagers don't normally come here, but if they hear something suspicious, they may come to check it out."

"But what about the car? We were supposed to have a car," I repeated as if asking for one would get me one. "If I don't leave Iran, they'll come looking for me."

By now the Aminis would be marshalling all their friends and connections to search for Farhad. They would have found out Kamal's address, perhaps through Jamshid, and discovered the house was sold. With that, they would have gone to the Komiteh who would have put out a bulletin asking all posts to keep watch for me and Farhad. And we were supposed to have been out of the country when all that happened.

"Don't worry," the Kurd said. "No one can find you here. The car is not too far away at the border. We can't go until it gets dark."

After trying unsuccessfully to glean more information from him, we set about to pass the time. Shery even took pictures of the women because they had never been photographed before. Occasionally we peeked through the wooden slats of the door. Outside was a magnificent blue day. The lush, green fields were patterned with delicate wildflowers and even from our closed-in perch we had a magnificent vista of hills and valleys. The brightness of the day contrasted sharply with the darkness of our refuge. The sight of such beauty beyond my reach made me feel even more a prisoner.

Throughout the day, various Kurds came to confer with the smugglers, including a friendly young man who talked to us for hours in Turkish. Kamal, who did not understand the language, paced restlessly, smoking cigarettes one after another and complaining about the long delay. Farhad enjoyed the exuberance of the storytelling, even if he missed the actual meaning, and he sat enthralled, watching the young man's performance. The Kurd was squatting happily on the floor, recounting some fighting exploit against Khomeini's forces, when a woman burst through the door and grabbed him by the arm.

"The Komiteh has come to the village. They're asking for you."

The young Kurd explained to us that the villagers were dependent on the government for food coupons. But in order to get the coupons, they had to give the local Komiteh their birth certificates. "They use the certificates to keep an eye on us. We needed the food, so I let my family give them my card. But now they know I am old enough to go to war and they want to know why I am not fighting at the Iraqi front."

Evidently used to dodging the Komiteh, he decided to spend the rest of the day in the hut with us until the revolutionary committee men left. I could not believe that we had come so far only to be caught because of someone else on the run. All we could do was wait. After four interminable hours, during which the Komiteh searched the dozen or so houses in the village but ignored our humble stable, the same woman returned to tell us that the guards had finally left.

As soon as it was dark, true to their word, the Kurds we had met in the village came to lead us to where the horses were tethered. Already the night air was chill and, seeing us in our thin summer clothes, the older Kurds took off their huge jackets and threw them over us. We hugged and kissed and they wished us a safe journey. Not long after we set off, a heavy rain began to fall, and within minutes we were soaked. We ran for half an hour, most of it uphill, and I could hear Shery panting as she tried to keep up with us. We blessed the gifts of those Kurds and we promised to send the jackets back with the riders. At the meeting place were three men with three horses waiting for us. Again, Farhad and I mounted together on one horse with its rider, my son on the neck, I on the back, the two most uncomfortable positions on the horse. Because our horse was also carrying our bags, my legs were spread over them in a strained position. We set out for what turned out to be a four-hour ride at full gallop. I have no idea how the Kurds were able to make their way in the deep darkness. They seemed to sense the way ahead, rather than see it. The ride was a nightmare for all of us. Farhad was in such pain from the pounding that he kept begging me to let him off the horse.

My rider warned, "Shut him up. Voices travel in the mountains. Shut him up or I will."

I tried to calm Farhad even though my own body felt lacerated.

Occasionally, in the darkness, I could hear Kamal complaining. "We have to stop. My ulcers. My stomach. I am going to be sick. Let me off. My legs have gone numb."

Shery said nothing, but I knew she must be suffering, a woman of sixty who had a history of ailments.

"We can't stop. Move it," was all the Kurds usually said. Occasionally, to shut me up, one of them would say, "The car is nearby. Just a few minutes more." At one point, our horse threw his head back and hit Farhad full on the nose. He started to scream in pain and the rider just clamped his arm over Farhad's mouth and said, "I told you to shut up and I meant it.'

"Farhad, please," I begged, "we'll soon be there." Farhad must have been so frightened that he did not make another sound, but occasionally I could hear a little whimper and I knew that he was quietly crying all those hours.

At about 1:30 A.M. we arrived at a spot where five more Kurds were waiting with six horses. It was so dark that we could barely see the outline of the horses, and as we got a little closer I realized that the men had wrapped their head-scarves right around their faces so that only their eyes showed.

"You're going with them," my rider said.

"What's happening? Where is our car?" I demanded.

"It's a little further up," he answered, and he just picked me off his horse and transferred me to another. With so many horses available, each rider took one of us and they gave a horse to Kamal to ride on his own because he was a man and expected to be able to ride well. But Kamal had never ridden much and he was shaking uncontrollably from the cold and complaining about the numbness in his legs.

Shery whispered to me, "We have to watch him. He might have a heart attack."

When I heard that, I felt even more devastated. I had found the contact and set up the trip. It was supposed to be so easy, and now I had endangered all our lives.

Shery and I got off our horses and started to massage Kamal from head to toe to get his circulation going. With all the concern about Kamal, we could spare no time to see to Farhad and check that his nose was not broken. The Kurds were anxious to get going and they ordered us to remount.

Unable to face another horseback ride, especially on his own, Kamal just sat down on the ground. "I'm not going," he said. "Go on without me. I'm staying here. I can't bear it anymore."

Without much ceremony, the Kurds grabbed Kamal, propped him on his horse and started off.

"He's on the best horse," my rider said. "And we're not taking chances by putting another person on that horse and maybe straining its legs."

I offered them any amount of money to put a rider on with Kamal, but the Kurds would not listen.

We made our way higher and higher into the mountains over narrow little trails that ridged sheer drops and crossed over fast-moving streams. We were wet, cold and exhausted. When I saw how sheer the steep sides of the mountain trails were, I began to press my rider to take Farhad on with us. If we were going to go tumbling down, I wanted him close to me so that I could help break his fall. After about an hour of constant complaint, my rider grabbed Farhad as he rode past and put him once again on the neck of my horse.

It was a frightening journey, plodding up and up into the mountains, the air becoming colder and colder, penetrating to our bones. Once or twice, when there was a break in the clouds revealing the stars, I caught sight of Kamal lurching along and I could see that he had fallen asleep from exhaustion, almost ready to fall off to certain death. I called to him, but he turned to look at me with an unfocussed stare, then shut his eyes again. Fortunately, his horse seemed to know the way and followed the one in front. Shery and I had left our *chadors* behind with the Kurdish women in a moment of liberation — we had hoped we would never need them again — and one of the women had given Shery a Kurdish dress to wear over her trousers to keep her warm. Now those *chadors* might have been useful, but nothing we could have worn could have prepared us for such a cold, wet night, high in the Zagros.

The path zigzagged back and forth ever higher, and I tried to keep from looking down as the ground dropped sharply away into what I imagined were hidden valleys and dark gulleys, hundreds of feet below. The path was strewn with rocks that the horses stumbled over. I held on tightly to my rider, determined that if I should fall, so would he. In the middle of all that danger, when every sense had to be alert to stay alive, my rider started to rub his hand up and down my leg. I felt like hitting him, but I dared not do anything that might anger him and cause him to hurt my son and me. Instead, I gently took his hand each time and placed it back on the reins where it belonged. My anger was all the greater because I could do nothing to fight back.

At one point on that journey, three of the riders headed off towards a village that lay lower down a slope and we were left with two riders and three horses. After several hours of riding non-stop, we came across another group of five Kurds on horseback, their faces carefully covered and further obscured by the darkness, who appeared suddenly and menacingly out of nowhere. They rode alongside us for a few minutes and then dropped off. If the Kurds had planned to terrify and disorient us with such sudden appearances and disappearances, they could not have done it in a better way, because now we trusted no one. We no longer had any sense of who were our guides. We were in the hands of men with no faces, whom we could never recognize, even if we saw them again.

My rider eventually explained to me who the men were who had come and gone so eerily. "They've just taken two Iranian men over the border. We were all supposed to go over together, but we were a couple of hours late, so they went ahead."

As we continued, the terrain got rougher, and we had to dismount and walk our horses across cold streams and up muddy banks. Our jeans were stiff with mud. Every now and then I called out softly, "Farhad, are you all right? Kamal? Shery?" I would be reassured by their faint replies in the total darkness. But beyond that, we were not allowed to speak.

We rode all night, and by 6:30 A.M., when it was getting light, we looked around and saw that we were above the snow line and the ground was white. Suddenly the riders stopped and one of them said, "This is it. This is the border with Turkey."

As I looked around, I realized that I had arrived there on a different horse and with a different rider than I had started out with. Kamal was no longer even on a horse — he had walked the last half-hour. I had no idea when the changeover had taken place. I simply did not remember it. Exhaustion, confusion, shadows passing by us in the darkness—they had taken their toll on me.

The rider's words finally reached me. I jumped off the horse, picked up Farhad and hugged him until he could no longer breathe.

"We're free, Farhad, we've made it. We're out of Iran. You won't ever have to go back to the Aminis again. We're going to go and live in a free country. Nobody is going to come and arrest me anymore."

For two days and two nights, Farhad had never once asked where we were going. Perhaps he hadn't dared to hope. But now he asked, "Mummy, does that mean that I can live with you? That I don't have to go to my aunt and uncle's place anymore?"

"No, luvijun," I said, "never again. We're going to go to Europe and to America. And remember all those things I told you we would do? Like going to Disneyland and visiting all of our relatives in Canada and the United States? We're going to do all that."

How strange to be talking about Disneyland on top of a desolate, snow-covered mountain in Western Asia. But there was no time to consider the odd quality of that moment. It appeared that we were now with two Turkish Kurds: big, heavily built men, with stubbly beards and heavy frowns. Another equally difficult phase of our escape was about to begin. Contrary to all the promises made to us, now that we were at the border, tired, hungry and incredibly thirsty, there was still no car. There was no road. We were miles away from even a cart track, and now we had to slowly descend the other side of the mountain that we had climbed.

Right away a difficulty presented itself. The mud track heading down was too steep to ride on, and we had to walk the horses. As the older Turk, who seemed to be the leader, pushed ahead, he slipped and fell because the ground was so wet. Not wanting to risk a chance fall that might result in death, we sat on our bottoms and slid down single file for about half an hour. Suddenly, from behind, I heard Shery scream.

I turned to see her banging her head into her lap, hitting her head with her fists, pulling her hair and crying loudly.

"I've lost everything, everything. I'm not going on. I'm not moving anymore. Just leave me here. I don't care anymore."

After making my way carefully back up to where she sat, mud-splattered and tear-stained, I finally elicited from her what had happened. After the theft of my Turkish lire, she had put her handbag with all of her valuables in a black bag she kept constantly at her side. But because the bag did not zip up properly, somewhere along the way her wallet had fallen out. She had lost $25,000 in foreign currency — all she had — her passport and her around-the-world airline ticket. Apart from some jewellery that she had stitched into the hem of her skirt, she had lost everything she had been able to take out of Iran.

"Where can I go without a passport?" she asked. "Just leave me here."

"Don't be crazy," admonished the younger Turk. "We're right near the border. We have to move. They'll shoot us if they find us anywhere near here."

I tried to cajole Shery into continuing with us, promising that we would solve all our problems together once we got to Turkey, but she refused to budge until one of the Kurds suggested that he would go back and look for the wallet.

"There is a fresh horse waiting for us farther down the mountain, away from the border area. I will go back and find it for you. It's black. It will show up well in the snow. Now let's move."

With that promise, Shery continued to slide down the hill. We slid for another hour before, as promised, we found two fresh horses tethered to a stone on the ground. The Turk galloped back up and we continued, Kamal in a daze, saying nothing, Farhad exhausted but marvelling at our surroundings, I was so fatigued that I thought every step would be my last, and Shery . . . I looked back at her as we trudged along, her once-proud figure bent over under a filthy horse blanket one of the Turks had given her, the heels of her shoes broken and twisted into crazy angles, the Kurdish dress she was wearing muddied to the waist. At that moment, more than ever, I hated Khomeini and everything he had done to my country. Once, Shery had been internationally known for her work with the handicapped, had dined with presidents and prime ministers. She had spent a lifetime helping those who could not help themselves. And her payment had been continual harassment by Khomeini's thugs and, finally, this forced escape.

We walked in silence for about two hours. Then I heard Shery's voice softly singing a favourite song of schoolchildren in Iran: "Where are you coming from and where are you going and how will you get there," she sang over and over again.

What spirit, I thought. What incredible determination to be able to keep singing when she has lost everything and can look forward only to a future as an exile. But then I realized that she was repeating the refrain over and over again, mechanically, as if she had got stuck and could go no further. Shery was still walking, but something inside her had stopped back at the mud slide.

Eventually, the Turk who had gone off in search of Shery's

wallet came galloping past, shouting as he went, "I couldn't find it. Keep moving. I'm going on to tell them to get the car ready for you."

Shery and I exchanged a long, empty look. "He has found it. I know it. And now he is going to rob me." She said it without anger, with only a dead acceptance.

There was nothing I could say because I knew she was probably right and yet what could we do? If the Turkish Kurds chose to abandon us, we might be lost for days on the mountains.

As tired as I was, I could not help but notice the beauty of nature all around us: the hills covered with yellow and purple flowers, their breathtaking fragrance everywhere.

After a while, we reached a small plateau from which we could see a village below. "We wait here," the Turk said. "This is where the car is going to come. A couple of Iranian men are coming, too."

"What do you mean, the car is going to come?" I asked in exasperation. "There isn't even a road. We're on top of a mountain. How do you expect to get a car here?"

He shook his head mulishly. "It's coming. You have to give me all your bags. I'm going to hide them under some hay. You have to lie down so that the villagers don't see us."

By now it was morning, about 9:00 A.M., and far below we could make out signs of movement: farmers walking in the fields, shepherds wandering with their flocks, plumes of smoke rising lazily from miniature mud huts. The air was still chill and damp, even though the sun was breaking through the early morning haze. We bundled ourselves up close together to share our warmth, the horse blanket our only protection from the cold ground. Suspecting further treachery from our guide, I found an excuse to gather our bags and move them right beside us instead of near where the Turk was keeping watch a little farther down. Soon he ordered us to change our position and we walked over a ridge so that now we could look over into another valley, hidden by a low, makeshift, stone wall that the smugglers had obviously rigged to protect their cargo from the eyes of villagers below. Twice a bruising cold mountain rain fell heavily on us, and we had to lift our blanket off the ground and use it as a covering. After waiting, cramped and cold, for four hours, I finally rebelled.

"Look. We're tired, cold, hungry and thirsty. We haven't slept properly in almost three days. We haven't eaten in eighteen hours. We want to go down to the village and wait for the car there."

"No," he shouted angrily. "We're smugglers. It's risky for us to go down there. Just wait. There will be a car soon." Relenting a little, he added, "When the other man gets back, I'll send him to get some water."

After we had waited for what seemed like hours, the other Turk returned, offering no explanation for his dash past us or where the promised car might be. But he did go to get us water. The Kurds drank first, using a dirty, chipped metal cup which they then passed on to me. I was too thirsty to be squeamish. My lips were cracked and my tongue felt swollen from lack of fluids. I held the water in my mouth, savouring the taste and feel of the cool mountain water. No matter how much I drank I could not get rid of my thirst.

I began to suspect that the car did not exist, that it had, in fact, never existed. With a sun offering feeble warmth, I took off Farhad's shoes, socks and trousers and spread them out on the ground in an effort to get them dry. I coaxed Shery and Kamal to do the same. Both had fallen into a stupor and seemed incapable of doing anything for themselves. After a while, Kamal and Farhad fell asleep while Shery and I kept a nervous vigil. As I watched Farhad, I could see his little body twitching, whether with cold or fear I could not tell. Then a sweat formed on his face and he started to roll around fitfully as if in pain. With a start, he sat up, his eyes open but not seeing. He started to cry out, "I don't want to go on the horse. Don't make me go on the horse. I don't want to. My feet hurt. Leave me alone. Leave me alone." His screams echoed on the hillsides and I could see the two Turks look nervously around, but I was afraid to wake Farhad up too rudely. I wetted a cloth in the water, applied it gently to his forehead and spoke softly.

"Farhad, luvijun. You're not on the horse anymore. You're just having a bad dream. Soon you'll wake up and you'll see there is no horse. You're here beside me."

Shery leaned over and said, "It's best not to wake him. Let him get it out of his system. He's overtired." Together we bathed his face, and after crying uncontrollably for a while, he again fell into a deep sleep.

As the morning and then the afternoon wore on, I became increasingly frightened. Why were they stalling? Were they just going to wait for nightfall and then kill us and rob us? Far below I could make out a road. Why weren't they taking us there? Soon it would be dark and we were in no shape to spend another night without food or good protective clothing in below-freezing temperatures. Our last hope was to get down to that road before nightfall.

After a quiet discussion within our group, I announced to the two men, "If you have no intention of taking us down, we're going down ourselves. We're not waiting for you anymore."

When they saw how determined we were — even Kamal was somewhat revived—the Turks became agitated. "All right. All right. Wait for a moment," the leader yelled. The other grabbed our bags and strapped them onto the horses. As we began our descent, thick clouds again rolled in and showered the mountains. With the renewed rain, the farmers out in the fields headed back into the village and our guides again became nervous.

"We can't go down this way," the leader said. "We have to go back up a little. There is a cave. We can wait there for a while until the villagers have gone home. Then we'll move again."

When we had settled in the small cave that barely held us, Shery noticed that Kamal was shivering badly. Once again we massaged him vigorously. Kamal was barely able to talk, but he did make a few attempts to light a fire. Unfortunately, anything that could have served as kindling wood was wet. The two Turkish Kurds had found a spot for themselves a short distance away from us. But when I saw that Kamal was not getting any better and that Farhad was still wet through, I ran out into the rain. I felt like a wild creature, with my face bathed in rain, my clothes smelling of the forest. I started yelling out loud at the two Turks, not caring how they reacted. We had to get down to that road somehow. To stay where we were was death.

As my screams bounced around the valley, the Turks came running up. "What are you doing? Are you crazy? They can hear you all the way down to the village," the leader hissed.

"I don't care. We're frozen. We're leaving."

"All right. We'll take you down."

This time they meant it. We walked down muddy paths for close to two hours before we hit a small dirt road that a car could have used. Although it was getting darker, there was still no sign of a vehicle.

"The car that was supposed to be here hasn't made it," the older Turk said finally. "But if you're willing to pay another $2,000, we'll get you a car."

It was blackmail. I spluttered, "What do you mean? We've paid for all this. We're supposed to be driven to Istanbul. What are you talking about?"

"Look. That's the way it is. If you want a car, it will cost you $2,000."

On the way down, the Turks had said we were only half an

hour away from a town by car. But with Farhad whimpering with exhaustion and Kamal dropped to the ground with fatigue, I knew that we would never make it on foot. I would have to give in to them. I started to bargain to get the price down, but they remained adamant. After a lengthy argument, they told us that we would soon be meeting up with the two Iranian men who had been smuggled out shortly before us. Perhaps they would be willing to split the cost of the ride with us.

After remounting, we rode down the track to a small valley enclosed by sheer rock faces. But when we reached the valley bottom, I noticed that Shery and her rider were no longer with us. Over and over again, I called out her name. There was no reply. Terrified, I imagined the worst: that she had fallen off or that the Turks were beginning to divide us. Every time I called her name, my rider hissed at me to stay quiet. It seemed like a full hour later when she came riding up beside us again. At the time, we were approaching a dilapidated stone barn. No explanation was offered as to why her rider had hung back.

Outside the barn, several tired horses were tethered. They lifted their heads lazily to inspect us. Smoke rose lazily from an open door, promising at least minimal warmth. I dismounted quickly and ran into the barn. There, in the centre of the draughty structure, sat two young Iranian men and eight Turkish Kurds tranquilly warming themselves by a fire.

"Do you want to share the cost of a car to the nearest town?" I hurriedly asked the Iranians without so much as an introduction or a greeting. "They want $2,000 to get us a car. We just can't go on anymore."

Looking up at me somewhat bemused, the two young men seemed so much calmer and saner than I. I realized how strange I must have appeared to them, my wet hair flattened to my forehead, my jeans caked in mud, the Kurdish jacket stained and filthy. Kamal, Farhad and Shery walked in behind me, lost, dishevelled travellers from a much-too-distant land.

"Come, sit down by the fire," the one I later came to know as Mahmoud said to us. "We've just made tea. Please have some."

"We're just students," added the other, Sina by name. "We don't have any money to pay for a car. We've paid half the cost of our transportation and they are supposed to take us to Istanbul, where we will pay for the other half. So we are just staying here with them until they decide to take us."

Our two guides joined the Kurdish men in their circle and a discussion ensued in their language. After we had warmed ourselves a little, taken off our muddy shoes and socks and set them out to dry, I made a suggestion to the students in Persian, so that the Turks would not understand.

"Listen. I'm going to tell them that we've decided, all of us, to take the car. We'll pay, not you, but I don't want them to know it after all the bargaining I did."

When they agreed, I turned to our leading guide, the older Turk who had seemed to be in charge, and said, "We will pay the two thousand. You can go and get the car now."

He looked at me as if I were crazy.

"What car?" he asked, shifting his gaze nervously to the other Turkish Kurds. "There is no car. I never promised you a car. We'll have to wait a while and then get back on the horses again."

Our guides had intended to rob us after all. They would have extorted a bit more money from us and kept us up in the hills until night-time when they could just abandon us. But my cries, and their fears that the villagers might come up in daylight to investigate, had forced them to bring us down to the valley. In front of their fellow smugglers, who were perhaps more honest than they, the two were much more careful. There was lively talk among the Kurds. Then, one of them stood up and told us that they had decided to move us right away rather than wait any longer. He ordered us all to pack up and move quickly.

At the mention of horses, Farhad started to cry. He was desperate not to have to ride again and, no matter how I tried to explain, I could not make him understand that there was no other way. It took force to get him back on the horse. Much as I hated the Turk who had tried to cheat us—he gave his name as Ali to the other Turkish Kurds—I knew he was a good rider and had the best horse. I insisted that he take me and Farhad together.

Outside, night had closed in precipitously. The clouds were so thick that we did not even have the moon and stars to light our way. Quietly, with only the gentle sounds of the horses rising about us, we moved along muddy mountain trails. The rain started up, a raucous battery of sounds in the still mountain air, and at one point threatened to wash away the path just where it was most narrow. There were many times when we had to prod the horses to jump over a rushing stream. Each time, Ali took the lead because his horse was the best jumper and he could best gauge if the others could make it. Before every jump, the horses would rear up and become skittish. Even when they made it to the other side, they often bogged down in the mud and had to struggle to free themselves and scramble back up onto firmer ground. Ali's horse, carrying a heavy load of three riders, often had to jump over and then back again because Ali had decided that the others would not be able to follow. Then we would set off in search of another, less dangerous spot to cross over the water. I kept yelling at Farhad to hold on and I grabbed Ali even more tightly around the waist, determined to stay with him and keep Farhad steady. All the others, the Kurds and the Iranians in the group, at one time or another, fell off their horses into the stream that night, but my determination to keep Farhad safe was such that we never once fell, even though we took the most chances.

Later, before leaving us, Ali said to me, "You are a good rider for a woman." That was quite a compliment coming

from a brigand and a master of the rough mountain trails —
but not one that I relished at that moment.

All night we rode on. Occasionally I saw Kamal sitting
dazedly on his horse, not even bothering to hold on to his
rider. When I called his name, he did not look at me. I pestered
him to hold on tightly, but he was beyond fear, and somehow
the spills he took did not seem to hurt him.

When we finally reached a wide, flatter stretch of land, we
heard in the distance the yelping of a pack of wild dogs. The
baying came closer and closer until it seemed to be all around
us. With a break in the clouds, I saw that there were dozens
of dogs running with us, jumping up, snapping at our heels,
yelping excitedly as if chasing prey. There was no way to
lift our legs out of danger because at the speed we were moving we would have become unbalanced and perhaps come
tumbling down. I had to fight every instinct to pull my legs
away from those snapping mouths. Even the horses were nervous, running furiously, taking wild chances as they strained
to escape. The dogs chased us for more than half an hour
before dropping away, perhaps having reached the borders
of their territory. All I know is that suddenly they were no
longer there. But neither was one of the Iranian students,
Mahmoud. When Sina saw that his friend was missing, he
refused to go on.

"I'm going back," he insisted. "I'm not leaving him behind."

The Kurds discussed the situation. Having come to some
common decision, Ali hurled me and Farhad to the ground
and took off at a gallop back in the direction of the dogs.
Soon he returned with Mahmoud. They stopped just long
enough for Mahmoud to tell us what had happened.

"My horse reared and I fell off," said Mahmoud, still shaken
by the experience. "I kept trying to climb back on, but the
dogs kept closing in and my horse just kept dancing around.
I threw rocks and I whipped the dogs but the horse was too

scared. I'd been at it for a while when Ali showed up. I thought for sure those dogs were going to get to me before he did."

Again we mounted the horses. The Kurds yelled at us to hurry because the car was supposed to be waiting for us on the highway. But the running through the night seemed to go on forever. Never once did Ali listen to Farhad's pleas to let him get down to urinate. Then, when we were slightly ahead of the group, I persuaded Ali to stop on the side of the stream that we had just jumped so that I could take Farhad to pee nearby. We were just preparing to remount when I heard Shery scream in the darkness and then shout my name.

In the total blackness of the night, I could see nothing. With arms outstretched I stumbled in the direction of Shery's desperate moans. As I got nearer, I could hear the thrashing of a horse in the water. I waded into the gelid stream. The two Iranian students and Kamal had also dismounted and I could hear them moving towards her. We found Shery lying on her back, her head and shoulders just out of the water. Her rider, who had fallen on top of her, was just pulling himself up. The horse had managed to right itself and was jumping nervously onto dry land. It was evident that Shery had taken the brunt of the fall. Breathing with some difficulty, she held both hands to her chest as if in great pain while Kamal and the students lifted her and carried her to the side. The Kurds made not a single attempt to help us.

"I have broken my ribs, Sousan, help me," she cried. Her Kurdish dress was a muddy tangle around her.

Barely able to see what I was doing, I stripped her of the wet Kurdish dress while Mahmoud searched through his bag to find her the extra jacket that he was carrying. Sina offered a pair of trousers. Hours before, Shery had discarded her own shoes for a pair of Kamal's running shoes, but in the chaos of the fall, they had disappeared. Although he must have had as much difficulty as we in the darkness, Farhad got down on his hands and knees and somehow came up with both running shoes.

But Shery was no longer rational. She demanded a pair of her high-heeled shoes and she started to take off the dress she had been wearing under the Kurdish one. Her movements reassured me that she had probably not broken her ribs, despite her discomfort. The dress she was removing contained the rest of her jewellery in its hem. Shery herself had carefully sewn into it the gold chains and bracelets that she hoped to be able to sell once she got to freedom.

Trying to keep my voice from being heard by the Kurds, I said, "Shery, don't take that dress off. You may need it. Remember?"

But she was beyond understanding. Her expensive Chanel shoes, which she was now stuffing her feet into, were ludicrously small for her: her feet were not only muddy, they were also swollen horribly. She gave up trying to put them on and tossed them aside. Then she pulled her dress off despite my protestations and threw it on the ground.

Impatient and growing more nervous with each lost minute, the Kurds started to mount their horses.

"Let's move," a voice whispered angrily. "We're not waiting anymore."

We rushed to finish dressing Shery. Coming to her senses, she said quietly to me, "Sousan, my dress. Make sure you pack it."

With not a glimmer of light to guide me, I felt the ground with my hands. I came across one shoe and a dress which I quickly stuffed back into her bag. I handed the bag up to her driver so that he could strap it onto the horse. Within seconds we were gone, and although we asked the Kurds over and over again to give Shery one of their thick jackets (even the one that the student had given her was not enough to fight off the cold), they refused. They relented only enough to give her the old horse blanket that Ali, Farhad and I had been riding on.

We rode for three more hours bareback — every moment of it a nightmare for Farhad, who asked repeatedly when we were going to stop. Then, just as abruptly as we had started, the riders halted and announced that we had arrived. It was the middle of the night, with not a village light or a road to be seen, not a sound of domestic pets or farm animals — nothing. Just a dirt track good enough for a tractor on a fairly flat stretch of land in the middle of nowhere.

The students and Kamal immediately protested. Sina and Mahmoud refused to get off the horses. But we were outnumbered and were forced to dismount.

"You're five minutes away from a town. Just walk in that direction," said Ali, pointing to the left. The Kurds' main concern seemed to be to return to their villages before their neighbours woke up and discovered they had been away for the night. Not all Kurds approved of smuggling, it seemed.

As a final insult after all the lying and cheating, the Turkish Kurds demanded that we give them the jackets that the Iranian Kurds had so generously lent us and that had probably saved our lives on that cold journey. Kamal offered to pay them for the jackets — it was freezing and Shery was still drenched — but they ripped them from us. At full gallop, they rode off, leaving us stunned and silent by the side of an unknown track near an unknown town, somewhere in Turkey.

After walking for about ten minutes, carrying our bags, with Kamal and one of the students supporting Shery between them, we decided that we could not go on. Just when we had lost all heart, from well down the road came the rumbling sound of an approaching tractor. It could be a Turk who would turn us in to the police and we might find ourselves back in Iran in front of a firing squad. Or it could be a farmer who might be glad to help a miserable group of escapees. We had no choice. We had to take a chance and flag the tractor down.

Of the two of us who could speak Turkish I was the only one with any strength left, so it was decided that I would try to hitchhike while the others hid in the ditch by the side of the track. It was a wild thing to do. Turkey has a reputation even among other Moslem countries for being unsafe for a woman on her own. But I stood in the middle of the track, waving frantically and shouting to be heard above the din of the motor as the single light of the tractor beamed down at me.

The driver stopped and I ran to the side. As soon as I stepped out of the blinding light of the tractor, I could see that it was not just one farmer, but many heading out early for fields far from their home. There were three men on the tractor itself, but a wagon attached to the tractor carried about five people.

"Please, can you tell me how far the highway is from here?" I asked the startled driver. "I am trying to get to the bus to Van." As I spoke, the rest of our party gathered around the tractor. I could see the man getting a little nervous.

"Well, let me see . . . it's about forty-five kilometres."

"We'll never make it there. Please, could you give us a lift there?"

The driver looked at our group and then at his own and finally said, "No, we can't do that. We're on our way to work."

"We'll just go as far as you are going. Look, we have a child with us and a sick old woman. You must help us."

Again he looked around, and this time he agreed to let Shery and Farhad ride in the back along with our luggage. But we could not allow them to become separated from us along with all our valuables. We also could not allow this miracle — this tractor come out of nowhere — to slip from us.

In Persian I told the others just to jump on board. Then I made a great show of thanking the driver. Within seconds we were all on board. The decision having been made for them, the Turkish farmers — Kurds by the looks of them — just shrugged, and we trundled off.

With a cold wind blowing relentlessly, we rode for two hours on that tractor. The wagon was carrying a load of bundled wheat, which became a hard, wet seat for us. Mahmoud and Kamal used their bodies to shield Shery from the worst of the wind. At about 6:00 A.M., when the driver announced that he was going to have to turn off the track and drop us off, I was almost grateful because at least we would get out of the wind.

After he had insisted that the highway was just ten minutes away, I gave the driver a generous payment for his help. He had helped us survive. The temperatures at night were below zero. Wolves roamed freely in the mountains and foothills. We had no food and no drink. I was sure that without his help we would not have made it through the night. Had it really been only three days and three nights since we had started off so full of hope?

And now it seemed that just as we were getting close to our destination—the town of Van was only thirty kilometres away—our forces would not hold out. Shery could not walk on her own strength, and Mahmoud and Sina each grabbed one of her arms and carried her along. With their free arms they carried their luggage. Kamal, who grudgingly took a bag, fell farther and farther behind. Farhad held one of my hands tightly while I carried my bag in the other hand. Farhad never once complained. He never once asked for things he knew I could not give him. At three points we had to cross cold, slippery streams. After I had helped Farhad across I had to go back and lead Kamal. Each time, Kamal threatened to stay behind and meet whatever fate befell him and I cajoled him into taking a few more steps. With no sleep, and with my lower back grindingly painful after the hours of riding, I somehow found reserves of strength I did not know I possessed. I started to play the game we had called upon throughout our escape every time things became unbearably depressing. "Remember when we get there, we will find the best hotel on earth. We will have a long bath, then we will sleep on clean sheets. We will eat a sumptuous meal—anything that strikes our fancy . . ." My voice travelled without conviction along the Turkish mud track.

Twenty minutes later, the sun was well up when we finally reached the highway. Like a group of castaways, we dropped to the ground, exhausted and grateful to have reached secure land. After a while, we tried to clean ourselves up as best we could without water and soap; we did not want to be too noticeable when the bus came by. It was then that Shery made her terrible discovery. The dress that I had stuffed back into her small suitcase was not the one carrying her gold — the last of her valuables — but the worthless Kurdish dress. Her wails filled the air but we could offer little comfort. Even her Chanel shoes, which she now searched out in a crazy attempt to make herself once again into the respected, well-dressed woman she once was, were useless. There was only one left, and even that one was muddy.

While we waited, Farhad fell asleep by the side of the road and once again he relived his nightmare ride through the mountains. When he finally woke, he looked at me ashen-faced and asked weakly, "Could I have some water? I'm so thirsty. Just a little water." I felt dreadful knowing that it might be hours yet before I could get him food and drink.

It was still early, and the road was quiet. Only the occasional car passed. The farmers had told us that a bus would come by to take us to the city, but we had no idea of the direction in which the bus would be travelling. So that our group would not be too large and noticeable, the two students left us and walked down the highway to wait at a different location.

We discussed how we would deal with any inquiries about where we were from. Because Shery was the only one of us who spoke Turkish without an accent, we decided she would pretend to be Turkish. She would do most of the talking and I would be introduced as a relative who had lived a long time in Iran (to account for my Iranian-accented Turkish).

"Kamal, you will have to pretend to be deaf," said Shery, "and Farhad can pretend to be sleeping or just bored."

The suggestion was an affront to Kamal. "I will not act the part of a deaf person."

"But you have to," I insisted. "It's the only way." I was getting a little angry with his inflexibility. Why should he care about such a thing, anyway? It was just pride.

Finally, a small public bus, probably from one of the side-roads, came by and deposited a couple where we were waiting. It turned out that they, too, were there to catch the bus to town and we were indeed on the right side of the road. After striking up a conversation, we found out from the man that there was a fresh-water spring not far away and that we would have time to go there before the bus arrived. Even though the thought of walking a few paces was daunting, we made the ten-minute hike to the spring and took gulps of cool, wonderful water, our first in hours.

When we returned, the couple became quite friendly and began to ask us about ourselves. We said we were from the vicinity, but I am certain they became suspicious when they asked us what village we were from and we could not name it. Then, when the man tried to ask Kamal a question, Shery told the stranger he was deaf.

"Poor man," the woman said. "He's such a handsome man as well, isn't he?"

To prevent Kamal from exploding in anger and giving us away, Shery asked the man, "We are beyond the army checkpoint here, aren't we?"

"Oh, no," he answered. "The checkpoint is just up ahead."

We looked at each other in dismay. If we were stopped at the checkpoint, the authorities might yet send us back to Iran. We decided to tell the couple a little of the truth.

"I am Turkish," said Shery, "but my friends here are Iranians and I am trying to get them to Istanbul. Will they ask for identification at the checkpoint?"

The man did not seem at all surprised. Instead, he started to think up ways to get us safely through the checkpoint.

"My wife and I both have birth certificates. I could give mine to your friend here and she could give hers to the woman. Nobody will ask the boy and you can pretend you're too old to pay any attention to them. Nobody will suspect us because we come from around here. Shall we try that?"

It was such a generous offer, given so freely by the side of that dusty road. The kindness a few people showed us at the worst times during our escape still astounds me. We gratefully accepted, but before long another crisis presented itself. A car pulled up and Shery asked the occupants if they knew when the next bus was expected.

"Wait a moment," the driver said, "you're Iranians, aren't you?"

Badly frightened, Shery realized too late that the men were probably plainclothes policemen. She started to edge away from the car, but two men sitting in the back seat of the car started to call out to her.

"Don't be afraid," said one of them. "We're Iranian, too. The police will arrest you, but then they'll let you go."

One of the policemen told the Iranian to stop talking, and the car sped off.

We had had no time to consider the meaning of the episode when a truck pulled up. Soldiers jumped out, surrounded us and pointed their rifles at us. At the sight of the armed men, the man and woman who had been so helpful ran off and hid. We sat immobilized in the circle of rifles.

"Into the truck," ordered a soldier who seemed to be in command.

Without a word, Shery, Farhad and I stepped up into the front cab of the truck and Kamal joined the soldiers in the back. As we headed off to the army checkpoint, I despaired completely for the first time during our escape. After all our efforts, we had failed to escape Khomeini's reach. The soldiers would probably send us back to the Iranian border and there a firing squad would be waiting for us. Shery tried to comfort me, but I could no longer bear to listen to empty words of encouragement. Our long fight was over.

Within minutes we arrived at the police station situated at the checkpoint. We sat down before the local commander who scrutinized us carefully. Who were we, he wanted to know. Where had we come from? Where had we been intending to go? To Paris, eh? When he heard our story, he got up from behind his desk. Well, this is it, I thought. Then he walked over purposefully to us and — shook our hands!

"Welcome to our country," he said with a broad smile beneath his wide moustache. "I wish you luck."

Was I hearing right? Was this man who had just arrested us at gunpoint actually wishing us luck? I was so disoriented that at first I could not believe what was happening.

"Bring these people some tea," he ordered an assistant.

"Do you mean to tell us that you won't send us back?" I asked incredulously.

"Yes, I'm welcoming you. And if I could I'd go and personally kill Khomeini. I feel very sorry for all you people."

When I saw how sincerely he meant his words, I started to cry. They were the tears I had held back during the terrifying hours on horseback; when Farhad had asked for drink and I could not give it; when I had watched Shery disintegrate before my eyes; when I had seen Kamal turned senseless by fatigue. Now I could allow those tears to fall.

"Nothing will happen to you," the commander continued. "We are simply going to take you to police headquarters in Istanbul where they will ask you a few questions, and then you will be free to go anywhere in the world."

"Oh, and by the way," he added, motioning to the next room, "a couple of your friends are here."

When I peeked into the next room there stood Mahmoud, who was waxing his shoes, and Sina, who was shaving. Once again, I was amazed at how cool the two students were.

Everything went as the commander had predicted. After being interrogated at the police station, we were taken to a hotel in the nearby town of Van, where we stayed for two weeks while awaiting transportation to Istanbul. The hotel was a way-station for displaced Iranians — rich and poor alike. For the first two days we did nothing but sleep, but later I came to know many of the Iranians and heard their harrowing stories of escape. One family had been caught in the mountains for a month while the Komiteh and their Kurdish guides fought it out with rifles. Another group was still waiting for its suitcases: its guides had promised to deliver them later, but six weeks had gone by and there was still no sign of them. There were pregnant women about to give birth and old men about to die — yet all of them had wanted to escape badly enough that they had braved the uncertain journey. Many were Jews who had found life impossible under Khomeini.

One young woman was travelling with two young children: a little girl of two and a baby barely three months old. When I asked her how she had braved such a difficult trip on her own, she explained to me that it was the only way the family could leave Iran. Her husband, a businessman, had been permitted to make a working trip to West Germany. The authorities were confident that with his wife and children held safely in Iran, he would be forced to return. It had been up to her to take the risk of an illegal exit so that they could be together in the West. Fortunately, her guides had been kind and her trip, although uncomfortable, had gone smoothly. And her husband was already waiting for her in Istanbul. We used to joke that the baby was the youngest escapee from Khomeini, but the pregnant women in the group always shook their heads in amazement at her courage. They had chosen to leave before their babies were born, knowing from the experiences of others that it was quite possible to go for days without food or water while trying to escape. They had preferred to bear the rigours of the trip themselves, no matter how awkwardly their bodies straddled the Kurds' horses, rather than place their babies at risk.

Throughout our stay Kamal was sick most of the time. Perhaps it was just the shock of the trip that made him so demanding. He complained about the food and never wanted to leave the room. Because he was so unwell, I suggested that for a few nights Farhad and I sleep in a separate room so as not to disturb him. But he came to demand his own room anyhow because he did not want a child around him.

We were all exhausted. We were all sick. I had discovered that the skin on my tailbone had been scraped off from the hours of riding on the horses. It was so painful that I could barely sit down, and it took two months for the aches in my arms and legs to disappear.

While Kamal hid away in a darkened room, Shery, Farhad and I explored the small town. There was not much there except a few restaurants and stores, but the three of us took delight in being able to sit down to a meal, however modest, and meeting other emigrés. Shery was still stunned, but she was slowly recovering with rest and nourishment. She no longer cried over her losses. She began to plan her future and how she would set about getting a new passport. Farhad rebounded the most quickly. He ran around making friends with other Iranian children, and the nightmarish trip became the source of whispered story swapping.

Right to the very last day in Van, I worried that we would be sent back to Iran. Perhaps we displaced Iranians were feeling unduly paranoid, but rumours swept our small transient community regularly. "The Turks think there are too many of us." "They send a group back every now and then." "Who knows when they'll get tired of us? Will we be among the ones sent back?" And on and on. I felt no peace even though there was no overt danger.

Eventually, the police arranged a convoy of forty cars and buses to make the thirty-eight-hour road trip to Istanbul. When we arrived after a painful, sweaty ride, Shery was able to call relatives living in the city and she went to live with them while her passport problems were resolved. At Kamal's insistence, we moved into the Hilton where we again took two rooms, even though I was becoming quite worried about the money we were spending. Kamal's intolerance of Farhad's presence in the same room with him did not bode well for a future life together. Farhad passed through the hotels and police stations as if our transient life was an adventure. But he, too, was becoming tired of perpetual change, and it was evident that he was longing for the stability of his own home.

Istanbul is a beautiful city with its domes and minarets and its narrow streets. But during the week that we spent there, we slept almost all the time. I was not yet savouring my freedom. I suppose that I did not truly believe that I was free. The visas that had been so difficult to get in Teheran were now the most valuable things in our possession. The hotels were full of stranded Iranians. I could not guess at how many were in the city in 1982. But early in 1987 a Turkish newspaper had put the total number of Iranians in the country at over half a million. Many of them were young men trying to evade the draft. The process of applying to the embassy of a Western country for a visa or permission to become an immigrant could take years. All that time, the exiled Iranians lived in limbo, supported by relatives in the West if they were lucky enough to have them, or living off the precious valuables they had smuggled out. I was so grateful that we would be spared that ordeal. We could fly off to a Western European country whose embassy employees in Teheran had been brave enough to help us. I will not reveal which country had so generously accepted us, for fear of reprisals against their embassy. But they helped us take the first step in finding a new home.

Finally, one morning, we headed for the airport. A local police chief who had been kind to us during our stay in the city drove us there personally and escorted us onto the plane. I will never forget his courtly manner, his kind smile when he saw us off.

"Allah be with you," he said, waving us off. "May you have better luck in your new home."

As the plane lifted off, I looked back. But it was not Turkey that I was seeing. It was the sun turning the snowy peaks of the Alborz into diamonds above Teheran, the ruby-red tulips growing wild in the valleys of Azerbaijan, villages of red mud brick facing inward, away from the wind on the desert plain and the turquoise sky brilliant over Sabbalon. It was Iran, the country of my birth, the land of my father and my mother.

And still, every day, I make fresh my memories.

Epilogue

The Moving Finger writes; and, having writ,
Moves on: nor all your Piety nor Wit
*   Shall lure it back to cancel half a Line,*
Nor all your Tears wash out a Word of it.

OMAR KHAYYÁM

 And now I, like so many others, live the life of an exile. Displaced Iranians are to be found everywhere: the middle class avoiding the conscription of their sons into a bloody war that cannot be staunched; the wealthy who escaped to stay alive now trying to find meaning in what they are left with; the intellectuals and professionals chased out by intolerance. In Turkey, Spain, France, Switzerland and England, but mostly in the United States and in Canada, there are large new Iranian communities.

For Kamal, Farhad and me, the first six months after our escape were sad ones. We settled in Paris where Kamal's parents were living and took a small studio apartment. The first shock came when Kamal went to dealers to sell his old stamps. He had been told they were worth about $300,000. Instead, they fetched only about $6,000. He had been badly cheated by a fellow Iranian. Then, just days after our arrival in Paris, I received bad news: my father had been arrested by the Komiteh and his remaining property confiscated. For three weeks I waited, dreading to hear reports of his death, until finally they released him without explanation. Just as I was beginning to settle down again, I heard from my Uncle Fayegh that he had had a recurrence of cancer. He died not long afterwards.

There was other news from Iran. When Farhad had failed to return to them at the appointed time on the Friday afternoon of our escape, the Aminis had reacted swiftly. Within hours every Komiteh man and border guard was looking for us. They badgered my uncles and aunts. They made threats against my family and they swore that no matter where we had gone they would send assassins after us. We took their threats seriously. Even now, I keep my address and my identity secret.

The Aminis got most of what they wanted, including my house, the villa, Farhad's millions in cash, and many other things. But while they still use the villa, the house was eventually confiscated by the Komiteh. As far as I know, they use it as a local headquarters. Both gardeners still live off the fruits of the orchard, and Jalal Agha and his wife, the traitors within my own home, are still there, enjoying the house they chased me from.

In Paris, Kamal, Farhad and I had to learn to live much more modestly than we had been used to doing. I had no right to use my son's apartments in Europe. His properties even now remain tied up in legal wrangling because he does not have right of control over them until he turns eighteen, five years from now. And I had trouble selling the carpets I had smuggled out because so many other Iranians had done the same thing and the market was flooded. Soon the pressures of living in cramped quarters and with much less money took their toll on our shaky marriage. Like many Iranian men, Kamal was having a hard time adjusting to the loss of his social status, his profession and properties, nor could he decide on a new career. Under the strain of our escape and continuing troubles, everything seemed to irritate him. He became morose and introspective and spent most of his time by himself at cafés. No doubt I was as irritable and demanding in those sad, disjointed days.

I managed to enroll Farhad in a private school, and of the three of us, he adapted the most quickly to our new circumstances. But as each day passed, I became more and more distracted. I worried about events back home and I missed my family deeply. We were living on some savings that I had sent out of Iran months before, and I was still counting on selling some of my jewellery, which I kept safely hidden in suede pouches in the oven. In that small apartment, it was the only hiding place I could think of. One day, when I was particularly dejected, I decided to cook a roast to cheer us up. I worked all day to make a lovely meal and, for a change, Kamal ate with some appetite. It was not until the next day when I went to put on one of my gold chains that I realized I had forgotten to remove the jewellery before I put in the roast. I rushed to the oven and found a gooey mess, and ashes where pearls had once been. The gold had melted and the diamonds were blackened from the suede pouches. I wept.

On another occasion I actually left my passport — my precious official identity—behind at a photocopying shop. I rushed back but never found it again. It took the intervention of Shapour Bakhtiar, the last prime minister under the Shah, himself an exile in Paris, to persuade the French authorities to give me travel documents. The Iranian Embassy in Paris, now under the control of the *mullahs*, would certainly not have done so.

Not long afterwards, I made the difficult decision to leave Kamal. I applied and received permission to move with Farhad to Canada, where my Uncle Ardeshir and Aunt Guity had settled in Toronto. A year later, I returned briefly to Paris to obtain a divorce.

For the formerly wealthy and powerful of Iran, adjusting to being modestly equipped outsiders has not been easy. Hamid and Sufi both told me stories of former American business colleagues who had been buddies while the two of them were still men to be reckoned with in Iran, but who snubbed them as soon as they made it to the West. This was partly because we bore the brunt of American anger after the 1979 hostage crisis. And it was partly because many people simply blamed the *taghouti* for the revolution.

My friends are now widely dispersed. Shery finally managed get out of Turkey, again thanks to Bakhtiar, who helped her obtain a French visa. She now lives in the United States. She had dreamed that the foreign social workers and international foundations she had worked with while she was in charge of the schools for the handicapped in Iran would help her find a job. But those who had once been so friendly refused to return her calls. She lives on little money.

I have not seen Hamid again. When he heard of my marriage to Kamal, he married and now lives happily in California, where he is slowly building a new business.

Sufi is with his wife in Europe and he remains my constant and true friend. Paul, my embassy friend, and his wife Anna left legally, happy to move back to their own country. And even Jamshid, my husband's partner, eventually took the Turkish route out rather than be caught for having smuggled carpets.

Chloe and Darvish are still together in California. My cousin Firouzeh and her husband divide their time between the United States and England, where they continue to live well. And the students who joined us on the last gruelling part of our escape finally made it into the United States after spending months in Spain. Mahmoud is studying and Sina is working and helping to support him. They are inseparable as always.

As for me, I am finally making a life for myself on my own, with Farhad. I design and sell jewellery and find that I can support us that way. I hope to remarry, for love and not out of necessity, but I am in no hurry. I want a man who will respect my rights and will accept my child. I want a marriage that will last.

Perhaps Farhad is the one who has gained the most from these difficult changes. He speaks English well and is adapting at school despite his past troubled life. It was the right decision, I think, to take him out of Iran—even though there is a good chance that he may never be able to return there. As long as the war continues and conscription takes away the young and strong, it will not be safe for him to go home and claim his rightful inheritance.

I always think of my country. The tragedy that has overtaken Iran spreads so far, touches so many lives and so many countries, that my own grief is lost in a larger sorrow. Every time I pick up the newspaper, I read of fresh horrors. The war with Iraq is at a bloody stalemate. The president of the United States is embroiled in a scandal involving the sale of arms to Iran. And there seems to be no question that Iran is supporting radical groups in Lebanon which use human lives for barter. Those of us who are moderate, whether we live in exile or are still imprisoned in Iran, can see no end in sight for Khomeini's regime. Daily, Iran turns in on itself even more, becoming more and more distrustful of the outside world. Anyone who tries to come near becomes ensnared by its national paranoia.

I have lost all hope of returning. I take to heart the words of our poet, Mollah-Beli Vidadi, "The day will come, you will think of home and weep."

Futura now offers an exciting range of quality titles by both established and new authors. All of the books in this series are available from:
Sphere Books,
Cash Sales Department,
P.O. Box 11,
Falmouth,
Cornwall TR10 9EN.

Alternatively you may fax your order to the above address. Fax No. 0326 376423.

Payments can be made as follows: Cheque, postal order (payable to Macdonald & Co (Publishers) Ltd) or by credit cards, Visa/Access. Do not send cash or currency. UK customers and B.F.P.O.: please send a cheque or postal order (no currency) and allow £1.00 for postage and packing for the first book, plus 50p for the second book, plus 30p for each additional book up to a maximum charge of £3.00 (7 books plus).

Overseas customers including Ireland, please allow £2.00 for postage and packing for the first book, plus £1.00 for the second book, plus 50p for each additional book.

NAME (Block Letters) ....

ADDRESS ....

....

☐ I enclose my remittance for _____

☐ I wish to pay by Access/Visa Card

Number ☐☐☐☐☐☐☐☐☐☐☐☐☐☐☐☐

Card Expiry Date ☐☐☐☐